A HISTORY

OF

THE ENGLISH PURITANS.

BY

W. CARLOS MARTYN,

AUTHOR OF "THE LIFE AND TIMES OF JOHN MILTON," "A HISTORY OF THE HUGUENOTS," AND "THE LIFE AND TIMES OF MARTIN LUTHER."

PUBLISHED BY THE
AMERICAN TRACT SOCIETY,
150 NASSAU-STREET, NEW YORK.

ENTERED according to Act of Congress, in the year 1867, by the AMERICAN TRACT SOCIETY, in the Clerk's Office of the District Court of the United States for the Southern District of New York.

PREFACE.

THIS book makes no pretensions. It often falls below what Dryasdust would call "the dignity of history," and is satisfied to be considered simply an accurate daguerreotype of the men and manners of a heroic past.

The English Puritans have always labored under the disadvantage of which the lion in the fable complained so bitterly. Though they were the conquerors, their enemies were the painters. They have come down to us in the distorted lineaments of hostile pencils. If one may borrow the clever illustration of Grainger, the performances of most of their historians remind us of the paintings of Brueghel, who had so accustomed himself to paint witches and imps, that if he tried to paint a man, he was sure to make him like a devil.

But it has been well said, that in history the law of optics is reversed:

> "Our souls much further than our eyes can see."

Society now perceives that the Puritans were earnest, honest, devout men, anxious mainly to inaugurate the *régime* of vital godliness and of civil liberty—*sub libertate quietem.* Their great effort was to *purify* society. Puritanism was a protest against formalism; it was an insurrection of the soul against the body. And their pithy theology, their stern devotion to duty, their unfaltering heroism, have combined to crown them as the teachers of their own time and as the apostles of the Christian future.

Posterity is concerned to know precisely how such men lived and acted, "at what a forge and what a heat was shaped the anchor of their hope." A volume which shall tell this story, and tell it fairly, which shall

> "Nothing extenuate,
> Nor set down aught in malice,"

is certain to receive a welcome not only from the descendants of the Puritans, but from good men who do not see eye to eye with those uncompromising heroes.

The materials for such a work are vastly more copious than the mere casual observer would imagine; they not only fill the highways of English history, they choke the bypaths. From the reign of Elizabeth up to the Act of Toleration under William of Orange, there is hardly a private memoir or a diary which does not have something to say about the Puritans. English chroniclers and foreign *savants* alike noted their impressions of them. Puritanism was not merely of local interest; it expanded into European importance, and forced men, whether they would or not, to investigate and to judge it.

The distinctive name *Puritan* was not applied

until the reign of Elizabeth, but the *spirit* existed long before the name was born; so also did the great struggle which gave rise to it. It is impossible to understand Puritanism unless we comprehend what preceded it. Therefore this sketch antedates the nominal rise of the Puritans under the maiden queen. Going back to the introduction of Christianity into Britain, it has compressed into two or three score pages the ecclesiastical history of twice seven hundred years before the Reformation, and ends the rehearsal at the year 1688, the epoch of definitive toleration. This is a broad field to traverse, but an honest effort has been made to glean the harvest; and at the same time that saying of the Grecians has been borne in mind, that "the best books are those whose covers are least far apart."

For the authority of this volume, the marginal notes must speak, and an appeal is made to them.

With the Puritans every enterprise commenced with God; it is eminently proper that the benediction of heaven should be invoked upon the record of their labors. To His favor this book, a feeble but sincere tribute to the spiritual heroes "who kept the faith so pure of old," is reverently commended.

NEW YORK, January, 1867.

CONTENTS.

CHAPTER I.

CHAPTER II.

CHAPTER V.

CHAPTER VI.

CHAPTER VII.

CHAPTER VIII.

CHAPTER IX.

CHAPTER X.

CHAPTER XI.

CHAPTER XII.

CHAPTER XIII.

CHAPTER XIV.

CHAPTER XV.

CHAPTER XVI.

CHAPTER XVII.

CHAPTER XVIII.

CHAPTER XIX.

CHAPTER XX.

CHAPTER XXIII.

CHAPTER XXIV.

CHAPTER XXV.

CHAPTER XXVI.

CHAPTER XXVII.

CHAPTER XXVIII.

CHAPTER XXIX.

CHAPTER XXX.

CHAPTER XXXI.

CHAPTER XXXII.

CHAPTER XXXIII.

CHAPTER XXXIV.

CHAPTER XXXV.

A

HISTORY OF THE PURITANS.

CHAPTER I.

A RETROSPECT.

WE have reached the epoch of Christian democracy. In the nineteenth century ideas rule; empty titles do not domineer. Christendom is under a government of opinion and morning newspapers. Popes and kings no longer mark the ages. Luther and Calvin, Faust and Fulton, Howard and Bentham shape the ethics and mould the material interests of society. Churches and open Bibles represent the controlling influences of modern times. Thrones and the Vatican are "twin relics of barbarism;" they serve as milestones, and show how far civilization has travelled.

This record is especially true of the Saxon race. The remote East still gropes, like a blind Samson, for the pillars of its prison-house. The Romanic races only slowly emerge from the dungeons of the Inquisition. But enough has been gained to show that Christianity now strikes the diapason of human affairs. The Papacy may never more fetter lips and taboo progress. The wave of tyrannical rule shall never sweep so far westward as to fill once more with miniature tyrants the robber-castles of the Rhine. Upon the future God sets the seal of his apostleship. The race to this goal has been run for, "not without heat and toil." Thought, the earthquake of conscience, has shaped a unique era. The Titans heaving beneath the mountains have thrown up the soil of a new *régime.* The distinctive trait of this age is a puissant and evangelized individuality. At length Christianity teaches the inestimable value of every human soul. The toil of eighteen hundred years cries, "Eureka! I have found the diamond of an immortal soul and an equal manhood."

This grand truth was born of the Reformation, and it is the outgrowth of the New Testament. Its sturdy growth in England and in America is due to the persistent nurture of the Puritans, those lineal descendants of the reformers of the sixteenth century. For "Puritanism was the natural, inevitable fruit of the Reformation. Henry VIII. was the remote author of the Bartholomew act. Baxter was the true representative of Cranmer; and the ejected clergy of the reign of Charles II. were the spiritual successors of the martyrs of Smithfield under the rule of Mary."*

Lord Bacon, as he takes his march down the centuries, may lay one hand upon the telegraph,

* Stowell, Hist. of the Puritans in England, Preface, p. 12.

and place the other upon the steam-engine, and say, "These are mine, for I taught you to invent." So the Puritans, peering through the misty centuries to catch a view of the garnered fruit of their pain and sacrifice, the overflowing lap, the cunning fingers, happy labor vocal on every hill-side, commerce whitening every sea, societies for the amelioration of mankind taking up the four corners of the globe, the press largely evangelized, a Christian literature, whole continents dotted with school-houses and churches, may echo of these elements of modern civilization, "You too are ours, for we taught you to believe in God."

It is quite the fashion now in certain circles to vilify Puritanism; pigmies run up and down its sides striving to measure it with their yard-sticks. Dizzy *savants* mock and sneer. Infidel letters snarl and sputter. The votaries of an emasculated Christianity, who "run after strange gods," growl and snap. Men of latitudinarian principles and selfish greed, "lewd fellows of the baser sort," debauchées, the scum of corner groggeries, exhaust their vile rhetoric and shout themselves hoarse in denouncing the Puritans.

But they are not original in their abuse. Laud abused them as cordially more than two hundred years ago. The names of the Puritans were linked with epithets of hatred, generations before the birth of these "latter-day saints" of materialism. The Puritans withstood the onset of the profane wits of the Restoration. Dryden and the rest could not lampoon and laugh them out of existence. Tipsy cavaliers, pausing after each fresh glass to hiccough curses upon them, could not blast their fair fame. Is their posthumous reputation to be tarnished by the empty wind of modern scoffers?

Undoubtedly many good men on either continent earnestly dissent both from the distinctive religious tenets and from the political philosophy of Puritanism. But these do not stoop to retail the exploded gossip of coffee-houses and the effete slander of bagnios. The more candid of them readily recognize that there is in the annals of the Puritans much of truth to enlighten the mind, much of romantic beauty to kindle the imagination, much of Christian heroism to thrill and renovate the heart.

At all events, the Puritans were the creators of moral America; and it is not fit that they should be suffered to go down the ages clothed in the distorted history of heated foemen. Who shall object, if fair historic statements assist them to emerge from the vulgar pillory of misconception in which the malice of a beaten monarchy and the spite of a Romanized priesthood have held them with patient vindictiveness through two hundred years?

It has been well said, that in the pursuit of truth blind partisanship should be excluded, and that in this case it is quite possible to conclude, on the evidence of facts, whether the Puritans were essentially right or wrong. Whatever decision may be reached, it is momentously important to familiarize ourselves somewhat minutely with the vivid and checkered story of those "sane giants and giants gone mad," who have played so central a part in the history of twice a dozen decades,

> "The dead but sceptred sovereigns who still rule
> Our spirits from their urns."

"In order that this study may be useful, it should have a character of universality. To confine the history of a people within the space of a few years, or even of a century, would deprive it both of truth and life. We might indeed have traditions, chronicles, and legends, but there would be no history. History is a wonderful organism, no part of which can be retrenched. To understand the present, we must know the past. Society, like man himself, has its infancy, youth, maturity, and old age. Ancient pagan society spent its infancy in the East, in the midst of the anti-Hellenic races, had its youth in the animated epoch of the Greeks, its manhood in the stern period of Roman greatness, and sheltered its old age under the decline of the Empire. Modern society has passed through analogous stages; at the time of the Reformation it attained its legal majority."*

These slow and distant preparations form one of the distinctive characteristics of history. Cuvier said, borrowing the idea from St. Hilaire, that the whole bony structure of every animal grew from the idea of a single bone. Grant him that, and he could complete the whole bony structure. That is what preparatory eras are in history; they may seem

* D'Aubigné, Reformation in England, p. 18.

insignificant, but they are the primal bone; they are at once the prophecy and the guaranty of the completed future.

The birth of Christianity in England is shrouded in tradition.* In the absence of authoritative *data*, it is only possible to guess more or less shrewdly at the hidden fact. It has been conjectured that "in the second Christian century, vessels frequently sailed to the savage shores of Britain from the ports of Asia Minor, Alexandria, and the Greek colonies in Gaul," and that "among the merchants busied in calculating the profits they could make upon the merchandise with which their ships were freighted, there would occasionally be found a few pious men from the banks of the Meander or the Thermes, conversing peacefully about the birth, life, death, and resurrection of Jesus of Nazareth, and rejoicing at the prospect of saving by these glad tidings the pagans towards whom they were steering."†

Through some such apostleship as this, nominal Christianity was introduced into Britain.‡ The island had been known to the Phœnicians, those earliest navigators, several centuries before the Roman conquest;§ nor was it *terra incognita* to the Carthaginian and the Grecian merchants.‖ The most ancient inhabitants of Britain are believed to

* Gibbon, Decline and Fall, vol. 1, chap. 1. Lingard, Hist. Eng., vol. 1, ch. 1. Hume, vol. 1, ch. 1.

† D'Aubigné, Reformation in England, p. 19.

‡ Bede, Eccl. Hist., lib. 1, cap. 23.

§ Hist. of the Anglo-Saxons, vol. 1, book 1.

‖ Ibid.

have sprung from the Cimmerian and the Celtic stocks, and to have wandered thither through Gaul.*

Of the singularly wretched condition of primeval Britain, historians give striking instances. Nor did the introduction of the Roman civility suffice in any marked degree to elevate the Britons. The heathenism of the Druids was simply supplanted by the more polished paganism of the classic mythology, that one-eyed leader of the blind. Then at an indefinite period an anomalous Christianity swayed a feeble and irregular sceptre; but with the wane of the Roman rule, the restless energy of Druidism began to encroach upon the ill-defined domain of the new ethics, and where Christianity was not absolutely swallowed up, it was fatally distorted by the hideous aboriginal superstitions. Of the vicissitudes of this struggle no authentic history remains to us. The most careful antiquarian, as he bends over the relics of this fabulous past, can decipher naught but the idle records of a legendary and portentous hagiology.†

A little later came the Saxon invasion. The resistless barbarians streamed from their German forests, bringing with them the Tartaric idolatry of the North. The grim superstition of the Druids, the obsolete paganism of Rome, the venerable forms of Christianity, all were absorbed, or at least beaten back, and joining hands with the genius of

* Bede, lib. 1. Punchard, Hist. of Congregationalism.

† Webb, Life of Wickliffe, p. 63.

British independence, they retired to impenetrable retreats and mountain solitudes. The island was abandoned to the spirit of Odin, and for upwards of a century the gospel was lost to the kingdoms of the heptarchy.*

The reintroduction of Christianity was effected by Gregory, surnamed the Great. Before his assumption of the tiara, he chanced one day to stand in the market-place of Rome. While idling there he observed several youthful Saxons chained in the slave-gangs. Struck by their beauty and intelligence, he demanded of them their name. "*Angles*," was the reply. "*Angels*," exclaimed Gregory, "you truly are, and you ought to be joined to the celestial company." On being told that they came from the province of Deïra, he cried, "Aye, *de irâ* indeed; *from the wrath* of God they must be plucked." When he learned that Ælla was the name of their king, he instantly replied, "Alleluiah! Alleluiahs must be chanted by them in the dominions of their sovereign."†

The design which was born of this solemn trifling never dropped from the prelate's mind; and when in after years he was advanced to the pontifical throne, he dispatched an ecclesiastical commission of forty monks, headed by a Roman priest named Augustine, to the shores of Britain.‡

* Hume, Hist. of Eng., vol. 1, ch. 1, passim. Bede, lib. 1, cap. 23.

† Bede, lib. 1, cap. 23. Grey, Epist., lib. 10, epist. 56.

‡ Bede, lib. 1, cap. 23. Spelman, Com., p. 82.

A *point d'appui* already existed. Bertha, a Frankish princess who had married Ethelbert king of Kent, was devoted to the Christian faith. Augustine took advantage of this, and it was not long ere the cenobite dispatched to Rome glowing accounts of his multitudinous spiritual conquests; while the pontifical court exulted as much over these peaceful trophies as their ancestors had been wont to do over their most sanguinary triumphs and splendid victories.*

But it must not be thought that the Christianity with which the eldest kingdom of the heptarchy was so quickly inoculated, sprang pure and unsullied from the primitive fountain. The transition from apostolic simplicity to papal corruption had already commenced.

The first danger which beset the gospel was from the spirit of paganism. Both the schools of philosophy and the haunts of vulgar superstition were pervaded by elements at mortal variance with the simple essence of Christianity. From the wisdom of the heathen world, the new religion had accordingly to encounter either the peril of fierce opposition, or the still more dangerous and insidious offer of coalition. If the earth-born philosophy of the age were unequal to a conflict with the truth of God, it might at least scheme to hold a divided empire; and with this view it stretched forth the right hand of fellowship. The result was that the faith of Christ was gradually transformed

* Hume, vol. 1, p. 27.

into the likeness of a human science, wherein the intellect of man might freely and boldly take its pastime.

Still more infectious were the gay ritual and the imaginative mythology of paganism. Had an apostle revisited the earth at the end of a dozen decades from the period of his ministry, and looked at nothing but the outward church, he might have been tempted to fear that the truth for which he had pleaded, perhaps died, had been transformed into a gorgeous spectacle, a mystic pageantry, its painful and laborious evangelists into pompous actors, its places of worship into splendid theatres.

In primitive times the chalices were of wood and the ministers of gold; now the church was content with golden chalices and wooden priests.

Spirituality died out of religion with a shriek. The subtle essence of Christianity was frozen in formalism.* Religion became an incarnate Pharisee. The restless wit of man invented exorcisms for demons, absolutions for sin, and the thousand absurdities of the ceremonial law, and then, pausing with self-satisfied blasphemy, rebaptized the impious progeny of his own distempered brain with the sacred name of Christianity.

From these abuses grew the edifice of the papacy, whose corner-stone was blasphemy, whose pillars were spiritual death, and whose crowning arch was arrogant worldliness. "From the midst of this temple a portentous spectre was seen to arise, an

* See Milton's essay "On the Reformation of England."

apparition habited in the robes of priesthood, and surrounded by all the attributes of majesty, holding in one hand the rod of worldly power, and in the other a flaming sword which turned in every direction to guard the citadel of spiritual dominion. For ages did this stupendous phantom continue to spread out before the astonished and awe-struck nations, until its feet seemed to rest upon the earth, while its head towered among the stars."*

Such a Christianity, propagated among pagans, could be little else than a change of superstitions. Remembering these things, it is not difficult to accede to the statement of a recent historian, that while "it would be too much to assert that there was no intelligent piety in Britain in these ages, it is still perfectly apparent, from the history of the times, that Christianity had little else than a name to live, while it was dead. Flowing to the Saxons from the corrupted fountain-head of papal usurpation, it must have been the waters of death, rather than of life, to the ignorant islanders.

"The church history of the heptarchy is a loathsome story of papal imposition on the one hand, and of ignorant and superstitious devotion on the other. Many of the putrescent abominations of Rome were incorporated into the Saxon church. Reverence for their sovereign lord the pope was the first article of the Saxon creed. A devout regard for all that wore the sacerdotal habit stood next in order. The worship of relics and

* Webb, Life of Wickliffe, p. 39.

saints was held to be scarcely less important than the worship of God himself. The payment of 'Peter's pence' would purchase pardon for a thousand sins. A pilgrimage to Rome, the establishment of a monastery, a gift of property to the church, would cover the most flagitious crimes."* Christ was lost sight of. He was replaced by the Virgin. In Milton's phrase, "nearly all the inward parts of worship, which issue from the native strength of the soul, ran lavishly to the upper skin, and there hardened into a crust of formality."†

Upon the canvas of this picture is painted the story of British Christianity through a thousand years. The essential situation was unchanged by the fierce onslaughts of the Danish freebooters. Even in the enlightened reign of Alfred the arrogance of ecclesiasticism was as unbridled as in the darkest ages of the heptarchy. That energetic and accomplished prince either dreaded to provoke a conflict with the seeming omnipotence of the papacy by attempting to stem the torrent of abuses, or he had no disposition, absorbed in political reform, to trench upon what was universally esteemed to be the domain of Rome.

The great gain under Alfred's reign was the impulse which was given to learning. Since the Saxon invasion, the Greeks and Latins, and even the converted Goths, had looked upon the island with unutterable dread. "The soil," said they, "is

* Punchard, Hist. of Congregationalism, vol. 1, pp. 208, 209.

† Milton, On Reformation in England.

covered with serpents; the air is thick with deadly exhalations; the souls of the departed are transported thither at midnight from the shores of Gaul. Ferrymen, the sons of Erebus and Night, admit these phantoms into their boats, and listen with a shudder to their mysterious whisperings." Britain, whence light was one day to be shed over the habitable globe, was long esteemed the trysting-place of the dead.

In Alfred's age this superstitious notion was only slowly dying away. He found "the monasteries burned, the monks butchered or dispersed, the libraries destroyed."* He himself complained that "not a priest south of the Thames could translate Latin or Greek into his mother-tongue."† Britain floundered in the Serbonian bay of ignorant barbarism; he assisted his country to emerge and stand upon high land. Schools were everywhere established. The venerable university of Oxford was founded, endowed with many privileges, and supported by appropriate revenues;‡ while celebrated continental scholars were invited to make his court their home, and such as came were magnificently recompensed.§

Thus the future was secured to liberty. Schools insured churches. Learning was the *avant-courrier* of reform.

* Hume, vol. 1, p. 74. † Ibid. ‡ Ibid.

§ Spelman, Life of Alfred, ed. 1709, p. 120.

CHAPTER II.

AN OASIS IN THE DESERT.

After the death of Alfred, in the first year of the tenth century,* the heterogeneous elements which his plastic hand had moulded into seeming unity crumbled to pieces. Political and ecclesiastical affairs were all in confusion.

The chief agent of this ruin was St. Dunstan. The history of superstition can scarcely present another name so infamous for brazen abuse of vulgar credulity and a prodigal application of the grossest machinery of imposture. His whole progress from an anchorite cell at Glastonbury to the primacy of England is one perpetual atrocity and fraud. His grand object was to erect the Benedictine order on the ruins of the national church, and to consign to monks the entire government of the state.†

His commanding genius was well suited to this pernicious enterprise, and the success of his machinations was astounding. His career forms a monument of unscrupulous ambition such as might have appeared extravagant and monstrous even in the pages of romance. That his portrait has not been overcolored however, we may know from this, that his biography has been written, not by calumnious adversaries, but by admiring and contemporary

* Spelman. Hume. Chron. Sax., p. 99.

† Osborne in Anglia Sacra. Webb, p. 72.

chroniclers, while the gratitude of Rome has preserved his name to this day on her rubric of canonization.

The struggle thus inaugurated marked one age and moulded the succeeding. The blazing embers of the quarrel were only quenched by the Norman conquest. When William the Conqueror passed the channel into England, he commenced a new *régime*. The unlawful raid of the Norman robber had been sanctified by the special benediction of pope Alexander II.* Still, when he learned that Hildebrand assumed to lasso both spiritual and temporal Europe to his feet, the Conqueror's haughty spirit refused to succumb. He refused to do fealty for his kingdom to the see of Rome; and for once the crafty pontiff was foiled by a temper as resolute and arbitrary as his own.

However, it was in this reign that Lanfranc, an Italian who had been promoted by the Conqueror to the primacy of England, urged the infliction of celibacy upon the clergy. He also introduced into the Saxon church the doctrine of the corporeal presence in the sacrament.† But Lanfranc's‡ mind, lofty as it was, was not powerful enough to "rebuke the genius" of his master, and it still remains true that the main drift of William's reign ran counter to the supremacy of "the pope's proud prelacy."

* Hume, Webb, Punchard, D'Aubigné, etc.

† Webb, Life of Wickliffe, p. 73.

‡ Lanfranc succeeded Stigand, who was the last of the Saxon prelates.

The gigantic scheme of Hildebrand for the erection of St. Peter's chair into the throne of Christendom, and thus effecting the restoration of Rome to her old position of mistress of the world, is recorded in the blots which deform the history of mediæval Europe.

The march of usurpation was for a time diverted from England by the inflexible sternness and rigor of the Conqueror, by the reckless obstinacy of Rufus,* and by the intelligent firmness of Henry Beauclerc.

But Rome could afford to bide her time, sure that a crop of more pliable kings would eventually spring up. She knew that the Beauclercs did not come in large bodies, nor march in battalions: they stray through the centuries, now and then one; and he is the salt of a generation.

In the mean time letters continued to advance. The learning of that epoch was not altogether healthy; and Burke laments that "the infancy of British learning was suckled by the dotage of the Roman." Still, a monkish literature was better than none; and gradually expanding beyond the sullen walls of the monasteries, it somewhat smoothed the shaggy barbarism of the age.

Through all these years the papacy, not satisfied with maintaining old privileges, constantly clamored for new ones. Its hungry maw no sops could satisfy; and at length, when the reign of the first of the Plantagenets dawned, Rome claimed,

* See Fox, Acts and Monuments, p. 211.

through the lips of Becket, the total immunity of ecclesiastics from the secular jurisdiction.* The controversy which ensued was long and bitter. How disastrously it ended for the interests of liberty history records.

"It is the first step that costs," says the proverb; and when England began to yield, she made no pause, but flung herself recklessly into the abyss. King John, the most despicable of crowned heads, the butt of his contemporaries' sarcasms, the strangler of his nephew, of whom his subjects said, "You are not a king, nor even a *kingling*"—*fuisti rex, nunc fex*—once a king, now a clown—became the pope's vassal, was his armed missionary, and even stooped to do homage to the pontiff's legate on his bended knees for his kingdom, and to pay tribute.†

So low had the papacy brought England.

Then came a phase of resistance to these usurpations. Grostête protested, Bradwardine argued, Edward III. actively resisted Rome, and Wickliffe was the John Baptist of the English Reformation.

England, weary of the yoke of Rome, grew restless and began to fret. Wickliffe was the father of this dissent from Rome. Wickliffe was also the progenitor of the Puritans.

It becomes of interest therefore, to glance briefly at the salient characteristics of his career. His era was an oasis in the desert. His words were

* Webb, Life of Wickliffe, p. 75. D'Aubigné, Ref. in Eng.

† Matthew Paris, p. 231. Hume, Lingard, etc. Also Roger of Wendover's Flowers of History, vol. 2, Bolen's ed., pp. 215, 271.

the first breath of healthful doctrine which had passed over England for many a weary day.

John Wickliffe was born in 1324.* He was cradled in a Yorkshire hamlet;† but of his boyhood little is known.‡ In 1348 he was attending lectures at Oxford, where he sat at the feet of Bradwardine.§

At the outset, Wickliffe, like all who aspired to eminence in those days, devoted himself to scholastic philosophy; and with such success, that his contemporary and opponent Knighton has acknowledged that he was "second to none in philosophy, and that in scholastic subtlety he was altogether incomparable."‖

He was also learned in the civil and the canon law; and he had grasped the municipal laws of England.¶ There was no domain of knowledge which he did not lay under contribution; there existed no peak of learning which the towering genius of this "admirable Crichton" of divinity did not impel him to scale.

"It was well," remarks one of his biographers, "that Wickliffe went forth to his achievements sheathed in the panoply of the intellectual knight-errantry of his day; that he was master of 'the nice fence and the active practice' of the schools, as well as potent to wield the two-edged sword of the Spirit. This happy combination of accomplish-

* Webb, Life of Wickliffe, p. 99. Also Lewis, and other biographers. † Ibid. ‡ Punchard, vol. 1, p. 237.

§ D'Aubigné, Ref. in Eng., p. 84.

‖ Knighton, De Eventibus Angliæ, col. 2644.

¶ Webb, Life of Wickliffe, p. 102.

ments served to win him the respect of all parties. It secured him the reverence of his followers, who must have seen with justifiable pride that their teacher was foremost among the sages and doctors of his time. It silenced the voice of disdain; and effectually disabled his adversaries from attempting to cast discredit upon his cause by ridiculing the ignorance and incapacity of the advocate."*

Wickliffe having mastered the human sciences, next turned to the Scriptures.† Whatever study he commenced he aimed to exhaust. Of this study was begotten his conversion. He marked the fatal departure of the papacy from the biblical paths. The truths which he had discerned he determined to proclaim. The new moral world which he had discovered, the great Columbus of ethics felt constrained to make known.

"He commenced with prudence; but being elected, in 1361, warden of Baliol, and in 1365 warden of Canterbury college also, he began to set forth the doctrine of faith more energetically. His biblical and theological studies, his knowledge of theology, his penetrating mind, the purity of his life and manners, and his unbending courage, rendered him the object of general admiration. A profound teacher, like his master Bradwardine, and an eloquent preacher, he demonstrated to the learned through the week what he intended to preach, and on Sunday he preached to the people what he

* Webb, Life of Wickliffe, p. 105.

† Punchard, vol. 1, p. 240.

had previously demonstrated. His disputations gave strength to his sermons, and his sermons shed new light on his disputations. He accused the clergy of having banished the holy Scriptures, and he required that the authority of the Bible should be reëstablished in the church. Loud acclamations crowned these discussions, and the crowd of vulgar papists trembled with indignation when they heard the shouts of applause."*

Wickliffe's public life had four phases.

The first was political.

The larger part of his life was spent in the reign of Edward III., one of the most vigorous and statesmanlike of the English kings. King John had alienated the kingdom, and paid tribute to the pope.† The money had always been paid irregularly. Latterly all payments had ceased. Pope Urban V., heedless of the laurels won by the conqueror at Crecy and Poitiers, summoned Edward III. to recognize him as the legitimate sovereign of England, and to forward the annual rent of a thousand marcs.‡ In case of refusal, the king was cited to appear at Rome.

The conqueror of the Valois, irritated by this insolence of an Italian bishop, convened a Parliament. The papal arrogance stirred England to its depths. In 1350 the statute of *Provisors* was passed. It was rendered a penal offence for any

* D'Aubigné, Ref. in Eng., p. 85. † Chap. 2, p. 39.

‡ Ranke, Hist. of the Pope's Pontificate of Urban V. Hume; Lingard.

one to procure a presentation to a benefice from the court of Rome.* By the subsequent statute of *Præmunire*, any person who carried a cause before the pope by appeal from home jurisdiction was outlawed.†

"If the statute of *mortmain* put the pope in a sweat," says old Fuller, "this of *præmunire* gave him a fit of fever."‡

Through all this controversy, Wickliffe was active. At once an able politician and a fervent Christian, he vigorously defended the rights of the British crown against Romish aggression. His tracts upon this momentous question are profound and statesmanlike. They created a sensation; and attracting the attention of the king, he made Wickliffe one of his chaplains.§ That act rang the death-knell to the papal claim to the sovereignty of England.

The second phase of Wickliffe's ministry was, the preaching of the gospel to the poor.

During the heat of the controversy on the sovereignty of Great Britain, Wickliffe had been dispatched on a mission to the pope at Avignon. On his return, he was given the cure of Lutterworth;‖ and from that time a practical activity was added to his speculative and academic influence.

"At Oxford," says D'Aubigné, "he spoke as a master to young theologians. There he had earned

* Hume, vol. 1, p. 371, Reign of Edward III. † Ibid.
‡ Fuller, Chh. Hist., cent. 14, p. 118.
§ D'Aubigné, p. 86. ‖ Lewis, Webb, etc.

the honorable and unique title of 'The Gospel Doctor.' In his parish he addressed the people as a friend and pastor—a new and beautiful relation."*

The third phase of his beneficent career was the translation of the Bible into English. Scholasticism had placed the Scriptures under ban. Rome assumed to be the infallible oracle; and she padlocked the evangelists in musty Latin. Wickliffe unlocked the dungeons of the imprisoned gospel, and set it free.

The effect was prodigious. Minds were everywhere enlightened; souls were everywhere converted; the birth of a new era was hailed with acclamations. But the priests snarled and threatened. "Master Wickliffe," said the monks, "has, by translating the Bible into English, rendered it more acceptable and intelligible to laymen, and even to women, than it has hitherto been to the learned. The gospel pearl is everywhere cast out and trodden under foot of swine."†

Theology was Wickliffe's fourth phase; and in the cloister of Oxford he began to inculcate the distinctive doctrines of Protestantism—salvation through faith in Christ, and the sole infallibility of the sacred Scriptures.‡

Europe heard this brave preaching aghast. The mendicant friars, who swarmed in England, listened

* D'Aubigné, p. 87.

† Knighton, De Eventibus Angliæ, p. 264.

‡ See the various biographies of Wickliffe; also Punchard's Summary of his Doctrines, vol. 1, pp. 269-310, passim.

in agony. "I should suspect," says Fuller, "that his preaching had no salt in it who made no galled horse wince."

Wickliffe did not tread on flowers. He was more or less persecuted throughout his whole career; but during the life of Edward III., the favor of that gallant prince sheltered the bold reformer; the throne of England was his ægis. On Edward's death, in 1377, it seemed certain that the Roman court would avenge itself; but the notorious papal schism which immediately succeeded, occasioned by the election of two pontiffs to the vacant throne of Gregory XI., once more saved Wickliffe. Through the remainder of his life, the scandalous quarrels of the rival popes at Avignon and at Rome so occupied the attention of the church that the great Englishman enjoyed comparative immunity.

The story of Wickliffe's life reads like a page culled from the chapter of romance. But through all vicissitudes, he lived to see his sixty-first year; and he died in the very service of the altar.*

Had Wickliffe completed that reformation which he only inaugurated, the Protestantism of England might have been moulded in the form of the Protestantism of republican Geneva; for "it must be plainly confessed," remarks a modern English critic, "that there is a close resemblance between Wickliffe and at least the better part of the Puritans who troubled our Israel in the reign of Elizabeth and her successors. The likeness is sufficiently strik-

* Lewis, Webb, Fox, Vaughan, etc.

ing to mark him out as their progenitor and prototype."*

Singularly gifted, ripe in experience, a profound teacher, a pure iconoclast, a luminous Christian, an enlightened patriot, Hampden and Milton need not blush to take Wickliffe, the one by the right hand, the other by the left, and say, "Behold our father!"

* Webb, p. 325.

CHAPTER III.

THE DAWN OF DAY.

It has been said that William of Normandy, Edward III., Wickliffe, and the Reformation, are the four ascending steps of Protestantism in England. Up three of these the gospel had already climbed; it now stood on the last, and prepared to hurl the papal usurper from the throne of the island.

Even within ten years after the death of Wickliffe, Britain appeared to have been revolutionized. Lollardism* seemed about to new model the church. To the licentious ostentation of the papal clergy, Wickliffe's disciples opposed a Christian humility;

* The true definition of the word *Lollard* has been the subject of no little controversy. Like the terms *Huguenot*, *Puritan*, and *Methodist*, conferred in later times, it seems to have been originally bestowed as a contemptuous nickname. Fuller appears to think that the Lollards were so called from *Walter Lollardus*, one of their German teachers. Church History, p. 163, folio edition. Speed, quoted in Walsingham, p. 588, folio ed., says that "Wickliffe's followers were, in the phrase of those dark days, called *Lollards*, (*lolium* signifieth *cockle* and such weeds;) whereas, in truth, they endeavored to extirpate all pernicious weeds which, through time, sloth, and fraud, had crept into the field of God's church." Mosheim thinks that the name was derived from the German word *lullen* or *lollen*, which means *to sing* softly, whence our English word *lull;* and this because the Lollards made great use of singing in their worship. Cent. 14, pt. 2, ch. 2, n. 68. See also Punchard, vol. 1, pp. 314–316.

to the degenerate asceticism of the mendicant orders, a spiritual and free life. "Every minister," said they, "can administer the sacraments, and is competent to confer the cure of souls equally with the pope."* The Lollards recognized a ministry independent of Rome, founded, not on the permission of popes or the decrees of councils, but on the Scripture text.

Around these pure teachers all classes crowded; grim-visaged men-at-arms listened sword in hand, ready to defend them; the nobility began to take down the images from their baronial chapels;† even the walls of the cathedrals were placarded with parchments satirizing the friars and lampooning the vices which they defended.‡ Indeed so strong did Lollardism feel itself to be, that, in 1395, a petition was presented to Parliament urging a radical reformation.§

Nor was the agitation confined to the island. The gospel breeze swept across the Channel, across the Netherlands—those countries which the plodding patience of ages has wrenched from the ocean and dedicated to civilization and religion—across Germany, across Bohemia.‖ Sleepers were awakened. The shroud of souls was riven. Wickliffe's pamphlets were received with enthusiasm. Mediæval Europe, blind and shackled as it was, half stag-

* Walsingham, p. 388.

† Knighton, De Eventibus, etc., lib. 5, p. 2660. ‡ Ibid.

§ Lewis, Life of Wickliffe, p. 338; Webb, and others.

‖ Waddington, Ch. History. Gillett, Life of Huss.

gered to its feet to salute the new tenets. Huss was Wickliffe's spiritual son; the lurid fire of Constance was kindled in England. The exiled Vaudois, driven by the fierce harries of the Roman crusaders from fair Languedoc to seek shelter beneath the crags of mountainous Bohemia, hastened, under the influence of Wickliffe's inspiration, to reorganize that ancient church which the Inquisition had failed to choke.

But while the Continent was thus stirring, England was torn by persecution. The papacy had long followed the scent of heresy with keen nostrils, but with muzzled jaws. It had quitted its lair, and, like a long-leashed and hungry hound, it now sprang at the throat of its victim.

Richard II., the weak successor of Edward III., was formally deposed, and a usurper bought the crown by steeping himself to the lips in oaths to suppress Lollardism.

Rome, ever watchful to take advantage of revolutions, had engineered this one. Arundel, a cunning priest and an astute politician, was then primate of England. He advised Henry IV. to consolidate his mushroom power by conciliating the papacy. The king, remembering that a former pontiff had sanctified the robber-raid of the Norman conqueror, esteemed Arundel's advice to be good, and he muttered, "Persecute."*

Then martyrdom succeeded martyrdom. The Lollards, baring their heads to "the pelting of the

* Fuller, Ch. History, p. 153.

pitiless storm," could only wail out their agony in God's ear; they sobbed themselves to sleep in Jesus.

The persecutions covered a large part of a century. The hunted reformers hid themselves among the lower classes, preached in secret, burrowed in English catacombs,* or bore stout witness to the truth in massive dungeon-keeps and "Lollard towers."† Even the sanctity of the grave was violated; and by a decree of the Council of Constance, Wickliffe's mouldering bones were disinterred and burned, while the ashes were thrown into a neighboring brook.‡ "The brook," says Fuller, "did convey his ashes into Avon, Avon into Severn, Severn into the narrow seas, they into the main ocean, and thus the ashes of Wickliffe are the emblem of his doctrine, which now is dispersed all the world over."‡

The intervention of the civil wars of the "Roses" in the latter half of the fifteenth century, somewhat blunted the edge of persecution. Between the embattled ranks of the houses of York and Lancaster the demon of religious bigotry stood disarmed. Indeed, scarred and barbarized by war, civility itself seemed at its last gasp. "The sound of bells in the steeple," remarks an old historian, "was drowned by the noise of drums and trumpets. And yet this good was done by the civil wars, that

* See Raynauld, Ann. 1414, and onwards. † Ibid.

‡ Lewis, Life of Wickliffe; Webb; Punchard, etc.

§ Fuller, Church History.

they diverted the prelates from troubling the Lollards; so that this very civil storm was a shelter to those poor souls, and the heat of these intestine enormities cooled the persecution."*

Still, that quaint old martyrologist, Fox, informs us, that "from the time of Richard II. there was no reign of any king in which some good man or devoted woman did not suffer the pains of fire for the religion and true testimony of Christ Jesus."†

Marked by these vicissitudes, the generations hastened by on winged feet. In 1485, the internecine struggle touched its climax on the fatal plain of Bosworth; that subtle and enigmatic tyrant Richard III. was hurled from his stolen throne into an untimely grave. The Lancastrian conqueror was proclaimed king under the title of Henry VII., and this title-deed to the kingdom, substantiated by battle, was in the following year rendered doubly valid by a marriage which seated the representatives both of the White and the Red Roses on the throne.‡

Then the first of the Tudors began to exhibit the intolerant spirit which had animated his ancestors. He showed the same subserviency to the clergy; he manifested the same unchristian malignity.§

* Fuller, Church History. † Fox, Acts, etc.

‡ Hume, Reigns of Richard III. and Henry VII.

§ For a striking account of the persecutions under Henry VII., see Fox, Acts and Monuments, vol. 1, p. 882, and onwards, passim.

But the hour of vengeance was already in God's heart. It hurried forward with speedy but stealthy feet. "Retribution," it is said, "has a foot of velvet, but a hand of steel." In the midst of the moaning of God's children, an arm was uplifted which was soon to smite the scalp of this gigantic and godless oppression.

In the tenth year of the sixteenth century the reign of Henry VIII. commenced—an event for ever memorable. It was the beginning of modern history. In that new era "all those events happened, and all those revolutions began," says Bolingbroke, "which have produced so vast a change in the manners, customs, and interests of European nations, and in the whole policy, ecclesiastical and civil, of these parts of the world."*

In morals, as in physics, after an ebb comes the full tide. A calm, devout, suffering, but patient protest against the prevalent corruptions of religion had been uttered in England since the death of Wickliffe. Now the invention of printing, the circulation of books, the dispersion of learned men, and the persuasive teaching of Continental reformers united to give that worn protest fresh life and emphasis. Across the yawning chasm of a hundred years men stretched their palms to join hands with the Lollards of the age of Wickliffe. A new light dazzled in the horizon. Luther launched the Reformation in Germany. Zwingle awoke the joy-

* Bolingbroke, Letters on the Study and Use of History, letter 6.

ous echoes of the Swiss Alps by the repetition of the magic words, "Religious Liberty." Tyndale once more unchained the Bible through an English translation.

A host of devout, learned, and ingenious men in England labored to effect a reformation. Every weapon which honorable men could use was brought out from the intellectual armory and pressed into active use. The universities were early revolutionized. Bilney, converted by reading Erasmus' Greek Testament,* began to preach. Latimer arose, and he maintained from the Cambridge pulpits that the Bible ought to be read in the vernacular.† "The Author of Holy Scripture," said he, "is God himself; and this Scripture partakes of the might and eternity of its Author. There is neither king nor emperor that is not bound to obey it. Let us beware of those by-paths of human tradition, full of stones, brambles, and uprooted trees. Let us follow the straight road of the word. It does not concern us what the fathers have done, but rather what they ought to have done."‡ Then came Barnes and Frith, the bosom friends of Tyndale, and the two Ridleys and Cranmer followed. These men, the fathers of the English Reformation, were all illustrious scholars, and they had most of them been eminent either for zeal or piety in the Roman

* Fox, Acts, etc., vol. 4, p. 633.

† D'Aubigné, p. 247.

‡ Latimer's Sermons, Park. Soc., vol. 1, p. 70, Sermon on the Plough.

communion. Their opposition to the papacy was the result of their intimate knowledge of the vulgar errors of the holy see. This acquaintance with the Babylonish mysteries added fresh pungency to their epigrams and gave new point to their satires.

"Do you know," said Latimer, "who is the most diligent bishop in England? I see you listening and hearkening that I should name him. I will tell you. It is the devil. He is never out of his diocese; you shall never find him idle. Call for him when you will, he 's ever at home, he is ever at the plough. You shall never find him remiss, I warrant you. Where the devil is resident, there away with books and up with candles; away with Bibles, and up with beads; away with the light of the gospel, and up with the light of wax tapers, yea, at noonday; down with Christ's cross, up with the purgatory pick-purse: away with clothing the naked, the poor, the impotent; up with decking of images and gay garnishing of stones and stocks; down with God and his most holy word; up with traditions, human councils, and a blinded pope. Oh that our prelates would be as diligent to sow the corn of good doctrine, as Satan is to sow cockle and darnel."*

The grand distinctive principle of Tyndale, of Frith, of Latimer, of the Ridleys, of Bradford, was the divine authority and sufficiency of the sacred

* Latimer's Sermons, Park. Soc., vol. 1, p. 70, Sermon on the Plough.

Scriptures, and the consequent rejection of the earth-born authority of popes, councils, fathers, and kings, in all matters that pertained to religion. The Bible was their standard, as it was Luther's and Bucer's; to that touchstone they brought every thing. If the Scripture approved it, well; if not, then away with it.

It was this principle which gave emphasis and color to their apostleship, as it did afterwards to that of their descendants the Puritans. It was this which sustained Tyndale in his weary exile—this which enabled Latimer and Ridley and Bradford at a later day to brave the awful fire.

But in the mean time this healthy stir was frowned upon by the government. Cardinal Wolsey, who really controlled England, was a determined and unscrupulous enemy of the Reformation. The king himself had entered the lists against Martin Luther, and in grateful return for his services, the pontiff had crowned him *Defender of the Faith.** In 1521, Henry fulminated a decree against home heresy.† Up to the year 1527, the record of the Bluebeard king was that of the most blind and unscrupulous adhesion to Rome.‡

Then occurred a strange event: a question of divorce broke the chains which bound England to the papal throne.

Soon after his assumption of the purple, Henry

* Froude, Hist. Eng., Henry VIII.

† Strype, Eccl. Mem. Burnet, vol. 1, part 1, book 1, pp. 18, 19.

‡ Ibid.

VIII. married his brother Arthur's widow, Catharine of Aragon. Many circumstances combined to render the nuptials ill-omened. The lady was the young monarch's elder by six years.* Henry disliked her; and when first told that the union was under consideration, he formally protested against it.† "Very many, both cardinals and divines, did oppose it" on scriptural grounds.‡ Henry VII. himself, the originator and chief promoter of the match, is said, when on his death-bed, to have become convinced of its illegality, and to have charged his son not to consummate it.§ Yet, spite of these objections, any one of which might have been esteemed sufficient to checkmate the plan, political reasons crowned it with success. Catharine was the daughter of Ferdinand and Isabella; she was also the aunt of the emperor Charles V., the Charlemagne of his age, and she brought the kingdom an immense dowry.|| It was thought also that the marriage would strengthen and enrich the island, bind England and Spain in indissoluble bonds, and chain both to the Roman see.¶ These potent argu-

* Herbert's Henry VIII., pp. 7, 8. Burnet, Hist. Ref., vol. 1, part 1, book 2.

† Ibid. The protest is dated June 27, 1505.

‡ This text in Leviticus was cited against the marriage: "If a man shall take his brother's wife, it is an unclean thing; . . . they shall be childless." Lev. 20:21.

§ Herbert, Burnet, and others.

|| Her dowry was 200,000 ducats, equivalent to $480,000 in American gold. This was doubtless one grand reason why Henry VII., the most miserly of kings, was anxious to secure the marriage.

¶ Punchard, vol. 2, p. 39.

ments might not be resisted; so a papal dispensation ratified and legalized the union.*

The royal couple lived together during eighteen years. In that time Henry, who was passionately desirous of children, lost no less than six in rapid succession.† But one lived, the "Lady Mary" of bloody memory. Some time in 1527 the king also saw and became enamoured of Anne Boleyn, one of the beauties of his court.‡

Urged equally by love and the death of his children, which he regarded as a providential punishment upon his unlawful and incestuous marriage,§ Henry, in the fall of 1527, demanded a divorce, and he dispatched an ambassador to Rome to obtain the papal dispensation.

Queen Catharine was of course bitterly opposed to a divorce which would illegitimatize her children, and convict her of having lived in adultery eighteen years. She poured her griefs into the ear of her nephew Charles V. The emperor naturally sided with his aunt. He was then in the full flush of his military triumphs on the Continent, and holding the pontiff in the hollow of his hand, he forbade the issue of a dispensation.‖

Consequently, when Henry's ambassador reached the Roman court, he was met by equivocations, beguiled by words, put off by promises. Clement

* Herbert; Burnet; Hume; Froude, etc.

† Froude, Hist. Eng., vol. 1, pp. 115–118.

‡ Cavendish, Life of Wolsey, pp. 118–134. Herbert's Henry VIII., p. 284.

§ Froude, vol. 1, p. 115.

‖ D'Aubigné, chs. 9–12, passim.

VII. dared not comply with the English king's imperious order.

In the mean time Henry began to chafe. Wolsey sent courier after courier to implore the pope to hasten, picturing the anger of the king, the spread of heresy, and the imminent danger of losing the island to the church in case of the alienation of the monarch.*

The pope was between Scylla and Charybdis; on either side his boat would be dashed to pieces. But Charles V. was nearer than Henry VIII.; he was also more dreaded. So Clement continued to procrastinate. Through five years of chicanery the divorce dragged.†

Then Henry lost patience; he hurled bitter oaths at the pope; he cursed the college of cardinals; he disgraced Wolsey;‡ and taking the divorce into his own hands, he had it decreed by a home tribunal;§ then he barricaded Rome out of England by statutes.

The great minister's prediction was verified—Britain was lost to the Roman see.

As for Wolsey, broken and discrowned, like the effete faith whose representative he was, he retired from his gorgeous palace into a hovel to die. He could only sigh,

> "Farewell, a long farewell, to all my greatness."

* D'Aubigné, chs. 9–12, passim.
† D'Aubigné, pp. 301–518, passim.
‡ Hume, Froude, Lingard, Cavendish, Life of Wolsey.
§ Ibid. Herbert, Life, etc., of Henry VIII.

He could only mutter between his sobs,

> "Oh, how wretched
> Is that poor man that hangs on prince's favors!
> There is, betwixt that smile he would aspire to,
> That sweet aspect of princes, and his ruin,
> More pangs and fears than wars or women have;
> And when he falls, he falls like Lucifer,
> Never to hope again."

CHAPTER IV.

THE TWO DIVORCES.

It is not necessary in this *résumé*, if we may borrow the striking simile of Hooker, to "uncover the cup of all those deadly and ugly abominations wherewith this papistical Jeroboam hath made the earth so drunk that it reeled under our feet." We may accept Fuller's summary: "Seeing that the complaints of the conscientious in all ages against the errors in the Romish church met with no other entertainment than frowns and frets, and afterwards fire and fagot, it came seasonably into the minds of those who steered the English nation to make use of that power which God had bestowed upon them; and seeing that they were a national church under the civil command of one king, he, by the advice and consent of his clergy in convocation and the great council in Parliament, resolved to reform the church under his inspection from gross abuses which had crept into it, leaving it free to other churches either to follow his example or to continue in their old condition; and on these terms the English Reformation was first advanced."*

From the downfall of Wolsey to the Act of Supremacy, the Reformation swept on with regular and triumphant steps. In 1532, Henry VIII. and

* Fuller, Church History, vol. 2, p. 50.

Anne Boleyn were married.* In 1533, Parliament erased from the statute-book many of the barbarous laws against Lollardism; reiterated former acts restraining the payment of ecclesiastical dues to Rome; enacted that church dignities should be conferred, not by the pope, but by deans and chapters or priors and convents, under the license of the king; and made provision for the conduct of religious matters within the kingdom, without resort to the Roman courts.† Besides all this, the power heretofore exercised by the "apostolic chamber" over religious houses was transferred to the king.‡

But while the law was thus active in severing England from the holy see by statute, the press and the pulpit were not idle. The press groaned under the load of pamphlets daily issued against the papal claims. The pulpit proclaimed that the pontiff had no authority, ecclesiastical or civil, in England.§ Even the dead verbiage of the statutes grew eloquent in the defence of liberty. The press seemed animated by the glowing spirit of the Lollards. The pulpit appeared to be but an echo of the resurrected soul of Wickliffe.

While the Parliament was busy in chattering law against Rome, a convocation or ecclesiastical assembly was in session; and here too several remarkable events occurred. The clergy, under a pressure from the throne, not only acknowledged

* Herbert, Life of Henry VIII.; Burnet; Froude.

† Statutes, 25 Henry VIII., ch. 20. ‡ Ibid., ch. 21.

§ Burnet, vol. 1, p. 130.

that their convocations might only be assembled by the king's writ, but they addressed the monarch as the "protector and supreme head of the church and clergy of England"—a title which he exacted, and which was a little later ratified by an act of Parliament;* and they promised also, *in verbo sacerdotii*, that they would never make nor execute any canons without the royal assent.†

It may interest some readers to learn how it was that this convocation, composed largely of bitter Romanists, came to make such fatal concessions to Henry VIII.

When the king began to weary of the arrogance and chicanery of Wolsey, he sought for a pretext to decree his downfall. The eager and cunning lawyers of the court instantly opened the musty statute-book; and pointing out the statutes of *Provisors* and *Præmunire*, which enacted that no Englishman should receive bulls from Rome, or exercise legative authority in Britain, they reminded Henry that Wolsey had transgressed the law in both these respects. The king seized the half-forgotten law, and Wolsey fell, smitten by the statutes of *Provisors* and *Præmunire*.‡

The clergy long refused to recognize the supremacy of the king. Then Henry once more bethought him of his statute-book. He again had recourse to the *Provisors* and *Præmunire*. If Wolsey had exer-

* Burnet, vol. 1, pp. 214, 228.

† Statutes, 25 Henry VIII., ch. 19.

‡ Burnet, Hist. Ref., vol. 1.

cised the legative authority, so had the clergy recognized the legitimacy of that clearly unlawful power. An action would therefore lie against them. Henry could put them out of his protection, confiscate their property, and imprison their persons: such was the penalty which awaited the infraction of the act. This the contumacious clergy understood; and fully aware of the unmerciful character of the king when his own ends were to be subserved, "they were only too happy," says Burnet, "to escape the full infliction of this whip of scorpions by compliance with the royal wishes."*

In 1534 the Act of Supremacy, from which has grown the church of England, was confirmed by Parliament; and this gave the papal authority in Britain its legal *coup de grace*.†

In the following year the memorable visitation of the monasteries began. These "religious houses," swollen with wicked prosperity, gorged with ill-gotten gains, and bloated with license, were suppressed: the lesser ones in 1536, contemporaneously with a parliamentary decree extinguishing the authority of "the bishop of Rome;" the larger ones in 1539,‡ the wealth so gained reverting to the state.§

A royal proclamation against holy days soon followed. Clerical trickery was uncloaked; Thomas

* Burnet, Hist. Ref., vol. 1. We know of no one who has so admirably analyzed this page of history as Burnet.

† Statutes, 26 Henry VIII., ch. 1, anno 1534.

‡ Statutes of the Realm, 27 Henry VIII., chs. 27, 28; Fuller; Burnet.

§ Froude, vol. 2, ch. 10. Hume.

á Becket's shrine was demolished, and the Roman play-house began to lose its baby-clothes.

Then came what has been finely called "the Bible era" of the Reformation. In 1537 the first royal proclamation in favor of the English Bible was issued.* Good men were at the helm of government. Thomas, lord Cromwell, a sagacious statesman and a hearty reformer, became vicar-general of England; Cranmer, archbishop of Canterbury, a prelate of brilliant learning, devout spirit, but somewhat vacillating in action, ably and cordially supported the reform—sometimes took the initiative.

The floodgates of divine truth were now fairly opened, and no power, royal, papal, or diabolical, was able to breast the gracious waters.† "It was wonderful," says Strype, "to see with what joy the book of God was received, not only among the learneder sort, but generally all England over, among all the vulgar people; and with what greediness God's word was read, and what resort to places where the reading of it was. Everybody that could bought the book, or got others to read it to them if they could not themselves. Divers elderly people learned to read on purpose; and even little boys flocked among the rest to hear portions of the holy Scriptures read."‡

But through all these momentous scenes the

* Fox, Acts, etc., vol. 2, pp. 324, 325.

† Punchard, vol. 2, p. 102.

‡ Strype, Life of Cranmer, vol. 1, p. 91, Oxford ed., 1840.

court of Rome was not quiet. In 1538 a papal bull was fulminated, which outlawed and damned king Henry, and which embodied "every prohibitory and vindictive clause invented by the most aspiring of the popes."*

There was in England a large, active, and scheming party which was devoted to Rome. At the head of this faction stood Sir Thomas More,† a statesman of brilliant acquirements, but a heated partisan. It also numbered among its adherents very many of the higher nobility; and below these swarmed a substratum of monks, who, robbed of their monastic nests by the Reformation, bore it an unrelenting hate, and who roamed through the island ubiquitous, intriguing, fomenting insurrection, and endeavoring to entangle England in foreign wars.‡

But the wings of the Romanist party were clipped; they could no longer soar to hawk at their quarry. For a time they were powerless—

> "Wicked but in will, of means bereft."

All this series of kaleidoscopic changes was the result of two divorces: one from a woman, and comparatively insignificant; the other from a creed, and therefore momentous.

It is an oft-repeated sophism, that Henry VIII. was the architect of the English Reformation. Oh, no; the corner-stone of that stately edifice was laid

* Bullarium Romanum, vol. 1, p. 704.

† See D'Aubigné's account of More, Hist. Ref. in England.

‡ Neale, Hist. Puritans, vol. 1, pp. 13, 14.

by the almighty Master-builder. *Other foundation can no man lay.* "The church of Christ, which was from the beginning, is, and continueth unto the end."

Unquestionably human elements, often unfriendly elements, entered into and helped perfect the work. The pride and the wantonness of Henry were the *occasion* of the break with Rome; but the *cause* lay behind the passion of the kingly puppet. Heaven put Henry to this use; and "it is usual with God's wisdom and goodness," says Fuller, "to suffer vice to sound the alarm to that fight wherein virtue is to have the victory."*

Still it is true, as D'Aubigné has reminded us, that "the Reformation in England, perhaps to a greater extent than that of the Continent, was effected by the word of God. Those great individualities with which we meet in Germany, in Switzerland, in France—men like Luther, Zwingle, Calvin—do not appear in England. What brought light into the British isles subsequently to 1517, and more markedly after 1526, was the Bible widely circulated. The religion of the Anglo-Saxon race, a race called more than any other to circulate the Scriptures throughout the world, is particularly distinguished by its biblical character."†

This Reformation was no easy, gala-day achievement. The actors in it were not masqueraders in a mimic war. It was born of infinite hard fights,

* Fuller, Ch. Hist., vol. 1, p. 51.

† D'Aubigné, Ref. in Eng., pp. 149, 150.

when if "Michael and his angels fought the dragon, the dragon fought, and his angels," also.

And this triumph is all the more remarkable when it is remembered that it was won against the shrewdest master-piece of human wisdom. "The experience of twelve hundred eventful years, the ingenuity and patient care of forty generations of statesmen had improved the Roman polity to such perfection that, among the contrivances which have been devised for deceiving and controlling mankind, it occupies the highest place."*

It has been well said, that among the wants of man may be reckoned an appetite for deception; a desire, inherent in our depraved nature, to bring into an agreement the claims of Deity with the indulgence of our pet frailties; a wild impatience for the conveniences and splendors of a religious structure in which the luxury of delusion may be enjoyed.

This Rome supplied. Ample and complete indeed was the apparatus which she provided for the accommodation of all the various passions and propensities of mankind. She "had a chamber for every natural faculty of the soul, and an occupation for every energy of the natural spirit. She permitted every extreme of abstemiousness and indulgence, of fast and revelry, melancholy abstraction and burning zeal, subtle acuteness and popular discourse, world-renunciation and worldly

* Macauley, Essay on Ranke's History of the Popes. Essays, vol. 3.

ambition. She embraced the arts, the sciences, the stores of ancient learning—adding antiquity and misrepresentation of all monuments of better times; and she covered carefully, with a venerable vail, that Bible which was able to expose the false ministry of the infinite superstition."*

The essence of Romanism is deceit and proselytism. The Romanist, says Macauley, is required to be "inflexible in nothing but in fidelity to the church. Their divines are described by some as the most rigid, by others as the most indulgent of spiritual directors. Both descriptions were correct. The devout listened with awe to their high and saintly morality. The gay cavalier who had run his rival through the body, the frail beauty who had forgotten her marriage vow, found in the Romanist an easy, well-bred man of the world, who knew how to make allowance for the little irregularities of people of fashion. The confessor was strict or lax according to the temper of the penitent. His first object was, to drive no person out of the pale of the church. Since there were bad people, it was better that they should be bad Romanists than bad Protestants. If one were so unfortunate as to be a bravo, a libertine, or a gambler, that was no reason for making him a heretic too."†

So subtle and flexible was the Roman *rationale*. It is not possible to combat a creed which accords

* Irving, Babylon, etc., Foredoomed, p. 238.

† Macauley, ut antea.

so well with the natural instincts of the heart with any mere human weapons. To say then that Henry VIII. overthrew the papacy in England, is to utter a self-evident absurdity. To the accomplishment of that, nothing was adequate but "the grace of God, powerful to the pulling down of strong-holds."

CHAPTER V.

THE FLOOD AND EBB TIDES OF REFORM.

THE age of Henry VIII. was the fly-leaf between the old and the new dispensations. The Reformation did not reach its legal majority in the reign of the second Tudor. Epochs are not cut short by dates.

It was a transition era. An old faith was unsettled; a new faith groped half blindly towards the dawning light. Each pulpit preached a different doctrine, impelled by individual belief or by caprice.* One chanted the mass, and proclaimed stiff popery. Another asserted that "holy water was juggled water;" held that "auricular confession, absolution, and penance were neither necessary nor profitable in the church of God," and planted itself on Scripture alone.† Babel seemed come again; all unity of faith seemed lost.

It was to establish unity in the English church that, in 1536, the king convened the first reformed assembly.‡

The convocation consisted of two houses: the lower, of the clerks and proctors, the deans and archdeacons of the several cathedrals and dioceses; the upper of the bishops, with the lord-

* Neale, History of the Puritans, vol. 1, p. 17.

† Fuller, Ch. History, vol. 2, pp. 71, 74. (List of erroneous opinions.)

‡ Neale, ut antea.

abbots and priors, or such of them as rated as barons in parliament.* Lord Cromwell presided in state as the king's vicar-general.†

The members of this unique assembly were a heterogeneous mass, some Romanists, some Protestants, some neither; but all were animated by a servile wish to do the royal bidding.‡

Almost the first thing they did was to confirm Henry's divorce from Anne Boleyn, "the papists willingly, the Protestants faintly, but all publicly." Fuller informs us that "no particular cause is specified in the sentence, still extant in the record; and though the judge and the court seemed abundantly satisfied of the reasons for nullifying the marriage, yet, concealing the same unto themselves, they thought not fit to communicate this treasure unto posterity, except they shut their coffers on purpose, because there was nothing in them. However, after ages take the boldness to conceive that the greatest guilt of Anne Boleyn was king Henry's better fancying of another, which made him, the next day after her execution, to mourn passionately for her in the embraces of a new and beautiful bride, the Lady Jane Seymour."§

Anne Boleyn wore the purple four years, not so long as it took Henry to win her. In that time she gave birth to a daughter, who afterwards reigned as queen Elizabeth.‖ Fuller makes this record of

* Fuller, vol. 1, p. 67. † Ibid.
‡ Fuller, Ch. Hist., vol. 2, p. 69. § Ibid., pp. 68, 69.
‖ Hume; Lingard; Froude, etc.

the unhappy lady: "She was a great patroness of the Protestants, a protector of the persecuted, the preferrer of men of merit—among whom was Hugh Latimer—and a bountiful reliever of the poor."*

After the consummation of this piece of servile rascality, the convocation addressed itself to the elaboration of a creed. Then the discordant passions of the members crystalized them into two radically opposed factions, one earnest to stand in the old ways, the other eager to achieve a complete reformation.

Latimer had opened the first session with a Latin sermon preached from this text; "The children of this world are in their generation wiser than the children of light." Fuller, with quaint humor, thinks that it would be cruel to quote these words *apropos* of the disputants in the convocation.†

The debates were warm and long continued; they ended, as is the pernicious custom in such cases, in a compromise on radical differences.‡ Oil and water were made to mix. Popery and Protestantism kissed each other. So they say the Romans could roast one half of a boar, and boil the other side. The convocation grew an ecclesiastical apple, one half pippin, the other half russet. They gave birth to a "twilight religion," whose essential tenets were these: the Scriptures, and the Apostles', the Nicene, and the Athanasian creeds—according to which the Bible was to be interpreted—

* Fuller, p. 68.

† Fuller, vol. 2, p. 75.

‡ Ibid.; Neale; Newell, etc.

the recognized standards of faith; the admission of the doctrine of justification by faith; four of the seven papal sacraments ignored; purgatory left doubtful; but auricular confession, transubstantiation, and the use of images and saints for certain specified purposes still retained.*

These articles gave very general dissatisfaction. The reformers thought that the cup was poisoned by the popish ingredients; and the Protestant princes of Germany, some months later, deputed three learned men to reason with the bishops and the king of England on behalf of a further progress in the reformation of the church.†

The Romanists treated the royal articles with undisguised contempt. They openly scouted the pretensions of Henry to ecclesiastical supremacy;‡ and the angered monarch had no redress but to slake his rage in the blood of the scoffers. Monks of the Charter-house and of the Carthusian order were executed; and to crown the holocaust, Fisher bishop of Rochester, and the ex-lord chancellor Sir Thomas More, were both beheaded within a fortnight of each other.§

But despite this severity, the *émeutes* broadened

* Fuller quotes the articles *in extenso*, as copied by his own hand from the convocation records, as do also Burnet and Collier. Neale gives an abridgment of them; so does Newell. The summary given in the text is a faithful transcript of the spirit of the articles.

† Newell, History of the Puritans in England, p. 72.

‡ Neale, vol. 1, pp. 17, 18.

§ Froude, Hume, Lingard, Herbert, Life of Henry VIII.

into rebellion. One insurrection of twenty thousand men was choked by a proclamation;* but another in the north of the island was only suppressed by battle.†

These commotions made the unstable and unprincipled monarch weary of pressing the Reformation. Frightened by the war-cloud in the north, and at heart still attached to the essential tenets of Rome, he appointed, on the 5th of May, 1539, a committee of the House of Lords to draw up new articles of agreement in religion.‡ The result was what Lingard styles that "severe and barbarous statute" of the Six Articles. The first of these affirmed transubstantiation; the second, communion in one kind only; the third, the celibacy of the clergy; the fourth, the observance of celibacy as an ordinance of God; the fifth, the continuance of private masses; the sixth, auricular confession.§

Sprinkling with holy water, the invocation of saints, images, and most of the other superstitious rites and ceremonies of the papal church were retained; and it was decreed that the act should be read by the clergy once a quarter, while those who spoke or wrote against transubstantiation were to be burned without any abjuration, and to forfeit their real and personal estates to the crown. Those

* Froude, Hume, Lingard, Herbert, Life of Henry VIII.

† Ibid.

‡ Neale, Newell, Burnet, Fuller.

§ These are cited in full by Fuller, vol. 2, p. 98; by Newell, pp. 73, 74; by Neale, vol. 2, p. 21, and by other ecclesiastical historians.

who spoke or wrote against any of the other articles were to suffer imprisonment during the king's pleasure, besides forfeiting their goods and chattels to the state, for the first offence; and on the second, they were to suffer as felons. It was also decreed that those priests who had married should be convicted of felony, unless they "put asunder" those "whom God had joined;" and it was made penal for any conscientious soul to absent himself from the confessional.*

Henry VIII. surrendered to Rome. England struck her flag to the Vatican. Romanism shrieked with frenzied joy when Parliament "framed this mischief by a law."

"Power and profit," says Fuller, "are the things which politic princes chiefly desire. King Henry had already obtained both by his partial reformation: power, by abolishing the pope's usurpation in his dominion; profit, by seizing on the lands and goods of suppressed monasteries. And thus having served his own turn, his zeal wilfully tired to go any further; and only abolishing such popery as was necessary to his design, he severely urged the rest on the practice of his subjects.

"Herein he appeared like to Jehu king of Israel, who utterly rooted out the foreign idolatry of Baal—fetched from the Zidonians, and almost appropriated to the family of Ahab—but still worshipped the calves in Dan and Bethel, the state idolatry of the kingdom; so our Henry, though banish-

* Burnet, Hist. Ref., part 1, pp. 258, 259.

ing all outlandish superstition of papal dependence, still reserved and maintained home-bred popery, prosecuting the refusers to submit thereto."*

Against the Six Articles Cranmer and Cromwell in vain protested;† and they were ere long sealed in the martyred blood of Lambert, a learned and amiable divine who had achieved wide fame as minister to the English congregation at Antwerp, but who, on returning to Britain, had ventured to tilt against transubstantiation.‡

Before Lambert's *auto da fé* the Reformation halted. Reformatory movements do not go backwards, but they oscillate. So now in England religious progress fluctuated. Henry VIII. had done his work; liberty waited for his death to leave room for the fresh young truth to grow.

In the mean time the king sternly enforced the law. Even Cranmer, his chief favorite, was compelled to send away his wife; while Latimer and Haxton not only resigned their respective sees of Worcester and Salisbury, but were both imprisoned for inveighing against the statute.§ The patient and thoughtful pen of old John Fox has preserved the names of many of the untitled victims of the king's "home-bred popery."‖

England had simply exchanged popes. "Henry VIII. was as much the pontiff of Britain as

* Fuller, Church History, vol. 2, pp. 97, 98.

† Ibid.; Newel; Neale, etc.

‡ Neale, vol. 1, p. 20.

§ Newell, p. 75.

‖ See his account of the sufferings of Testwood, Filmer, Anne Askew, etc.

Paul IV. was of Rome; and popery, under another head, still triumphed in its most obnoxious forms."*

In 1540 the fall of Cromwell occurred.† The astute statesman had provoked the ill-will of the shuttlecock king by the active share which he had taken in the promotion of the royal marriage with Anne of Cleves, a match which proved eminently unhappy.

Then Henry fell a complete victim to "the artifice and abject submission of Gardiner, Bonner, and other conforming popish bishops, who, by flattering his imperious temper and complying with his dictates, prejudiced him against the reformers added to which, his majesty's growing infirmities made him so peevish and positive, that it was dan-

* Brook, Mem. of Cartwright, Introduction, p. 4.

† Froude, vol. 3, p. 303; Burnet; Fuller, vol. 2, pp. 98-105. "There were eight charges in the bill of attainder against Cromwell, four of which related to his heretical character. This reveals the true ground of the enmity against him. He had risen by the force of his genius and capacity for business, from a very humble origin, to be the most powerful and influential subject in the kingdom. For this he was hated by the old nobility. But Cromwell's hatred of popery was undoubtedly his great offence. A forged confession and recantation was published after his death, as was done in the case of that gallant old Lollard, Lord Cobham, who was hanged and burned for his Protestantism a century and a quarter before Cromwell's death. The dying prayer of the great statesman contradicts the calumny that he recanted his faith in his last hours: 'Lord Jesus, merciful Lord, Christ Jesus, I see and acknowledge that there is in myself no hope of salvation; but all my confidence, hope, and trust is on thy most merciful goodness.'" Punchard, vol. 2, pp. 137, 138, note.

gerous to advise any thing not known to be agreeable to his sovereign will and pleasure."*

The fag-end of Henry's arbitrary, wayward, and contradictory career did not "bring forth works meet for repentance." Wrenched by disease, grumbling, and persecuting papists and Protestants alike, he hobbled to his grave, dying on the 28th of January, 1546. History ranks him "among the ill-princes, but not among the worst;" while it writes upon his tomb this acknowledgment, that God builded with him better than he knew.

* Neale, vol. 1, p. 20.

CHAPTER VI.

THE PROTESTANT INQUISITION.

"THE king is dead; long live the king!" so runs the formula of the old English law which proclaims with epigrammatic point the immortality of royalty. That last sad pageant of Henry's rule, his burial, was scarce concluded, ere his son and heir by poor Jane Seymour, Edward VI., stepped blithely into the vacant throne.

This boy—he was but ten years old when he began to reign—is the sphynx of English kings. Deeply learned, well versed in politics, precise in business, a shrewd observer, a careful critic, and yet a baby of ten, is it strange that posterity should wonder and laugh incredulously when it looks back across three hundred years and sees this royal prodigy?*

* Edward VI. was born October 12, 1537. He was proclaimed king January 31, 1547. Most Protestant historians dwell with reverent admiration upon his learning, piety, and talents; as, for instance, Burnet, Fuller, Neale. His teachers, says Strype, were "happily chosen, being both truly learned, sober, wise, and all favorers of the gospel." Cranmer, his god-father, superintended his studies. John Belonair taught him French. Dr. R. Cox, "a very reverend divine," instructed him in Christian manners. In Greek and Latin he was taught by "that accomplished scholar, Sir John Cheke, once public reader of Greek in Cambridge. . . . Other masters attended him for other tongues, but Cheke did most constantly reside with him." Strype, Eccl. Memorials, vol. 2, pp.

Henry VIII. left specific directions for the government of his kingdom during his son's minority;* but these were only partially complied with. The burly Tudor could not dictate so imperiously from the grave as he had been wont to do from the throne.

The sixteen executors to whom the government had been bequeathed appointed one of their number, the duke of Somerset, Protector, under certain restrictions; and it became his duty to act *in loco regis* until Edward should attain his legal majority.†

The administrators were composed in part of papists, in part of Protestants; but the reformers had the ascendency, and they immediately proceeded to initiate religious changes.

Cranmer became the leader of the Reformation.‡ The statute of the Six Articles was reversed. Many who had been forced by it to fly beyond the sea were summoned home; while others of its victims—Hooper, Coverdale, Rogers—were preferred to benefices in the church.§ Before the "open sesame" of the new *régime*, even the jail doors turned on

13, 16. Mr. Hallam remarks, "I can hardly avoid doubting whether Edward VI.'s journal, published in the second volume of Burnet, is altogether his own; because it is strange that a boy of ten years should write with the precise brevity of a man of business. Yet it is hard to say how far an intercourse with able men on serious subjects may force a plant of such natural vigor. . . . He treated his sister Mary harshly about her religion, and had, I suspect, too much Tudor blood in his veins." Con. Hist., p. 91.

* Burnet, vol. 2. Fuller, vol. 2. Newell, Hume, Froude.

† Ibid. ‡ Stowell, p. 80. § Neale, vol. 1, p. 27.

their rusty hinges; and Latimer, who had passed six weary years in the Tower, regained his lost *caste* and his unshackled lips.*

The council went still further: it invited learned foreign reformers to make England their home.† Several responded, among whom were the famous Peter Martyr and Martin Bucer.‡ The first of these was seated in the chair of divinity at Oxford; the other was preferred to a professorship at Cambridge.§

The government then proceeded to remould the loose and clumsy ecclesiastical system of Henry VIII. It was no part of the programme to introduce a radical reformation. The design was rather, as Burnet informs us, "to carry on the Reformation by slow and safe degrees; not hazarding too much at once;"‖ or, as Fuller puts it in his figurative style, they intended to imitate "careful mothers and nurses who, on condition they can get their children to part with knives, are content to let them play with rattles."¶

Instigated by Cranmer, the regents decreed a royal visitation, the object of which was to instruct the commons in the tenets of the Reformation.** This circuit was made by "six of the gravest divines and most popular preachers" in England.†† Cran-

* Punchard, vol. 2, pp. 155, 156. Wilkins, Concilia, 3.

† Burnet, vol. 3, p. 146.

‡ Punchard, ut antea. § Ibid.

‖ Burnet, Hist. Ref., Reign of Ed. VI. See the general spirit, passim. ¶ Fuller, Ch. Hist., vol. 4, book 8, sect. 3.

** Neale, vol. 1, p. 27. †† Ibid.

mer prepared twelve homilies for the enlightenment of groping souls; and these the government directed "all parsons, vicars, or curates" to read "every Sunday" in their respective churches,* to supply the absence of sermons, which the majority of the clergy, accustomed only to mumble the Roman formulas, were unable to compose.†

Conformity with this act was enjoined by pains and penalties.‡ Most of the bishops at once succumbed; but two of the stiffest of the Roman clergy, Gardiner and Bonner, refused to submit, and they were flung into the Fleet prison for contempt.§

But the visitation was a mere make-shift, intended to tide over a shallow spot. Notwithstanding the attempts at coerced unity made by Henry VIII., pulpit continued to clash against pulpit; nor were the laity less radically divided than the clergy.‖ The regents were anxious to melt these salient differences, which constantly threatened to inaugurate civil war, into a grand unity, "a consummation devoutly to be wished," but not sufficiently imperative to be entitled to dragoon every other desideratum into obedience.

The golden rule of toleration did not belong to what the Scotch call the "humanities" of that age of nascent Protestantism. This now well-recognized civil canon the twilight government of Edward VI. did not accept. The light still winked from the

* Burnet, vol. 2, p. 54. † Neale, vol. 1, p. 28.
‡ Ibid. § Collier; Strype; Hallam, Con. Hist.
‖ Neale, p. 30.

monastery windows; and if, groping in the era of tapers, Cranmer and his confreres often stumbled and fell, perhaps they are more deserving of pity than of too harsh censure.

In the first year of Edward's reign, a plan for the security of religious unity was digested;* and this was afterwards submitted to the Parliament for ratification. Parliament, anxious only to know and to execute the will of the court, readily enacted Cranmer's programme into law.

At one period in English history, Parliament stooped to be simply the attorney of the king. It was a clumsy scribe, esteeming its only function to be to record the will of despots. It would as soon have thought of decreeing the jury trial in Timbuctoo as of uttering an independent word, initiating a policy, or crying veto to the usurpations of a king. In a later age, Parliament took a juster view of its prerogatives, better understood its august functions, and stereotyped brave words into grand acts.

Still the Parliament just mentioned proved to be one of the most memorable in history; and it deserves to be called the *iconoclastic Parliament;* for it broke many idols. It struck down many of the oppressive statutes of the past; repealed the cruel enactments of Henry VIII.; decreed the removal of statues, crosses, and altars from the churches, the disuse of tapers, holy water, and incense; ordered the abolition of the worship paid the Virgin and the saints; left the doctrine of purgatory

* Burnet, Records, vol. 2, part 2, book 1, No. 7.

indifferent, though retaining the prayer for departed souls; decreed the discontinuance of auricular confession, the denial of the corporeal presence, the restoration of the right of marriage to the clergy; and to crown all, instituted a uniform order of prayer, and established the reformed liturgy.*

This was a glorious work, and jubilant Protestantism of all shades echoes the "well-done" of that age by the "Amen" of three centuries.

"The Book of Common Prayer of the Church of England" was not original with the committee of bishops and divines who prepared it. It was compiled from various local missals, the obnoxious popish features being omitted.† It was first published in 1548; but it was altered three years later, at the suggestion of dissenting foreign divines and their English adherents; when, in its amended form, it received the sanction of the Protestant Convocation.‡

The Liturgy, like the Prayer-book, was a form of public worship drawn largely from Romish sources and protestantized. It was intended to produce exact uniformity of doctrine; but became, from its rigidity—no discriminating latitude being left for tender consciences—the rock upon which the reformers split.§

With the salient features of the Liturgy, revised

* Statutes of the Realm, 1 Edward VI., chap. 2. Statutes 2 and 3 Edward VI., chap. 1. Parl. Hist., vol. 3, pp. 232, 235. Burnet, vol. 2, p. 192.

† Burnet, vol. 2, p. 192. Neale, vol. 1, p. 31.

‡ Newell, p. 82.

§ Neale, vol. 1, p. 32.

and changed from time to time, we shall become acquainted as this history proceeds.

The acceptance and use of the new service-book was enforced by harsh legislation. It was not only enacted that the clergy should make use of this, and of no other, but that if any parson, vicar, or spiritual person should speak in derogation of it, he should for the first offence forfeit a year's profits of one of his preferments, and suffer six months' imprisonment; for the second, lose all his preferments, and suffer twelve months' imprisonment; and for the third, suffer imprisonment for life.*

Substantially the same penalties awaited the layman who should ridicule the new form of worship, menace the clergy for adhering to it, or prevail on them to use any other.†

These enactments established that saddest, most illogical of farces, a Protestant Inquisition. It was the gospel turning persecutor. Religion attempted the *rôle* of Simon de Montfort.

To hoot such absurd legislation is not necessarily to reject the Liturgy. It would not be proper to force the Bible itself into unwilling hands by statute. The attempt to do this in England, in a certain sense wrecked the Liturgy before it was fairly launched. Nothing prejudices like compulsion. Thumb-screws and stocks are the most miserable of proselyters. This the history of the Inquisition proves. The most persuasive of preach-

* Statutes of the Realm, vol. 4, pp. 37, 38.

† Statutes, ut antea.

ers is liberty—the ability to accept or reject, as reason dictates. This the history of the nineteenth century demonstrates.

A reign of terror was now inaugurated. All who ventured to dissent from the governmental orthodoxy were proscribed, outlawed, or burned.* Conscientious men were transmuted into hypocrites by forced abjurations; or else, if they persisted in their creed, they were executed as contumacious heretics.

Among the victims of this unhappy persecution history has preserved the name of poor Joan of Kent, a maid who "maintained that Christ was not incarnate of the Virgin Mary, whose flesh being sinful, he could not partake of it; but the Word, by the consent of the inward man in the Virgin, took flesh of her." These were her words; a scholastic subtlety not capable of doing much mischief, and far from deserving so severe a punishment.†

Cranmer himself, the chief instigator of Joan's martyrdom,‡ had been by turns a papist, a Lutheran, and a Sacramentarian. In every change he was guilty of inexcusable severities. His own variations should have taught him to be more tender of the lives of those who rejected the governmental *dictum*.§

* Burnet, Fuller, Newell, Neale, etc.

† Neale, vol. 1, p. 36.

‡ Edward was disposed to pardon Joan, but "Cranmer at length overruled his objections. The king, as he put his name to the warrant, wept, and said to the archbishop, 'If I do wrong, it is in submission to your authority; you shall answer God first.'" Burnet, vol. 2, p. 112.

§ Neale, vol. 1, p. 35.

"His actions," says Burnet, "were much censured, as being contrary to the clemency of the gospel; and they were used by papists, who said that it was plain that the reformers were only against burning when they were in fear of it themselves."*

When the woful persecutions of the Marian era are pilloried in history, ought the example of king Edward's reformatory *régime* to be forgotten? The princess Mary herself would have been punished for non-conformity, had it not been for the active interference of Charles V.† Tumults everywhere occurred. Insurrection raised its hydra-head. "The new Liturgy did not sit well on the minds of the country people, who were for going on in their old way of wakes, processions, and church ales."‡

"Come we now," in the words of Fuller, "to the saddest difference that ever happened in the church of England, if we consider either the time, how long it lasted, the eminent persons therein engaged, or the doleful effects thereby produced. For now non-conformity in the days of king Edward was conceived; which afterwards, in the reign of queen Mary—but beyond sea, at Frankfort—was born; which in the reign of queen Elizabeth was nursed and weaned; which, under king James, grew up a tall stripling; but towards the end of king Charles' reign, shot up to the full strength and stature of a man, able not only to cope with, but to conquer the hierarchy, its adversary."§

* Hist. Ref., vol. 2.

† Newell, p. 83.

‡ Neale, p. 34.

§ Fuller, Ch. Hist., vol. 2, p. 329.

CHAPTER VII.

CHURCH AND STATE.

THE reign of Edward VI. is memorable because in it was cemented the union between church and state. "The Reformation was begun," says Burnet, "and carried on, not by the major part of the bishops and clergy, but by a few selected bishops and divines, who, BEING SUPPORTED BY THE KING'S AUTHORITY,* did frame things as they pleased, and by their interest at court got them to be enacted in Parliament; and after they had removed such bishops as opposed them, then they procured the convocation to submit to what was done."†

It was in that age the almost universal belief that government could as properly dictate in the realm of ethics as in civil affairs. Precedents were found in the Jewish state and in the Roman empire. When the clergy of Edward's day opened

* Strype says, "The papists cried out against Edward's doings, as being done in his minority, and done by others, the chief men about him. They would ordinarily say, 'Tush, this year will not tarry; 't is but my lord Protector's and my lord of Canterbury's doings. The king is but a child, and he knows not of it.' To which Latimer would respond, 'I will tell you this, his majesty hath more godly wit and understanding, more learning and knowledge at his age, than twenty of his progenitors that I could name had at any time of their life.'" Eccl. Memorials, vol. 2, p. 38.

† Burnet, vol. 2, Preface, p. 11.

the code of Justinian, they saw that the first law made by Theodosius, when he came to the empire, was, that all should everywhere, under severe pains, adhere to that faith which was received by Damasus bishop of Rome, and by Peter of Alexandria.*

Why then, queried they, may not the king give the like authority to the archbishops of Canterbury and York? They did not doubt the right; it did not even enter into their minds to divorce church and state. The ecclesiastical discipline of Europe at large was settled on that basis. Rome had always meddled with statecraft. The bishops who inaugurated the English Reformation thought that, in this, Protestantism should enact the *rôle* of Rome. So deep-rooted was this belief, that even a century later the stern ploughshare of civil war could not eradicate it. It was left for a brighter epoch and another country to explode the fallacy of "church and state."

In the church of England, Christ's vicar was the king. Under the Reformation the ancient ecclesiastical equipments were largely retained. The respective dioceses were still coextensive with the kingdom.† Cathedrals which had formerly echoed to the chanting of the mass, now resounded with the purer worship of the service-book; and the national church, like the papal church, continued to be supported by tithes gathered from the Channel to the Tweed.‡

* Justinian's Code; cited by Burnet, vol. 2, Preface, p. 11.

† Fuller; Burnet; Strype; Hallam, etc. ‡ Ibid.

While the Reformation retained, in some measure, the paraphernalia of Rome, it parted with the essence of papacy. Up to the reign of Edward VI., "the public services of the church had been, for the most part, said and sung in a language unintelligible to ninety-nine hundredths of the people. Even the Lord's prayer the poor suppliants had been compelled, until recently, to mumble over in Latin, not knowing the meaning of one petition which they uttered; and very many of the priests who officiated at the altars knew scarcely more of what they said or sung than the poor people whom they deluded with their ostentatious ceremonies.

"To gather together the mass-books and primers, cull from them the best bits, translate these into English, and so place in the hands of the people a book of prayer, administration of the sacraments, and other rites and ceremonies, which they could read and understand, and by means of which they could intelligently engage in acts of public worship—to do all these things was indeed a great and most praiseworthy work. It was to take a long and bold step towards reformation. And could the reformers have appreciated the true spirit of Christianity sufficiently to have left this reformed and intelligible service to find friends and to make its way in the world without enforcement by penal enactments, it would have saved their memory and the church of England from many stains, which no human hands can now fully remove.

"The fatal error of the church-and-state reformers was the delusive idea of enforcing *absolute uniformity*. The very title of the act which established the new service-book was, 'An Acte for Uniformity of Service and Administration throughout the Realme.' The attempt to compel unvarying uniformity, the refusal to grant any liberty to worship God otherwise than as the law prescribed—this was the great error of the reformers. In this matter of exact uniformity, the reformers even outran the very papists; for, previous to the passage of this act, there was no absolute uniformity in the English church, but a variety of forms of prayer and communion were tolerated, differing in different sections of the country. As the pope permitted this latitude, so Henry VIII. seems to have allowed the churches to disregard all the popish forms and prayers, and to use such others, even in English, as they preferred. So at least we infer from what Strype says when speaking of the variety which existed in England before the act of uniformity, that 'those who liked not any of these popish forms and Latin prayers, used other English forms, according as their fancies led them.' "*

The obstinate persistence of the government in enforcing uniformity even in non-essential points provoked, in the years 1550 and 1551, the initial controversy from which grew "many and tall branches of mischief."

Among other things, it had been decided to retain the old habits which had been worn by the

* Punchard, vol. 2, pp. 179–181.

Roman clergy in the service of the altar. These vestments were disliked by some of the reformers as the badges of the old serfdom to Rome; by others they were esteemed lightly, because in the minds of the papists they symbolized Latin orthodoxy.*

To this very general feeling John Hooper, a divine who was pronounced by king Edward to be "of great knowledge and deep judgment both in the Scriptures and in profane learning, as also a person of ready utterance and of an honest life,"† was the first to give public voice.

Hooper had quitted England in the latter part of the reign of Henry VIII. "He was residing at Zurich at the time when all Germany was in a flame on account of the Interim, which was a form of worship contrived to keep up the exterior face of popery. Upon this there arose an important question among the Germans concerning the use of indifferent or non-essential things. It was said, if things were indifferent in themselves, they were lawful; and that it was the subject's part to obey when commanded. So the old popish rites were retained on purpose to draw the people more easily back to Romanism.

"Out of this another question arose: whether it was lawful to obey in things indifferent, when it was certain that they had a bad tendency, and were enjoined with an ill design. To which it was re-

* Strype, Burnet, Fuller.

† Edward's Letter to Archbishop Cranmer.

plied, that the designs of legislators were not to be inquired into.

"This created a vast distraction in the country. Some conformed to the Interim; but the major part were firm in their principles, and were turned out of their livings for disobedience. The reformed were for shaking off the relics of popery, at the hazard of all that was dear to them in this world. This was especially the feeling at Zurich, where Hooper was; all were zealous against any compliance with the use of the old rites.

"With these principles, and fresh from the heat of that controversy, Hooper came over to England, and applied himself to preaching and explaining the Scriptures to the people. He was in the pulpit almost every day in the week, and his sermons were so popular that all the churches in which he preached were crowded. His fame soon reached the court, and with Dr. Poguet he was appointed to deliver all the Lent sermons. In May, 1550, Hooper was appointed bishop of Gloucester; but he declined because of the form of the oath of supremacy, and the vestments. The oath, "By God, by the saints, and by the Holy Ghost," Hooper thought impious, since God only ought to be appealed to in an oath. The young king, convinced that this objection was just, struck out the obnoxious words with his own pen. However, the scruple about the vestments was not so easily gotten over. The king and council were disposed to dispense with them; but Ridley and the rest of the bishops, who had worn them, were of another mind, saying the thing was indifferent, and therefore the law ought to be obeyed."*

Hooper's objections were substantially these: that the vestments and ornaments—the rochet, chimere, square cap, and the rest—were mere human inventions, having no countenance in Scripture, but brought into the church when in its most corrupt state, by tradition or custom; that they were not suitable to the simplicity of the Christian religion, and were condemned by the apostle as "beggarly elements;" and especially that they had been invented chiefly to give effect to the pompous and idolatrous celebration of the mass, and were so consecrated in the minds of the ignorant that they were considered essential to the due celebration of religious service. He affirmed his willingness to wear a decent, simple attire, different from the ordinary dress of a layman; but he was not willing to sanction the superstitious notions of the people, that the peculiar habits of the clergy were necessary to the efficacy of religious services, and that no priestly act was of any value unless performed in a priestly dress.†

Ridley was the main spokesman on the other side. He granted that the vestments were "neither things to be regarded as necessary to spiritual health and salvation, nor yet as if without them

* Neale, vol. 1, pp. 39, 40.

† The above summary of Hooper's objections is quoted from Punchard, vol. 2, pp. 195, 196.

the ministry might not be done;" but he argued "that, in matters of rites and ceremonies, custom was a good argument for the continuance of those that had been long used."*

It has been truly said that this argument proved too much; for if the ægis of custom shielded the *vestments*, then why not *all the other* rites and ceremonies—the gloves, the sandals, the mitre, the ring, the crosier, which had been so recently abolished?

This debate, seemingly of small importance, but which contained the germs of Puritanism, raged through two years. At the outset Cranmer was inclined to side with Hooper,† as did John Rogers,‡ Bradford,§ and the larger portion of the reformed clergy;|| but he at length opposed this "puritanical" move, urged thereto by his determination to enforce conformity even in trifles.

An appeal was taken to the famous continental reformers, Bucer and Martyr, then resident in England.¶ Both of these substantially agreed with Hooper; but in obedience to authority and to restore peace, they counselled submission. This also was the advice of the Genevan doctors, who, grieved that so eminent and learned a preacher should be silenced, urged him to comply, that he might be the

* Bradford, Writings, p. 375. † Neale, p. 41.

‡ Fuller, Church History, vol. 4, p. 62.

§ Bradford, Writings, p. 22.

|| Brook, Lives of the Puritans, Introduction, vol., 1, p. 9.

¶ Chapter 6, p. 81.

more capable, by his authority and influence in the church, of inaugurating a reformation.*

Hooper was long unwilling to obey, and his stiffness provoked his persecution. He was silenced, then committed to the custody of Cranmer, and finally thrown into Fleet prison, where, to the scandal of the Reformation, he lay for several months.†

At length the king determined to dispense with the vestments in Hooper's case, and his consecration was ordered to proceed. But so great was the reluctance of the bench of bishops to acknowledge themselves foiled, that the business dragged through six months after the royal order. Nor was it then settled without a compromise; Hooper consenting to wear the vestments at the ceremony of his consecration, on condition that he should be permitted to dispense with them ever after.‡

In after years both Ridley and Cranmer came to agree cordially with Hooper's estimate of the vestments; for Fox records that when in Mary's reign the papists, in their ceremony of Ridley's degradation from the priesthood, desired him to array himself in these very vestments, he refused; nor would he even put on the surplice, which they were themselves obliged to do, "with all the trinkets pertaining to the mass. And as they put it on, Ridley did vehemently inveigh against the Romish bishop, *and all that foolish apparel*, calling the pope

* Neale, vol. 1, p. 41. † Ibid., p. 42.
‡ Burnet, vol. 2, p. 218.

Antichrist, and the habit foolish and abominable, yea, too formal for a vice in a play, too ridiculous for a buffoon in a comedy."*

So when Bonner stripped off the vestments which had been placed on Cranmer, in order to degrade him preparatory to his martyrdom, he replied, "All this needeth not; I had myself done with this gear long ago."†

The "vestment controversy" was quieted in 1551. In that same year the articles which composed the doctrine of the English church were carefully revised;‡ and some things which had been incorporated in the original draft, in compliance with common prejudice, but against the convictions of the reformers, were now dashed out.§ In 1552 the convocation assented to the "Thirty-nine Articles" which form the basis of Episcopacy.‖ Under Elizabeth some of the articles were put into more general words,¶ but no essential alterations were made, and the service-book stands now almost precisely as it stood after Cranmer and Ridley had new-modelled it in the middle of the sixteenth century.**

* Fox, Acts, etc., vol. 3, p. 427.

† Fox, Acts, etc., vol. 3, p. 558. ‡ Burnet, vol. 2, p. 218.

§ Lathbury says, "There were various changes in the arrangement of the book; several rubrics were altered or omitted, and some were added; certain ornaments were enjoined in the first book which were dispensed with in the second; 'no copes or other vestures were required, but the surplice only.'" Lathbury. pp. 32, 35. ‖ Burnet, Records, No. 55.

¶ Ibid., Hist. Ref.

** Punchard, vol. 2, p. 214. Lathbury.

One of the marked features of Edward's reign was the honor paid to preaching. "Six eminent preachers were chosen out," says Burnet, "to be the king's preachers in ordinary; two of these were to be always in attendance at court; four were to be sent over England to instruct the people. Their names were Bill, Harley, Pern, Grindal, Bradford, and John Knox, who afterwards kindled the gospel light in the Scottish horizon. These, it seems, were accounted the most zealous and the readiest preachers of that time, and they were thus dispatched as itinerants, to supply the defects of the greater part of the clergy, who were generally very faulty."*

Since the year 1526 an organized club had existed in London, called, "The Association of Christian Brothers," whose object was the circulation of Bibles and religious books. "It was composed," says Froude, "of poor men, chiefly artisans, tradesmen, and a few, a very few, of the clergy; but it was carefully organized, was provided with moderate funds, which were regularly audited; and its paid agents went up and down the country, carrying Testaments and tracts with them, and enrolling in the order all who dared to risk their lives in such a cause."†

In its early years, before Henry VIII. broke with the papacy, the "Association" had a hard struggle for life. Its agents "were hounded from

* Burnet, vol. 2, p. 225.

† Froude, History of England, vol. 2, p. 26.

one place to another, compelled to disguise themselves, to hide their heads in friendly habitations or in the forests, to travel by night, and to resort to various stratagems by day to escape the bishop's hands; and with all their care they were not always able to elude the diligence and activity of their persecutors."*

The pious pen of Fox has traced in quaint old English the romantic stories of several of these pioneer *colporteurs;* and in thrilling interest and humble Christian heroism they glow and throb.†

In the days of Edward VI. the "Association" undoubtedly found it pleasanter sailing; and since their opportunities were broader, their work was probably grander. This was a Bible society and a Tract society; and since it was the first in English history, it deserves grateful remembrance. Could the old "Association" step from its grave three centuries deep, and shake hands with its mammoth descendants on either continent, it might be content to return once more to the tomb with the prayer of Simeon upon its lips, "Now, Lord, lettest thou thy servant depart in peace, for mine eyes have seen the beginning of thy salvation."

But dark days were coming on apace. The "black cloud no bigger than a man's hand" had already risen above the horizon. The fragile and devout young king, forced into unnatural maturity, broke and fell. His reign had been exceed-

* Punchard, vol. 2, p. 152.

† Fox, Acts, etc., vol. 2, pp. 438, 441.

ingly turbulent. His very counsellors had been proved to be traitors; his own uncles died under the hatchet of the headsman.

In July, 1553, Edward VI. expired. A satyr succeeded to Hyperion. With the removal of this royal breakwater, a vile flood of popery swept over England, while above the surging tempest wailed the cry of martyrs, and shrieked the joyous laughter of demoniacs.

CHAPTER VIII.

THE MARIAN EPOCH.

THE death of Edward VI. plunged England into chaos. "Brawls festering to rebellion" had scarred every month of his short reign. Those evils which history, speaking through a dozen familiar French instances and through half as many English, proclaims inseparable from the government of royal minors, were ubiquitous and rampant. The old chroniclers draw woful pictures of the men and manners of that epoch.

Strype makes this record: "How good soever Edward was, and what care soever was taken for the bringing in the knowledge of the gospel and restoring Christ's true religion, the manners of men were very naught, especially of a great sort of them. Among the grandees, and among the lesser noblemen, many were insatiably covetous. The truth of this appears not only in their grasping at the church lands, rents, and plate, but in their raising the rents on tenants, inclosing commons which had been for generations open pasturage for poor men's cattle, perverting of justice by intimidation or bribery, and by hoarding up all the gold they could get. To this pass had covetousness brought the nation, that every man scraped and pillaged from the other; every man would seek another's blood; every man encroached upon his neighbor. Covetousness cut away the large wings of charity, and plucked all to herself. She had clutched all the old gold in England, and much of the new."* Crime went brazen and unpunished; and "above all other vices, the outrageous seas of adultery burst in, and overwhelmed all the world."†

But "below this lowest deep, a lower deep still yawned." Into the "swept and garnished chamber" of the Reformation Satan came again, "with seven other devils worse than himself."

Henry VIII. had fixed it by his will, and had it enacted by Parliament,‡ that, in case of the death of prince Edward without issue, his daughter by Catharine of Aragon, the princess Mary, should succeed to the throne. Should both these die without issue, the sceptre was to be handed to his daughter by Jane Seymour, the princess Elizabeth.§

Henry had previously illegitimatized both Mary and Elizabeth by formal statute;‖ but his eventual decision in their favor was in exact accordance with the capricious character of the headstrong voluptuary.

In point of law, Mary's title to the throne was clean. Nevertheless her right was disputed. She was an open and bitter papist. The reformers feared that infant Protestantism, under such a governess, would be strangled in its cradle. It

* Strype, Eccl. Mems., vol. 2, pp. 131–137. † Ibid.

‡ Statutes, 35 Henry VIII. § Ibid.

‖ Hume, Reign of Henry VIII.

came now to be seen that an absolute supremacy over the consciences of men, lodged in a single person, might be prejudicial as well as beneficial to the gospel tenets.*

Edward, influenced by fear for menaced reform, and worked on by the ambition of Northumberland, his chief counsellor, was won, while resting under broken health, to sign a will settling the crown upon Lady Jane Grey, next in blood after the tabooed princesses, and a woman of rare purity, of singular genius, of profound scholarship, and a zealous adherent of the Reformation.†

To this unlawful testament—for the king was a minor, and therefore incapable of making a legal will—the royal council set their hands. Then, on Edward's death, the treason touched its climax in the coronation of Lady Jane Grey.‡

A variety of circumstances united to defeat the conspiracy. The young queen's relatives were unpopular, and this made the people either coldly indifferent or actively hostile to the new *régime*.§ Then the usurpation was so palpable, that even the most zealous of the reformers were forced to protest. Hooper openly proclaimed Mary to be the rightful heir.‖ Cranmer only half-heartedly opposed her claims.¶ It is impossible to rally the Anglo-Saxon race to the defence of a policy which they perceive

* Neale, vol. 1, p. 50. † Ibid., Fuller, Burnet, etc.
‡ Froude, Hume, Lingard, etc.
§ Burnet, vol. 2, pp. 456–458; Fox, Acts, etc., vol. 3, pp. 11–16.
‖ Neale, vol. 1, p. 53. ¶ Punchard, vol. 2, p. 272.

to be clearly in defiance of their fundamental precepts. There is more terror to an Englishman in the writ of a constable than in a thousand bayonets. The Anglo-Saxon is wedded to the forms of law; often so blindly enamoured of mere forms, that he has no eyes to see substantial law in any justice which is outside of the statute. 'T is the secret of Saxon progress—liberty regulated by law. This was why the "great rebellion" in the next century was only possible because the thinkers of Great Britain, Pym, Hampden, and the rest, had outgrown the monarchy. No war-cry ever stirred a generous people which had not in it much of truth and right.

The nascent government of Lady Jane Grey was seen to be the juggle of Northumberland; so it failed.

After considerable manœuvring, Mary, cordially supported by the Romanist element and reluctantly acquiesced in by the conscientious reformers, was recognized by the royal council, by the citizens of London, by England at large; and four weeks after the decease of her brother, without spilling a drop of blood, she was firmly seated on the throne, with Northumberland's shattered cabal beneath her feet.*

Thus the reddest, dreariest reign in English history began with a bloodless triumph. The Vatican bloodlessly subdued an *émeute;* then smeared the island with martyr gore in profound peace.

* Hume; Lingard; Neale, vol. 1, p. 52.

"No. faith is to be kept with heretics," says Rome. Mary hugged that ugly canon to her cruel heart, and set about illustrating it. Her bigotry had four phases.

When she skulked in Suffolk, a fugitive half-hopeless of the crown, she appealed to the yeomen of that Protestant county for support, assuring them that religion should be left by her, if she obtained her right, upon king Edward's basis.* It was this positive asseveration that won the too credulous Suffolkers to rally to her standard. History affirms that it was through their aid that Mary was eventually placed upon the throne.†

Her first step towards empire was taken on a lie; for a little later, after her acknowledgment, she not only released Bonner, Gardiner, and the rest of the popish bishops from the Tower, but she declared in open council that, "though her own mind was settled in matters of religion, yet she was resolved not to compel others, *save by the preaching of the word;*"‡ thus insinuating that the Roman creed was to be restored, but not by compulsion.

Mary's bigotry was of the nature of an intermittent fever; for nine days' further reflection convinced her that she had not gone far enough. Accordingly she published an inhibition forbidding all preaching without special license. In this document she declared herself to be of "that religion

* Collier, vol. 6, p. 6. Fox, Acts, vol. 3, p. 12. Burnet, vol. 2, p. 475.

† Ibid.

‡ Burnet, vol. 2, p. 490; Fox; Collier.

which she had professed from her infancy;" yet affirmed that "she did not compel any of her subjects to it *till public order should be taken on it.*"*

The inhibition was the first puff of the approaching whirlwind. Ere long the full storm burst. The Protestant pulpits were shackled; and when a delegation of Suffolk men waited upon her majesty, and presumed to remind her of her engagement not to change the basis of the national faith, "the queen checked them for their insolence; and one of their number chancing to mention her promise, he was pilloried for three days and had his ears cut off, for defamation."†

Gardiner and Bonner were restored to their recusant bishoprics. Hooper, Latimer, Rogers, Taylor, and a host of less distinguished worthies, were *bastiled.*‡ Peter Martyr, John à Lasco, and the foreign Protestants were commanded to quit inhospitable Britain;§ and so fierce grew the papist temper of the government, that a swarm of English reformers accompanied them, self-exiled, into foreign parts.||

"Eight weeks and upwards passed," says Fuller, "between the proclaiming of Mary queen and the Parliament by her assembled; during which time two religions were together set on foot, Protestantism and Popery; the former hoping to be contin-

* Collier, vol. 6, p. 12; Neale, Punchard, Lathbury, Fuller.

† Neale, vol. 1, pp. 52, 53.

‡ Ibid.

§ Burnet, vol. 2, p. 493.

|| Fox, Acts, vol. 3, p. 13. Fuller, vol. 2, p. 379.

ued, the latter laboring to be restored. And as the Jews' children, after the captivity, spoke a middle language betwixt Hebron and Ashdod,* so, during the aforesaid *interim*, the churches of England had a mongrel celebration of their divine services, betwixt reformation and superstition."†

Images were set up in various places; and the Latin ritual, though against the still unrepealed laws, was openly used.‡ In August, 1553, Gardiner was commissioned "to license such as *he thought* meet to preach God's word."§ This insured the exclusion of the reformed clergy.

In October, 1553, Mary was crowned by Gardiner, now become keeper of the great seal. The new lord-chancellor was assisted by ten other bishops, all in their mitres, caps, and croziers; and the ceremony was conducted with all the pomp of the Roman ritual.‖

From this time Gardiner became the chief of the reaction; he was to Mary what Cranmer had been to Edward.

A few days after the coronation, Parliament met. This Parliament outdid in servile meanness its base fellows of the reign of Henry VIII. It was packed by new members, elected by bribery and menace;¶ and the old members, yearning for "the flesh-pots of Egypt," were soon dragooned into servility. The

* Neh. 12:24. † Fuller, Ch. Hist., vol. 2, p. 375.

‡ Punchard, vol. 2, p. 277.

§ Burnet, vol. 2, p. 493. Fox, vol. 3, p. 12.

‖ Lingard, Froude, Neale. ¶ Neale, vol. 1, p. 51.

lackey Parliament commenced its work by affirming the lawfulness of Henry's marriage with Catharine of Aragon and Mary's legitimacy. It then proceeded to repeal all the religious enactments of the reign of Henry VIII.; to decree that "there should be no other form of divine service than that which was used in the last year of Henry VIII.," which was a resurrection of the "Six Articles;"* to fulminate severe penalties against such as should deface statues, abuse the sacrament, or break down crucifixes, altars, and crosses; and to make it penal "for any number above twelve to assemble for the purpose of altering the established creed;"† a statute which made the punishment of dissenters easy and legal.

As was the custom in those days, a convocation of the clergy sat with the Parliament; and this likewise was packed with the creatures of the court.‡ Care had been taken to exclude the Protestant divines; nevertheless, when Bonner, who presided, proposed that all subscribe to the dogma of transubstantiation, four members stoutly dissented, and debated the question through three days with such vigor and eloquence that the blustering prolocutor was obliged to cut short the disputation with the acknowledgment, "*You have the word, but we have the sword.*"§

It is not necessary to recite minutely the history of the various civil and ecclesiastical acts which,

* Chap. 5, p. 74.

† Statutes of the Realm, 1 Queen Mary.

‡ Neale, vol. 1, p. 51.

§ Ibid., p. 55.

in the reign of Mary, reconciled England to Rome. Suffice it to say that subsequent Parliaments, seduced by Spanish gold, sanctioned the queen's marriage with Philip II. of Spain;* confirmed Mary's resignation of her title of supreme head of the church to the pope; repealed all acts done since the twentieth year of the reign of Henry VIII. against the pontiff and his supremacy; sued on bended knees for the papal absolution, which was granted by cardinal Pole, the pontifical legate; and revived the barbarous statutes of the second Richard and the fourth and fifth Henries for the execution of heretics by fire.†

The dance of death now began. A *point d'appui* was gained; and those twin jackals of Rome, Gardiner and Bonner, commenced the hunt. Bonner was an ideal Thug; he was the hero of the blackguardism of his time. Gardiner was a keener, more polished knave. "He is to be traced like a fox," said bishop Lloyd; "and like the Hebrew, he must be read backward."‡

Lady Jane Grey and the other actors in the unhappy drama of the usurpation were executed in 1554.§ Sir Thomas Wyat, a Kentish knight who had taken arms to defeat the Spanish match, ascended the scaffold in that same year.|| And now that these political victims were in their graves, the

* Statutes of the Realm, 2 Queen Mary.

† Ibid., 3 Queen Mary. See Burnet, Records, vol. 2.

‡ Cited in Punchard, vol. 2, p. 208.

§ Hume, Reign of Mary, year 1554.

|| Ibid.

government, maddened by this taste of blood, determined to deluge heresy in gore.

A Court of Inquisition was set up.* A bureau of spies was formed.† England was put under *surveillance.* Letters were written to Lord North and others, enjoining them "to put to the torture such obstinate persons as would not abjure."‡

Thus it was that practised Rome dwarfed the clumsy and illogical persecution of the preceding Protestant *régime.* The Reformation stooped to kindle *autos da fé* with awkward, ill-dissembled terror; Rome did it with the graceful nonchalance of an adept.

In order to serve the twofold purpose of rendering them ridiculous and entrapping them in their own words, Cranmer, Ridley, and Latimer were "baited and abused at Oxford, under pretence of debating the sacramental question. They were ordered to appear separately each day before the gathered champions of popery. No conference with each other was allowed; but alone, with only such preparation as could be made within their prison walls, each was bidden to dispute on themes drawn up by their subtle enemies."§ A pimp named Weston, the congenial chaplain of Bonner, was procurator of this tumultuous assembly; and Fox tells us that the drunken bloat sat with "his tippling-cup at his elbow all the time of the disputation."||

* Hume, vol. 2, p. 697.
† Ibid.
‡ Punchard, vol. 2, pp. 287, 288.
§ Ibid.
|| Fox, vol. 8, p. 70.

It was no part of the design to secure a fair debate; accordingly these eminent men were hooted and pelted and insulted *ad libitum* by the vulgar crowd of Roman clergy. "There was great disorder, perpetual shoutings, tauntings, and reproaches," says Ridley in his account of the pitiable farce, "so that it looked like a stage rather than a school of divines."*

Yet despite the disadvantage under which they labored, the reformers "obliged the Romanists to avow that, according to their doctrine, Christ had, in his last supper, held himself in his hand, and swallowed and eaten himself."†

"Cranmer and Ridley were so hissed and derided, Latimer was so borne down by noise and clamor," that they all refused to dispute again. This gave the papists the desired opportunity; they declared the champions of the Reformation to be vanquished, and called upon them to recant. This of course all three refused to do. They were remanded to prison, and bidden to prepare for death.‡

In the following year, 1555, the government lighted an *auto da fé.* Hooper, Rogers, and Cardmaker, who had lain in prison for eighteen months without law, were taken out to be burned.

Rogers was the first martyr in the Marian death-dance. On the morning of the fourth of February he was ordered to be burned at Smithfield, an old

* Burnet, vol. 2, p. 562. † Hume, vol. 2, p. 685.
‡ Neale, vol. 1, pp. 56, 57.

suburb of London, and famous since the days of Wickliffe as the ghastly *rendezvous* of the fire goblins. The very memory of this quaint old suburb was long a terror. For a hundred years the Lollard had heard the word "Smithfield" only to shudder. Now the reformers listened to it, and felt their very flesh crawl. Smithfield was the torture-spot of Britain. It was as horrible to the island as the frightful prison of the "Bridge of Sighs" was to mediæval Venice. It was the fiery grave of "heresy."

It was to this spot that old John Rogers was led to die.

That morning crowds might have been seen gathering to gaze on a spectacle with which many had become sadly familiar. In an open space, in the midst of an old inclosure then devoted to the work of murder, stood the cruel pile, amply supplied with fagots, surrounded by barriers, and by officers armed to keep back the surging populace.

The tenements in a street then called Long-lane, built on both sides for "brokers and tipplers," yielded their contribution of thoughtless and profane idlers. Grave and more respectable citizens were wending their way through old Giltspur-street and other avenues, while from the windows of the fair inns and other comely buildings which adorned with their picturesque architecture the western side of ancient Smithfield, many a face looked out upon the dense masses in front of the church of Bartholomew Priory, whose tottering wooden steeple still rose to heaven, the memorial of a monastic house which, before the dissolution of abbeys in the time of Henry VIII., had stood there in its pomp and pride, one of the noblest architectural ornaments of London.

Suddenly there was a stir; some officers pressed through the throng, and, close to the stake, repeated a proclamation which had been already announced by placards on the city walls, near the archway of frowning Newgate prison, forbidding any one, under pain of imprisonment, to speak a word to the forthcoming martyr.

A band of serious persons yonder, standing close together, listened to these words with deep emotion, as men who had come to sympathize with the holy sufferer, and who were resolved that the expression of their sentiments by glance and countenance at least should not be enchained by the merciless edict.

Another stir announced the approach of the victim. A deep hush fell upon the multitude; while clear, serene, almost joyous, a sweet voice was heard reciting the fifty-first psalm: "Have mercy upon me, O God, according to thy loving-kindness: according unto the multitude of thy tender mercies blot out my transgressions. Wash me thoroughly from mine iniquity, and cleanse me from my sin. For I acknowledge my transgressions, and my sin is ever before me. Against thee, thee only, have I sinned, and done this evil in thy sight; that thou mightest be justified when thou speakest, and be clear when thou judgest. Make me to hear joy and gladness; that the bones which thou hast broken may rejoice. Create in me a clean heart, O God; and renew a right spirit within me. Cast me not away from thy presence; and take not thy Holy Spirit from me. Restore unto me the joy of thy salvation; and uphold me with thy free Spirit. Then will I teach transgressors thy ways; and sinners shall be converted unto thee. O Lord, open thou my lips, and my mouth shall show forth thy praise. Do good in thy good pleasure unto Zion: build thou the walls of Jerusalem. Then shalt thou be pleased with the sacrifices of righteousness, with burnt-offering and whole burnt-offering."

As these striking words resounded over Smithfield-square, the solemn stillness grew threefold more silent, while with intense interest all eyes were fixed upon the placid martyr.

He was quickly bound to the fatal stake; and just before the fagots were kindled, he was urged to recant, bidden to remember his wife and ten children, left wholly unprovided for, and promised a pardon as the reward of apostasy. John Rogers, for it was he, was firm. "God will care for my children," said he. The flames were then started. Higher, higher they leaped and laughed and crackled; while from the centre of the livid horror Rogers continued to exhort and "wash his hands in the fire," till God ended all, and took him to himself.*

The impression was deep and lasting. Men heaved a sigh; and as they turned from the scene

Burnet, Hist. Ref., vol. 2, pp. 385, 386; Fuller, Fox, etc.

in Smithfield, they mused on it in their heart of hearts. Often had the praise of heroism been there bestowed on some proud knight as he bore his lance in tilt and tournay, while his name had been inscribed with honor in the rolls of chivalry. But the praise of an infinitely nobler heroism belonged to this Christian martyr. His name was emblazoned on no herald's roll; but it was written in the book of God's remembrance: and he "shall be mine, saith the Lord, in the day that I make up my jewels."*

Five days after the martyrdom of Rogers, Hooper was burned at Gloucester, in his old bishopric.† He was not suffered to address the people; but no brutal *dictum* could prevent his addressing God. This he did with great fervor. When the flames were kindled, the wood was found to be green, so that the victim was "nigh three quarters of an hour in burning to death."‡ His legs and thighs were roasted, and one of his hands dropped off before he expired.§ But no racking pain could shake his serene trust; his last words were, "Lord Jesus, receive my spirit."‖

Some months later John Bradford, one of the most lovable and beautiful characters in ecclesiastical history, of whom it is said that his prison letters were grander even than his sermons,¶ ascend-

* Stoughton, Heroes of Puritan Times, pp. 17–20.

† Burnet, vol. 2, p. 386.

‡ Ibid.

§ Ibid. Neale, vol. 1, p. 69.

‖ Ibid.

¶ Fox, Acts, etc., vol. 3, pp. 232–300. Fox's account of Bradford is singularly full and affectionate.

ed into heaven in a chariot of fire. When he came to the stake at Smithfield, says Burnet, "Bradford fell down and prayed. Then he kissed the stake, and likewise took a fagot in his hand and kissed that, expressing thereby the joy he had in his sufferings; and he cried, "Oh, England, repent, repent; beware of idolatry and false antichrists!" But the sheriff hindering him from speaking any more, he embraced a fellow-sufferer, and prayed him to be of good cheer, for they should sup with Christ that night. His last words were, 'Strait is the way and narrow is the gate that leadeth into eternal life, and few there be that find it.'"*

From smoking Smithfield the *autos da fé* broaden over England. In the months of June and July of this same black year of 1555, "eight men and one woman," says Neale, "were burned in Kent; and in the months of August and September, twenty-five more suffered in Suffolk, Essex, and Surry. In October, Ridley and Latimer were martyred at one stake in Oxford. Latimer died presently; but Ridley was a long time in exquisite torments, his lower limbs being consumed before the flames reached his body. His last words to Latimer were, "Be of good heart, brother; for God will either assuage the fury of the flame, or enable us to abide it." And Latimer responded with characteristic vigor, "Be of good comfort; for we shall this day light such a candle in England as, I trust, by God's grace shall never be put out."†

* Burnet, vol. 2, pp. 401, 402. † Neale, vol. 1, p. 62.

It has been said that on this very same day Gardiner, the chief persecutor, was struck with sudden illness, which held him in great agony through thirty days, when he expired.* "He would not sit down to dinner till he had received news from Oxford of the burning of Latimer and Ridley, which came not till four in the afternoon; and while at dinner, he was seized with the distemper which ended his life."†

Burnet writes this eulogy upon Latimer and Ridley: "The one, for his piety, learning, and solid judgment, was held the ablest man of all that advanced the Reformation; and the other, for the plain simplicity of his life, was esteemed the model of a truly primitive bishop and Christian."‡

In March, 1556, Cranmer expiated his cruel abuse of power when he controlled the destiny of England, by meeting himself that martyrdom which he had awarded to others. Petty bickerings about the succession to his see of Canterbury had preserved his life thus far. Gardiner and Pole both desired it;§ now, since the death of Gardiner, every moment lost was an opportunity for misfortune. Accordingly it was decided to burn the broken and imprisoned ecclesiastic.‖ By much persuasion, and hoping thus to save his life, Cranmer had signed a paper abjuring his belief. "This was

* Neale, vol. 1, p. 62.

† Ibid. Other writers deny this version of Gardiner's death; but Neale's account is sustained by Burnet, vol. 2. pp. 409, 410

‡ Burnet, vol. 2, pp. 408, 409.

§ Ibid., pp. 418-425.

‖ Neale, vol. 1, p. 62.

quickly published to the world, with great triumph among the papists and exceeding grief to the reformers. But the unmerciful queen was still resolved to have his life. Accordingly she sent down a writ for his execution. She could never forgive him for the share he had taken in her mother's divorce,* and in driving the Pope's authority out of England. Cranmer, suspecting this design before the warrant came down, prepared a true confession of his faith, which he carried in his bosom to St. Mary's church on the day of his martyrdom.

"Here he was raised on an eminence, that he might be seen by the people while he listened to his own funeral sermon. Never was there a more melancholy spectacle; an archbishop, once the second man in the kingdom, now clothed in rags, and a gazing-stock to the vulgar multitude.

"Cole, the Romanist preacher, magnified Cranmer's recent conversion as the immediate hand of God, and turning towards his penitent, assured him that many masses for the salvation of his soul should be said. After the sermon, the archbishop was requested to declare his own faith; which he did with tears, professing his belief in the holy Scriptures and in the Apostles' creed. He then came to that which, he said, had troubled his conscience more than any thing else which he had done in his life, and that was, the subscription of his abjuration. This was done out of a fear of death and a love of life; therefore he affirmed his determination, when

* Chap. 4.

he came to the fire, of burning first the hand which had subscribed the paper."

The assembly broke up in confusion and disappointment; and the venerable and heart-broken prelate was led, shedding abundant tears, to the stake. On being tied to it, he did indeed stretch out his right hand to the flame, never moving it but once, to wipe his face, till it dropped off. He often cried out, "Oh that unworthy hand, that unworthy hand." And his last words, like Hooper's, were, "Lord Jesus, receive my soul."*

But this volume is not a martyrology; it is not therefore within its scope to go further into these sad details. Besides, it were needless to do so; for we may say with Fuller, that "this point hath been already handled so curiously and copiously by John Fox, that his industry herein hath starved the endeavors of such as shall succeed him, leaving nothing for their pens to feed upon. 'For what can the man do that cometh after the king? even that which hath been already done,' saith Solomon.† And Mr. Fox appearing sole emperor in this subject, all posterity may despair to add any remarkable discoveries which have escaped his observation. Wherefore, to handle this subject after him, what is it but to light a candle to the sun? or rather, to borrow a metaphor from his book, to kindle one single stick to the burning of so many fagots."‡

Suffice it then to say, that intolerance, without

* Neale, vol. 1, pp. 62, 63.

† Eccles. 2:12.

‡ Fuller, vol. 3, p. 390.

a gleam of charity, brooded over England. It has been claimed that cardinal Pole, the cousin of the queen, was opposed to the Sorbonne policy of guiding the erring by the fagot and the stake.* If it be so, "he showed the tameness of his spirit in this: that being against cruel proceedings with heretics, he did not more openly profess it; besides, he suffered both the other bishops to go on, and even in Canterbury, now sequestered in his hands and soon after put under his care, he left the martyrs to the cruelties of the brutal and fierce popish clergy."†

The fact is, that Rome can only be consistent when she persecutes. Three things force her to do so: she claims to be infallible; she denies salvation to heretics; she claims the subserviency of the civil powers as the ministers of her imperious will.

Consequently, "with Rome persecution has not been an accidental circumstance; it is the natural expression of her spirit, the consistent outgrowth of her principles. Other churches have fallen into the temptation of employing coercion in spite of their system; but hers has been a throne of iniquity which 'frameth mischief by a law.' The Protestant has fancied that he *might* persecute, the Romanist was persuaded that he *must.* The sword trembled in the hands of the reformer; it was grasped with terrible energy by the papist. It is inconsistent for Protestantism to persecute; it is

* Lingard. Hume, vol. 2, p. 693. † Burnet, vol. 2, p. 418.

inconsistent for Rome not to harry and bleed and kill."*

Still this very reign of Mary proves persecution to be impolitic, as well as unjust and unchristian. It did not choke heresy. On the contrary, the dissenting sects grew more militant—gained ground. "A sort of instinctive reasoning," says Hallam, "taught the people what the learned on neither side had been able to discover, that the truth of a religion begins to be very suspicious when it stands in need of prisons and scaffolds to eke out its evidences. Many are said to have become Protestants under Mary who, at her coming to the throne, had retained the contrary persuasion."†

Thus it should seem that the throttled truth still found proselytes, even under this fanatic government. "Be not deceived; God is not mocked." All were not devils, even in the pandemonium of this black, midnight reign.

* Stoughton, pp. 25, 26.

† Hallam, Const. Hist. Eng., vol. 2, pp. 104, 105.

CHAPTER IX.

THE EXILES.

PURITANISM, born in the reign of Edward, was nursed in the reign of Mary.

It will be remembered that, in the dawn of the Marian persecution, many "good men and true" quitted Britain, self-banished to the Continent.* Some passed into France; some settled in the friendly cities of Flanders; a few found refuge under the hospitable crags of republican Switzerland; others sought homes in the free towns of reformed Germany; and of these last the greater part came to reside in Frankfort-on-the-Maine.†

There the exiles were cordially received; the honest burghers vied with each other in the provision of suitable employment; and the Huguenot pastor of a French refugee church, drawn by the tie of a kindred misfortune, hastened to invite the English Protestants to share the chapel which the municipal government had kindly opened for their worship.‡

This arrangement was eventually sanctioned by the city senate through the active kindness of one of the senators, and it was agreed that the English should use the Huguenot chapel alternately with

* Chapter 8, p. 106.

† Troubles at Frankfort; Neale; Fuller; Burnet, etc.

‡ Ibid.

the French; but to avoid all occasion for bickering on forms, the grant was accompanied by this proviso, that all should assent to the French doctrine and ceremony,* based essentially on Calvinism.

After consultation, the English refugees assented to these conditions, although they necessitated a departure from their established ritual; and soon after they settled quietly and happily in the old "White Lady church," which had been originally a cloister dedicated to "the blessed Mary Magdalen."†

The exiles had arrived in Frankfort in June, 1554. By the middle of July all these preliminaries were arranged, and on the last Sunday of the month they held their maiden service. It was in some respects unique. Responses were interdicted. The Litany, surplice, and other ceremonies in service and sacraments, were omitted, both as "superfluous and superstitious." Instead of the English Confession, another, more appropriate to their banishment, was used. After the Confession, a psalm in metre was sung. A prayer succeeded the hymn; and that was followed by a sermon. The service was concluded by a general prayer for all states, and especially for England ending with the Lord's prayer, by a rehearsal of the old articles of belief, by another hymn, and the benediction.‡

So radical was the departure from the English

* Fuller, vol. 2, p. 407.

† Knox, Hist. Ref. Brook, Lives of the Puritans.

‡ Troubles at Frankfort; Fuller, etc.

ritual of the refugee congregation of Frankfort *Puritans.*

It has been well said, that "the communion of saints" never account themselves peaceably possessed of any happiness until, if it be within their power, they have also made their fellow-sufferers partakers thereof. Accordingly the innovating church wrote urgent and affectionate letters to the neighboring English congregations, inviting all to join them at Frankfort.* These missives were sent to Emboden, to Strasburg, to Zurich; and in them the reformers commended their new-modelled service, as approaching much closer to the primitive form than did king Edward's ritual.†

The Strasburg divines demurred; the Protestants at Basle exhibited no inclination to accede; the churchmen at Zurich refused to come.‡ Still, "let none say that Frankfort might as well come to Zurich as Zurich to Frankfort; for Frankfort was near England, and more convenient for receiving intelligence thence and for returning it thither. Besides, all Christendom met at Frankfort twice a year, the vernal and the autumnal mart; and grant that there was more learning at Zurich, there were more books at Frankfort, with greater conveniences for advancing in study. But chiefly at Frankfort the congregation enjoyed most ample privileges; and it was conceived that it would much enure to the credit and comfort of the English church if the

* Troubles at Frankfort; Fuller, Neale, Newell.

† Neale, vol. 1, p. 68. ‡ Fuller, vol. 2, pp. 408, 409.

dispersed handfuls of their exiles were bound up in one sheaf, united in one congregation, 'where they might serve God in purity of faith and integrity of life, having both doctrine and discipline free from any mixture of superstition.'"*

Strengthened by these reflections, and grieved, but not discouraged by the equivocal sympathy of the surrounding English churches, the *Puritans* of Frankfort walked in their chosen path; and casting their eyes towards Geneva, they selected stout John Knox, an exile from Britain like themselves, to be their minister.† "Let not men account it incongruous," says Fuller, "that, among so many able and eminent English divines, a Scotchman should be made pastor of the English church, seeing that Knox's reputed merit did naturalize him, though a foreigner, for any Protestant congregation."‡

Knox had hardly been installed ere a new difficulty arose. Those refugee congregations which adhered to the Established ritual refused to fellowship their non-conforming brothers in the faith.§ Grieved and anxious, the *Puritan* congregation forwarded the Liturgy to Calvin at Geneva for his judgment.‖ They had previously informed the conforming churches at Strasburg and at Zurich, when urged to model their church exactly after king Edward's ritual, that they did make no slight use of

* Fuller, vol. 2, pp. 408, 409.

† Knox, Hist. Ref., p. 84. McCrie's Life of Knox, vol. 1.

‡ Fuller, vol. 2, p. 410.

§ Newell, p. 100. Burnet, Fuller, Neale. Troubles at Frankfort.

‖ Ibid.

the service-book, but that, "as for certain unprofitable ceremonies, though some of them were tolerable, yet being in a strange country, and therefore free to choose, they could not submit to them, and indeed they thought it better that they should never be practised."*

Ere long Calvin's verdict arrived at Frankfort. "In the Liturgy of England," said he, "I see that there is not that purity which were to be desired. Those imperfections which could not at the outset be amended, were, since there was therein no manifest impiety, for a season retained and tolerated. It was lawful to *begin* with such rudiments, or *a-be-ce-daries;* but now it behooves the learned, grave, and godly ministers of Christ to enterprise further, and to set forth something more filed from rust, and purer."†

This letter caused some debate; but finally it was agreed to retain the larger portion of the Established ritual, and to add whatever might seem appropriate to the fluctuating state of the refugee church;‡ at the same time it was decided to refer all future disputes to the arbitration of Calvin, Musculus, Martyr, Bullinger, and Viret.§

So stood affairs at Frankfort when, in March, 1555, the harmony was rudely jarred by the arrival of Dr. Richard Cox, "a man of a high spirit, of deep learning, unblamable life, and of great credit

* Neale, vol. 1, p. 68.

† Calvin; cited in Fuller, vol. 2, p. 411.

‡ Knox, Hist. Ref., p. 31.

§ Ibid., p. 51.

among his countrymen, for he had been tutor unto Edward VI.," but who had been exiled under Mary's rule.

Cox had been prominent in the compilation of the English service-book;* naturally, therefore, he did not look with any favor on the Frankfort innovations; nay, he determined either to remould into conformity, or to destroy what he considered the mushroom ceremonies of the refugee congregation.

Accordingly he went, accompanied by a corps of equally zealous colleagues, one Sunday into the "White Lady church," and contrary to the settled order of procedure, answered aloud after the minister.† When admonished, he replied that he should do as he had been wont to do in England, and he further declared that the Frankfort church should have the face of an English congregation.‡

On the succeeding Sunday a still ruder breach of decorum occurred. One of Cox's company ascended the pulpit, and without the previous consent or knowledge of the church, intoned the entire Liturgy, while the interlopers in the pews responded aloud.§ This was in the morning; in the afternoon Knox sternly rebuked this insolence, which he said it "became not the proudest of them all to have attempted."||

Many animosities and intermediate bickerings between the two parties may well be omitted, espe-

* Newell, p. 101, note. Burnet.
† Troubles at Frankfort. Fuller. ‡ Ibid. Newell, p. 101.
§ Ibid. || Knox, Hist. Ref., p. 51.

cially at one conference, wherein Cox is charged with having come with his argument *ab auctoritate, Ego volo habere.** Knox's adherents finding themselves disturbed and ill-used, "got one voice on their side stronger and louder than all the rest, the authority of the senate of Frankfort. That magistrate who had befriended the refugees and procured them the chapel, announced that if the reformed order of the congregation were not observed, 'as he had opened the church door unto them, so would he shut it again.'"†

Beaten at fair weapons, the Coxians resorted to mean ones. They accused Knox of high treason against the emperor of Germany in this, that in an English pamphlet, entitled, "An Admonition to Christians," printed some years before in Britain, he had affirmed the emperor to be "no less an enemy to Christ than Nero."‡ The senate, alarmed—for Frankfort was "an imperial city, highly concerned to be tender of the emperor's honor"—requested Knox to quit the town, which, in March, 1556, he did, to the great grief of his congregation.§ "Strange," moralizes Fuller, "that words spoken years before, in another land and language, against the emperor, to whom Knox owed no natural allegiance—though since a casual and accidental one, by his removal into an imperial city—should, in this unhappy juncture, be urged against him by

* Fuller, vol. 2, p. 412. "By authority, I will have it so."

† Troubles at Frankfort, p. 40.

‡ Ibid. Knox, Hist. Ref. McCrie, Life of Knox. § Ibid.

exiles of his own religion, even to no less than the endangering of his life. Such too often is the badness of good people, that, in the heat of passion, they account any play to be fair-play which tends to the overthrow of those with whom they contend."*

Having now gotten rid of the chief obstacle to their programme, the jubilant Coxians at once proceeded to set up the service-book, which the magistrates permitted; they next ignored the old church officers, and elected new ones, and they crowned their reconstruction by the appointment of another pastor.†

The *Puritans* protested in vain; and the successful party refused to refer all difficulties to the arbitration of the reformed divines, "because, being already possessed of the power, they would not divest themselves of the whole to receive but part again from the courtesy of others. However, they lost much reputation by the refusal; for in all controversies, that side recusant to submit its claims to a fair arbitration, contracts the just suspicion either that their cause is faulty, or that its managers are froward and morose."‡

Yet, notwithstanding their determination to invoke no outside decision, the Coxians wrote Calvin, and urged him to sanction their proceedings, which of course he refused to do; on the contrary, "after a modest excuse for refusing to meddle in their affairs, he told them that, in his opinion, they were

* Fuller, vol. 2, p. 412. † Troubles at Frankfort, p. 52.
‡ Fuller, vol. 2, p. 414.

too much addicted to the English ceremonies; nor could he see to what purpose it was to burden the church with hurtful and offensive things, when there was liberty to have a simpler, purer service. He blamed their conduct towards Knox, which he said was neither godly nor brotherly; and he concluded by urging them to prevent divisions among themselves."*

Vainly did the great divine cry peace from Switzerland. "There was no peace."

With many tears the old congregation quitted Frankfort, and separated, some tarrying at Basle, others pressing on to Geneva, where a new church was formed under Knox, which "lived in great harmony and love until the storm of persecution blew over, at the death of Mary."† Those who had acted this unjust part at Frankfort did not find peace restored by the departure of the "come-outers." New tares were sown, and the church was fretted by endless contentions. But Cox, leaving the strife unmedicined, passed on, and provided himself with a less expensive abiding place.‡

These troubles were the earliest, infant cry of Puritanism; and we have gone thus into detail because "the pen-knives of that age grew into the swords of an older epoch."

When the Coxians flung after the dissenting party the epithet "schismatics," there arose a dispute as to whether that name could be applicable

* Neale, vol. 1, p. 70.

† McCrie, Life of Knox, vol. 1. p. 157. ‡ Ibid.

to those who, agreeing in doctrine, dissented only in superfluous ceremonies.* Some boldly affirmed that the reformers of king Edward's reign had no thought that they had settled definitively the ecclesiastical canons of the English church. It was said that the fathers of the English Reformation regarded their work as merely initiatory; and the opinions of Cranmer, Hooper, Latimer, and Ridley were cited in proof.† The assertion was openly made that these eminent theologians recognized but two orders of clergy as *jure-divino*—*bishops* or *ministers*, and *deacons*;‡ that Hooper, in his letter to Bullinger, in February, 1548, said, "The archbishop of Canterbury, and the bishops of Rochester, Ely, St. David's, and Lincoln, were sincerely set on advancing the purity of doctrine, *agreeing in all things with the Helvetic churches*;"§ that the churches of Dutch, French, German, and Italian Protestants, by whom the Reformation had been carried far beyond England, were encouraged by Cecil and by Cranmer, while the king granted them letters-patent "freely and quietly to use their own peculiar ecclesiastical discipline, *notwithstanding they do not agree with the rites and ceremonies now used in Great Britain*,"‖ and that the acts of the individual reformers showed that their object was not to anchor so near to Rome in outward observances, but to find harbor at a greater distance from the formulas of Latin ortho-

* Fuller, vol. 2, p. 414.

† Punchard, vol. 2, ch. 7, passim.

‡ Ibid.

§ Burnet, vol. 3, p. 201.

‖ Ibid.

doxy, as witness Hooper's position in the "vestment controversy," and Ridley's injunctions to his diocese in 1550.*

To crown all, it was urged that Martyr, Bucer, Fagius, and Tremellius, the eminent oriental scholar, all expressed views opposed to the existing Establishment; that Knox, an open non-conformist, received his salary as a royal chaplain till Edward's death; that all these thinkers regarded the Reformation as progressive; that upon their learning and judgment great reliance was placed throughout king Edward's reign; and that they all advocated a further departure from the state ritual towards apostolic simplicity.†

The opposite party held these views to be chimerical, stamped them as the idle or malicious tales of ignorant tradition, and believed, with a recent distinguished churchman, that "the work of the reformers was to restore, not to destroy; and that they intentionally stopped at that point at which they believed their object would be accomplished."‡

So early did the two great parties in the English church, the Progressives and the Conservatives, encamp on their respective theories. Even in banishment the champions on either side began to arm.

But "it may be inquired how these exiles were maintained, considering the vast numbers of them, and the poverty of many. God stirred up the

* Burnet, vol. 3, p. 305. † Newell, p. 85.
‡ Lathbury, pp. 120, 121.

bowels of the abler sort, both in England and in those parts where they sojourned, to pity and relieve them by very liberal contributions conveyed unto them from time to time. From London especially came often very large allowances; till Gardiner, who had his spies everywhere, got knowledge of it; when, by casting these benefactors into prison, and finding means to impoverish them, that channel of charity was in a great measure stopped. After this, the senators at Zurich, at the instance of Bullinger their superintendent, opened their treasures to them. Besides, those great ornaments of religion and learning, Calvin, Melancthon, Gualtier, Lavater, and others, sent them daily most comfortable letters, and omitted no duty of love and humanity to them throughout their banishment. Some of the persons of wealth and estate sent also their benevolences, among the rest the duke of Wittemburg, who gave at one time to the exiled English at Strasburg four hundred dollars, in addition to a larger sum previously given at Frankfort."*

But all did not subsist on charity. At Geneva, "a club of them" employed themselves in translating the Bible into English.† At Basle, "many poor scholars made shift to live in these hard times" by their peculiar care and diligence in correcting proof for the eminent printers of that city,‡

* Strype, Life of Cranmer, vol. 1, p. 519.

† Newell, p. 103. Fuller, vol. 2, p. 421.

‡ Humphrey, Life of Jewel, p. 87.

over which the shadow of Faust's printing-press seemed to rest.

But the hours even of the dreariest exile will pass. The year 1558 opened the hospitable continental prison-house. One morning the news of Mary's death flashed over Europe. If Rome heard it aghast, the Reformation heard it with hope. The refugees hastened to lay down the half-read proof-sheet, to close their open books, and with many a *vale* they set out for home.

CHAPTER X.

THE MAIDEN QUEEN.

ENGLAND awoke from her nightmare with a shudder and in a chill. The dizzy terror was passed. Men drew a long breath and heaved a sigh. Mary Tudor found few to regret her.* Her reign had been as disastrous in its foreign politics as in its domestic government. The people, ominously sullen, growled and muttered. The nobles were dissatisfied. Parliament had long been alienated from the court; its members had marked the determination of the queen to surrender the kingdom at discretion to Rome, her anxiety to elevate the clergy into undue importance, and the fierceness of her bloody faith.†

Troubled by these symptoms of royal fanaticism, Parliament peered doubtfully into the portentous future; England at large fretted and shuddered. Consequently the report of "Bloody Mary's" death occasioned only the most ghastly semblance of woe. Indeed Britain could hardly restrain a

* Mary died November 17, 1558, in her forty-third year, and in the sixth year of her reign. Her marriage with Philip II. had no issue. This increased the fierceness of her temper, and made her fret herself into the grave. "She was a princess of severe principles, and little given to diversions. She did not mind any branch of the government so much as the church, being entirely at the disposal of her clergy, and forward to sanction all their cruelties." Neale, vol. 1, p. 75.

† Burnet, vol. 2, p. 411.

shout of exultation. The masses, overlooking their theological disputes, expressed general and unfeigned joy that the sceptre had passed into the hands of Elizabeth.*

Elizabeth's succession was not contested. Parliament chanced to be in session on Mary's decease. Upon being apprized of that event, "scarcely an interval of regret appeared; and the two houses immediately resounded with the joyful acclamation of, 'God save queen Elizabeth!' The people, less actuated by faction, and less influenced by private views, expressed a joy still more general and hearty on her proclamation."†

Yet, though not a ripple stirred the placid sea, the keen good sense of the maiden queen was not misled. She knew that there was an under-current of dissent and hatred which ran swift and strong. She was an avowed Protestant; Romanism was the state religion. She was known to favor the Reformation; the clergy and the placemen of her sister's reign could not but be her foes.‡

Besides, England was at war with France, and she stood with a bankrupt treasury. The merchants on the Rialtos of the world refused her credit. The British arms, broken and demoralized, skulked before the victorious eagles of the French. All those conquests, which it had cost the nation so much sweat and blood to acquire, the dowry of two hundred triumphant years, were lost in less

* Hume, vol. 1, p. 710. † Ibid., p. 712.

‡ Lingard, Reign of Elizabeth.

than half as many weeks; while, bitterest mortification of all, Calais, the key to France, had, by the negligence of Britain, slipped from her girdle.*

So gloomy was the foreign outlook, so wrecked were the domestic fortunes of England when the youngest daughter of Henry VIII. came to ascend her father's throne. The times bade her beware; the least false step might precipitate her into the abyss.

Thus circumstanced, Elizabeth determined for the present to preserve the cautious *statu quo* of the old law; religious changes were adjourned; the government devoted itself to finance and foreign politics. The Romish clergy kept their livings; the ejected churchmen of the last reign were barred from their dioceses, and England still echoed to the celebration of the mass.†

Elizabeth stooped to dissemble. The pope had pronounced her illegitimate;‡ half the courts of Europe tabooed her royalty;§ Mary of Scots claimed the English crown‖—which the maiden queen never forgave, and one day revenged; but when her throne was consolidated, the imperious princess meant to dictate law not only to her island, but to Christendom.

Her first move on the chess-board of politics was wise. She had been not only ill-used, but often

* Fuller, Lingard, etc.

† Neale, vol. 1, p. 77; Burnet, Collier.

‡ Collier, Church Hist., vol. 2.

§ Ibid.

‖ Hallam, Cons. Hist.; Neale, Fuller.

in peril of her life, while Mary ruled. The counsellors of that policy were now in her hands, yet she forgave them, and buried the past in oblivion.* This was followed by a proclamation forbidding innovations, and legalizing the existing state of affairs until the convention of Parliament.†

In January, 1558, Parliament assembled at Westminster. It was stoutly Protestant, and cordially favored a reform.‡ The religious enactments of Mary's reign were repealed; the laws of Henry VIII. against the see of Rome were dug from the grave and placed again upon the statute-book; the acts of Edward VI. were resuscitated and reënacted.§

The title of supreme head "of the church of England" was omitted in all these acts, as being inappropriate, since "Christ alone was the supreme Sovereign of the church;"‖ but all loyal Englishmen were tied by oath to "acknowledge the queen to be the only and supreme governor of her kingdoms in all matters and causes, as well spiritual as temporal, all foreign princes and protestants being quite excluded from taking cognizance of causes within her dominions."¶

The ordinary convocation accompanied this parliament, but it "was very small and silent; for as it is observed in nature, when one twin is of an un-

* Hume, vol. 1, p. 710. † Ibid.
‡ Newell, p. 114; Burnet; Strype, etc.
§ Statutes of the Realm, 1 Elizabeth.
‖ Rainolds against Hart, p. 38. ¶ Fuller, vol. 2, p. 441.

usual strength and bigness, the other, his partner born with him, is weak and dwindled away; so here, this parliament being very active in matters of religion, the convocation, younger brother thereto, was little employed and less regarded."*

It was esteemed important that the papists who were still in possession of the episcopal sees should be verbally vanquished ere being ejected. Accordingly a disputation was appointed to take place, before the queen's privy-council and both houses of Parliament, between the champions of the two creeds, each side to be defended by nine debaters.†

This debate resulted in more noise than fruit; gave birth to more passion than reason, more cavils than argument.‡ Still there was something gained; for the Romanists, finding that the popular verdict was against them, broke off the dispute on the plea that their cause ought not to be submitted to such an arbitration.§ But in this they condemned themselves, for they had not scrupled to debate with

* Fuller, vol. 2, p. 443.

† Collier, vol. 2, book 6. Their names were, White, bishop of Winchester; Bayn, bishop of Litchfield; Scott, bishop of Chester; Wilson, bishop of Lincoln; Cole, dean of St. Paul's; Horpsfield, archdeacon of Canterbury; Chadsey, prebendary of St. Paul's; Langdale, archdeacon of Lewis, on the papist side; and Story, late bishop of Chichester; Cox, late dean of Westminster; Hern, late dean of Durham; Elmar, late archdeacon of Stow, and Messrs. Whitehead, Grinal, Guest, and Jewel, on the Protestant side. Collier gives the speeches at great length, vol. 2, book 6, part 2.

‡ Fuller, vol. 2, p. 447.

§ Collier, vol. 2, book 6; Neale, Burnet.

Cranmer, Ridley, and Latimer in the preceding reign, when the verdict was assured to them.* This was now remembered; and it was concluded that, since they had quitted the arena, their cause must be clearly indefensible—that "they only loved to have syllogisms in their mouths when they had swords in their hands."

The beaten Romanists were now commanded to take the oath of supremacy.† This the larger part did;‡ those who refused were summarily ejected from their livings, and several of the more prominent were imprisoned. Bonner was thrust into the Marshalsea, "a jail being conceived the safest place in which to secure him from the people's fury, every hand itching to give a good squeeze to that sponge of blood."§

So much being gained, it came now to be considered essential to secure uniformity of faith in England; for the Elizabethan epoch, grown no wiser in the lapse of time, was just as eager to mutter that shibboleth as the era of Edward or the age of Henry.

There now existed more perceptibly than ever, since the influx of the continental exiles, a large and influential party in England in favor of the service and discipline of the Genevan and Lutheran churches. They held the continental model to be purer and more nearly in accord with the primitive worship. These reformers began at this time to be

* Chapter 8, p. 110.

† Burnet, vol. 2.

‡ Newell, p. 116.

§ Fuller.

styled PURITANS, because they urged the establishment of a *purer* ecclesiasticism.*

Opposed to the Puritans was another large party who were zealous for the service-book of Edward VI.; who desired to divorce the English church from Rome only upon *doctrinal* points; who held rites and ceremonies to be indifferent, but who preferred those of the holy see because they were venerable and striking, and because old associations hallowed them in the hearts of the people.†

These parties agreed exactly in doctrine; they only quarrelled over forms.

But this may be said for the Puritans, that while their opponents held the ceremonies to be non-essential, *they* considered them to be of vast importance; for they bridged the chasm which yawned between Rome and the Reformation. Ignorant men, dazzled by the similarity in discipline, might not clearly perceive the radical difference in spirit; wedded to one superstition, this might breed others. It was best *to fix a gulf* between the island and the Vatican. As Protestantism was primitive in its creed, so ought it to be in its discipline.

"But the queen inherited the spirit of her father, and affected great magnificence in her devotions as well as in her court. She was fond of many of the

* Neale, vol. 1, p. 86. "Such as refused to conform and subscribe to the Liturgy, ceremonies, and discipline of the church, were branded by the bishops with the odious name of PURITANS." Fuller, vol. 2, p. 474.

† Ibid.

old rites and ceremonies in which she had been educated. She thought that her brother had stripped religion of too many of its ornaments—made the doctrines of the church too narrow on some points. It was therefore with difficulty that she was prevailed on to go even to the full length of king Edward's reformation;" it was plain that she never would smile upon Puritanism.

One of Elizabeth's earliest acts was to empower a committee of divines to revise the Liturgy. Substantially it was left unchanged, but some alterations were introduced to render the service more acceptable to the papal party.* Then the same parliament which had passed the act of supremacy, now placed upon the statute-book the twin law of uniformity.†

It was a clause of this statute which gave birth to those famous courts of High Commission and "Star-chamber," which make so prominent a figure in the history of a hundred years. The first of these tribunals possessed the authority which Henry VIII. had lodged in the single person of Lord Cromwell, "to visit, reform, redress, order, correct, and amend all errors, heresies, schisms, abuses, contempts, offences, and enormities whatsoever."‡

We shall discover how pregnant with evil this arbitrary court became. Standing without and

* Collier, vol. 2.

† Statutes, 1 Elizabeth. Camden, vol. 2, p. 372. D'Ewes.

‡ Ibid. Lingard, vol. 7.

above the common law,* calling in no intervention of juries,† alien to the spirit of the English Constitution,‡ irresponsible, stupendous, ominous, an incarnate fraud, this misshapen colossus of the law sported from the very outset in the most wanton acts of tyranny which no tribunal was empowered to curb.

Having now gotten the law settled and the courts arranged, the government set itself to enforce conformity. "Upon this fatal rock of uniformity in things merely indifferent, at least in the opinion of the imposers," says Neale, "was the peace of the church of England split. The pretence was decency and order; but it seems a little strange that uniformity should be necessary to the decent worship of God, when in most other things there is a greater beauty in variety. It is not necessary to a decent dress that men's clothes should be all of the same color and fashion; nor would there be any indecorum or disorder if in one congregation the sacrament should be administered *kneeling*, in another *sitting*, and in a third *standing;* or if in one and the same congregation the minister was at liberty to read prayers either in a black gown or in a surplice. The rigorous pressure of this act was the occasion of all the mischiefs which befell the church for above eighty years. What good end could it answer to press men into the use of a service without convincing their minds of its

* Macauley, Hist. Eng. † See the body of the act.
‡ Hallam, Const. Hist.

propriety? If there must be one established form, there should certainly be an indulgence to tender consciences. When there was a difference in the church of the Romans about eating flesh and observing festivals, the apostle did not pinch them with an act of uniformity, but allowed a latitude.* Had the reformers followed this apostolic precedent, the church of England would have made a still more glorious figure in the Protestant world."†

In 1559 the vacant sees were filled by Protestants;‡ Parker was preferred to the archiepiscopal see of Canterbury, and the ceremony was performed without gloves or sandals, rings or slippers, mitre or pall; even the episcopal vestments were omitted,§ and the consecration was by hands only. Strange that the archbishop should be satisfied with this in his own case, and yet be so zealous to impose the obnoxious garments upon the Puritans.‖ All the new bishops were confirmed in their diocesan dignities by an act of Parliament.¶

And now Elizabeth's government, civil and ecclesiastical, had "settled down into fixed ways." It began to dictate; it assumed to control.

Just here it becomes important to familiarize ourselves with the salient features of agreement and disagreement between the rising parties of the Conformists and the Puritans in the church of

* Romans 14:5.

† Neale, vol. 1, pp. 87, 88.

‡ Fuller, vol. 2.

§ Neale, vol. 1, p. 89.

‖ Camden, Neale, D'Ewes.

¶ Fuller, Burnet, Neale.

England. These Neale has admirably grouped, and we cite his *résumé:*

"The court reformers believed that every prince had authority to correct all abuses of doctrine and worship within his own territories. Actuated by this principle, Parliament submitted the consciences and religion of the whole nation to the disposal of the king, and in case of a minority, to his council; so that the monarch was sole reformer, and might model the doctrine and discipline of the church as he pleased, provided his injunctions did not expressly contradict the statute law of the realm.

"The Puritans disowned all foreign jurisdiction over the church equally with the court, but they could not admit of that extensive power which the crown claimed by the supremacy, apprehending it to be unreasonable that the religion of a state should be at the disposal of a single lay-person. However, they took the oath, with the queen's explanation that it only restored to her majesty the ancient and natural rights of sovereign princes over their own subjects.

"It was admitted by the court reformers that the church of Rome was a true church, though corrupt in many points of doctrine and government; that her ministrations were valid, and that the pope was a true bishop of Rome, though not of the universal church. It was thought necessary by some to maintain this, since their bishops thus derived their succession from the apostles.

"But the Puritans affirmed the pope to be antichrist, the church of Rome to be no church, and her ministrations to be superstitious and idolatrous; they renounced her communion, and dared not risk the validity of their ordinations upon an uninterrupted line of succession from the apostles through their hands.

"It was agreed by all that the Holy Scriptures were a perfect rule of faith; but the court reformers did not allow them to be a standard of discipline or church government, affirming that the Saviour and his apostles left it to the discretion of the civil magistrate, in those places where Christianity should obtain, to accommodate the government of the church to the policy of the state.

"The Puritans held the Scriptures to be a standard of discipline as well as doctrine, or at least, they thought that nothing should be imposed as necessary which was not expressly contained in Holy Writ, or derived from it by inevitable sequence. And if it could be proved that all things necessary to the government of the church could not be deduced from Scripture, they maintained that the discretionary power was not vested in the civil magistrate, but in the spiritual officers of the church.*

"The court reformers maintained that the practice of the primitive church, during the first four or five Christian centuries, was a proper standard of church government, and in some respects better

* From this it should seem that the Puritans thought that the civil magistrate might properly claim jurisdiction over all matters involving manifest breaches of the Scripture discipline.

than that of the apostles, which was only accommodated to the infancy of the church while it was under persecution, whereas theirs was suited to the grandeur of a national establishment. Therefore they only pared off the latter corruptions of the papacy, from the time the pope usurped the title of universal bishop, and left those institutions standing which they could trace higher, as archbishops, metropolitans, archdeacons, suffragans, rural deans, which were not known in the apostolic age, nor in those which immediately succeeded it.

"But the Puritans were for admitting no church officers or ordinances but such as are appointed in Scripture. They apprehended that the form of government ordained by the apostles was theocratic, according to the constitution of the Jewish sanhedrim, and was designed as a pattern for the churches of after ages, not to be departed from in its main features; and therefore they paid no regard to the customs of the papacy, or the practice of the earlier ages of Christianity, except in so far as these corresponded with the Scriptures.

"The court reformers maintained that things indifferent in their own nature, which are neither commanded nor forbidden in the Scriptures, such as rites, ceremonies, habits, might be settled, determined, and made necessary by the command of the civil magistrate; and that in such cases it was the indispensable duty of good citizens to observe them.

"The Puritans insisted that those things which

Christ had left indifferent, ought not to be made necessary by human laws. They affirmed that if the magistrate might impose things indifferent, and make them necessary in the service of God, he might dress up religion in any shape, and instead of one ceremony, he might load it with a hundred. Besides, it was urged that such rites and ceremonies as had been abused to idolatry, and tended to lead men back to popery, were no longer indifferent, but were to be rejected as unlawful.

"Both Puritan and Conformist agreed too well in asserting the necessity of uniformity in public worship, and of using the sword of the magistrate for the support and defence of their principles, of which they both made an ill use whenever they could grasp the power in their hands. The standard of uniformity, according to one, was the queen's supremacy and the statute law; according to the other, the decrees of provincial and national synods, allowed and enforced by the civil magistrate. Neither party admitted that liberty of conscience, which is every man's right."*

Such were the respective tenets of the Conformist and the Puritan parties. Neither made broad its phylactery, and inscribed thereon the golden rule of TOLERATION. Neither had yet grown wise enough to dare trust Justice. Neither maintained "the liberty of the children of God."

A swollen establishment on one side cried, Conform! Doubting consciences on the other side said,

* Neale, vol. 1, pp. 90–92.

No; and then struggled to acquire power, that they might, in their turn, play Sir Omnipotent, and dragoon churchmen into conformity with their idea. To say "toleration" in that age, was like hallooing in the midst of the avalanches. Still, the tendency of Puritanism was towards democracy. The courtiers recognized this, and perhaps that was one reason why Elizabeth so rudely curbed it. The Puritans believed in God; they also believed in the people. They disliked *caste.* Puritanism was the outgrowth of an interior life, the protest of a hungry conscience against dead forms; it was the insurrection of the soul against the body.

CHAPTER XI.

STAR-CHAMBER DECREES.

The sheet-anchor of peaceful faith is toleration. Civil and religious liberty, born of the New Testament, have at length won recognition. The struggle of eighteen hundred years touches its climax in a proclamation of divorcement between church and state.

In the United States we have placed two principles in our fundamental law:

Civil government is the protector of life, liberty, and property. It is the guaranty of political rights. Is a man wronged in person or in estate? there are the courts. It may not meddle with religious tenets, unless these breed gross acts of outward immorality; it cannot enforce a creed. Its single religious duty is to insure toleration. The jurisdiction of the state is merely political.

The kingdom of God is "NOT OF THIS WORLD." Therefore the jurisdiction of the church is purely spiritual. Her ordinances are spiritual; so ought her weapons to be. Her sword is Scripture, and her shield is reason. The pillars and the walls of her temple are exhortations, admonitions, reproofs. But the church may not dictate through civil penalties. She is tied to her functions precisely as the state is to its jurisdiction. The breakers of civil laws may be punished by weapons which affect their liberty and their property; the breakers of ecclesiastical canons may be disciplined by censure, or by the withdrawal of Christian fellowship. The courts of law take cognizance of the first species of offence; the court of conscience takes cognizance of the other. A citizen does not necessarily lose his civil rights when he changes his creed, or when he disqualifies himself for church-membership.

These two distinctive principles our ancestors could not understand. No party in the sixteenth century rose to the level of defending them. Not the papist, because his faith necessarily required intolerance; not the conformist, because he upheld the right of the government to dictate uniformity, even in non-essential things; not the Puritan, because he believed that the civil magistrate possessed the power to enforce whatever was agreeable to the Scripture text. Had these principles prevailed at the Reformation, truth and charity would have exorcised the spirit of discord, and there would have been no ground for the unhappy quarrel which eventually expanded from arguments into swords.

History teaches by example; and in the lurid light of such a past, we may read at once a warning and a prophecy.

But Elizabeth was tormented by no scruples. She assumed the power, if she had it not, to ransack consciences. She was prouder of her ecclesiastical supremacy than of all the rest of her royal prerogatives heaped together;* and her imperious

* Stowell, p. 122. Neale. Collier, vol. 2, book 6.

temper could ill brook contradiction in the realm of morals. Consequently when she discovered that, despite the statute of uniformity, the Puritans "refused to bow the knee to Baal," and that in their contumacy they were favored in great measure by her bishops* and by the chief members of her own council—by Leicester, by Walsingham, by the lord keeper Bacon, and by Knollys, whom Strype, with a spice of sarcasm, styles "the Puritan's chief instrument"†—when all this came to the ears of the impetuous princess, her rage bubbled over and blistered the offenders. "S'death, sirs," cried Elizabeth, "am I to be silent and easy while my very officers wink at impudent puritanical innovations which sap the foundations of the church?" The aroused queen then stirred Parker, archbishop of Canterbury, to invoke the rigors of the law against all non-conformists; and the frightened prelate, dropping the policy of delay, launched upon Puritanism the penalties of suspension, deprivation, sequestration, excommunication, and whatever other pains might from time to time seem meet to the Star-chamber court.‡

The ensuing persecution is rich in its record of steadfast devotion and Christian suffering. Hundreds bowed meekly to ejectment from their livings and to cruel imprisonment,§ confident that physical

* Strype, Annals, vol. 1, p. 117.

† Strype, Life of Parker, p. 152, and on.

‡ Ibid., vol. 1, p. 309.

§ Hopkins, vol. 1, p. 234. Soames, pp. 29, 30.

ills might be medicined, but aware that no human leech could cure the hurt of an undone conscience. Still, in spite of his utmost exertions, archbishop Parker discovered that a dozen rushed to occupy the post of every soldier whom he disarmed.* He was also much embarrassed by the lukewarmness of his fellow-bishops and of the queen's council. "If you remedy it not by letter," wrote Parker to the celebrated Cecil, Lord Burleigh, "I will no more strive against the stream, fume or chide who will."†

London was at this time the Gibraltar of Puritanism;‡ and the non-conformist clergy of the metropolis were enlightened, determined, conscientious, and eminently learned men.§ Elizabeth, provoked that Puritanism should be preached under the very shadow of her throne, nay, muttered in every corridor of her palace, issued another proclamation in 1565, peremptorily requiring uniformity; and under this, a number of the offending ministers were cited before Star-chamber commissioners, forbidden to utter a word in defence of their action, and called on to choose instantly between suspension and conformity. Thirty refused to subscribe, repeating the words of the apostles, "Whether it be right in the sight of God to hearken unto you rather than unto God, judge ye." The others submitted under protest, crying out as they quitted the court, "We are killed, we are killed in the soul

* Hopkins, vol. 1, p. 234. Soames, pp. 29, 30.

† Strype, Life of Parker, vol. 1, p. 318.

‡ Ibid., pp. 423, 427.

§ Newell, p. 121.

of our souls for this pollution of ours; for that we cannot practise our holy ministry in the singleness of our hearts."*

But the *desideratum* was outward conformity, not honesty of conviction; and in this hunt the wail of outraged consciences was little heeded. A stringent oath, binding the taker to unquestioning and patient obedience to the commands of the civil and ecclesiastical authorities, was framed, and this all clergymen were required to take before the cure of souls should be conferred upon them.† In every parish a bureau of spies was established, with orders to report at stated intervals to the Star-chamber court.‡ It was customary at that time for the archiepiscopal see to issue licences to the clergy. Without this authority, ministers might not preach. Now all old licences were cancelled; preachers were commanded to provide themselves with new ones; and in these a clause was inserted which bound the holder to submit to the control of his ecclesiastical superiors.§

This done, Elizabeth smoothed her ruffles, smiled complacently, cried, "Great is Diana of the Ephesians," and imagined that Puritanism had met both the first death and the last. But alas, non-conformity "would not down at her bidding." When she thought all avenues to the parish pulpits blocked

* Strype, Life of Grindal, p. 145.
† Ibid., Annals, vol. 1, pp. 131, 132.
‡ Ibid., Life of Parker, vol. 1, p. 431. Neale, vol. I, p. 240.
§ Ibid.

up, lo, one which might not be barred was still open. By a grant originally conferred by Pope Alexander VI. and confirmed by Elizabeth, the university of Cambridge had the right to license yearly twelve ministers. To the validity of the college license no diocesan assent was needed; the *imprimatur* of Cambridge was sufficient. Cambridge was at this time under Puritan influence; and therefore a number of stout dissenters were kept in the ministry despite the opposition of his grace of Canterbury.*

But in the main, the government achieved its purpose by the test-oath. The labors of a host of devoted ministers were stopped.† Hundreds of churches were entirely closed; for at best the supply of Protestant preachers was very limited;‡ and the Londoners, refusing to listen to the conforming chaplains, would not attend service at all, unless they could steal away and hearken to the exhortations of Coverdale, Sampson, Lever, and others of the disfranchised clergy who from time to time proclaimed the gospel to the poor from secret cellars and obscure dens, the catacombs of London.§

Gagged and expelled from the pulpit, the Puritans now had recourse to the press, that trumpet-toned avenger of the throttled truth. A war of pamphlets ensued; and the archbishop, beholding the popular attention which the controversy attract-

* Punchard, vol. 2, p. 452.

† Neale, vol. 1, p. 244. Strype's Parker, vol. 1, p. 380.

‡ Hopkins, Puritans, vol. 1, pp. 236–238. Collier, Eccl. Hist., vol. 2.

§ Punchard; Soames, p. 5.

ed, "became alarmed lest the silenced ministers should do, by means of their pens, what he had striven to prevent them from doing by preaching—convert the masses to Puritanism."

As the pulpit was chained, it was now determined to muzzle the press. Accordingly, in 1566, the Star-chamber issued a decree forbidding the publication of any book which criticised the state ritual under severe penalties, requiring bonds for the observance of this extra-judicial statute from printers, stationers, and booksellers, and placing the press under the supervision of the government, "that those in authority might see how books demeaned themselves."*

The Puritans were now reduced to an unhappy strait. The pulpit was tabooed; the press was padlocked. They lived under the ban and at the peril of the law. But they met the exigencies of their time with that faith which is able to "move mountains." They believed in God. *They actually believed in him,* just as much as if "the evidence of things not seen" stood demonstrated before their eyes. They calculated on God as astronomers calculate on the motions of the stars. Puritanism was incarnate faith.

It was in the year 1566 that the Puritans divided into two classes.† Hopeless of any consideration inside of the established church, some earnest, de-

* Hallam, Cons. Hist.; Strype, Annals; Neale; Fuller.

† Neale, vol. 1, p. 252; Hopkins; Burnet; Strype's Grindal, p. 168.

vout men determined, "after solemn consultation," that "it was their duty, in their present circumstances, to break off from it, and to assemble as they had opportunity in private houses or elsewhere, to worship God in a manner which might not offend against the light of their consciences."* These were called "Separatists;" and they based their church-government upon the principle of the individual independence of the churches.†

But by far the greater number of the Puritans still adhered to the church of England, and continued to do so for upwards of a century longer. These "would not use the habits nor subscribe to the ceremonies enjoined, as kneeling at the sacrament, the cross in baptism, the ring in marriage; but they held to the communion of the church, and willingly and devoutly joined in the common prayers."‡

Remembering this statement of so careful and competent an observer as Strype, the assertion of Fuller, that the Puritans "accounted every thing from Rome which was not from Geneva, and endeavored in *all things* to conform the government of the church of England to the Presbyterian reformation,"§ must be taken with some latitude, especially in view of the fact that the name "Puritan" covered all the dissenting evangelical sects of the time, the Baptist and the Lutheran, as well as the Genevan schools.

* Neale, vol. 1, p. 252; Hopkins; Burnet; Strype's Grindal, p. 168. † Punchard, vol. 2, chap. 13, passim.

‡ Strype, Life of Grindal, p. 168. § Fuller, vol. 2, p. 480.

But whether the Puritans were Separatists or church-of-England men, the government harried them with equal rigor, greedy to clutch all to the bosom of its uniformity.

During the soughing of this home tempest, Mary of Scots, expelled from her mountain-throne on account of her opposition to the Reformation in Scotland, came into England, and in 1568 claimed the protection of her royal cousin Elizabeth.*

Scotland, through the zeal of a corps of indefatigable preachers led by John Knox, had been gathered into the Protestant fold; but the northern reformation was modelled after the Swiss church, and it stretched the right hand of fellowship to the English Puritans.†

Ardently wedded to the old ways, Elizabeth could not but detest the Puritanism of Scotland; but rancorously as she hated the Scotch Puritans, she still more cordially detested the young and beautiful queen who now stood before her throne suing for protection. She had never forgiven Mary for assuming the arms of England and claiming the British crown on pretence of her bastardy.‡ Now, as power was in her hand, vengeance was in her heart; and from the hour of her first entrance into England, she had detained the queen of Scots in a gilded imprisonment which was baptized "protection."§

* Fuller, Burnet, Hume.

† Neale, vol. 1, pp. 128, 129.

‡ Chap. 10, p. 137.

§ Hume, vol. 1, p. 757.

The European sky was at this time portentous. Behind each cloud lurked a stealthy thunderbolt. Romanism, reorganized by Jesuitism, was making its reaction assault upon the Protestant idea. France, torn by internecine strife, bled at every pore. Each sigh she heaved seemed destined to be her last. She wallowed in Huguenot gore. That awful succession of puppet kings under the Machiavellian regency of Catharine de' Medici, who shall adequately paint its horrors? It was the jubilee of pandemonium.

The Netherlands, tortured by the cruel skill of the duke d'Alva, shrieked in concert with unhappy France.* Large parts of Germany were dragooned into sullen submission to the Vatican. It was the carnival of persecution. The Continent, drunk with blood, reeled in a ghastly *fête*.

In this wild foray upon the Reformation, England was not forgotten. Popish emissaries, Protean, intriguing, ubiquitous, swarmed over the island, manipulating fanatics into conspirators.† The popish party became an incarnate cabal. Jesuits were found under every disguise—scholars, physicians, merchants, conformist churchmen, Puritan preachers. True to their assumed character, they still preached ultra and absurd doctrines, whose tendency was to disgust and divide Protestants. Muttering their favorite shibboleth, "The end sanctifies

* See Mr. Motley's graphic history of the persecution in the Netherlands, in Rise of the Dutch Republic.

† Stripe, Life of Parker, vol. 1, p. 146 ; Hume, Fuller.

the means," they even married and took the oath of supremacy, when doing so promised to aid their machinations. There was no crime, strange, unheard of, unthought of before, which their prolific brains did not hatch and galvanize into busy mischief.

Books against Elizabeth and her government were scattered broadcast throughout Europe.* A papist league was formed, whose grand object was the dethronement of the maiden queen.† Romanist astrologers predicted the speedy occurrence of strange events. Popish conjurers juggled the ignorant into believing that the death of Elizabeth and the overthrow of Protestantism might momentarily be expected by the miraculous intervention of the heavenly powers.‡

"Having no place in England wherein to recruit themselves," the Romanists established colleges upon the Continent for the express purpose of educating "missionaries" to effect the reconversion of their country.§ The first of these nurseries of priestcraft was erected at Douay, in Flanders. There were others at Rome, Valladolid, Ghent, St. Omers, and Madrid.|| To these schools, where deceit and murder were taught as sanctified morality, the Romanist gentry of Britain dispatched their sons to be educated. The immense sums of money collected

* Strype, Annals, vol. 1, p. 92; Neale; Hopkins.

† Ibid. Life of Parker, vol. 2, pp. 1–5.

‡ Ibid.

§ Fuller, vol. 2, p. 485; Neale, Collier, etc.

|| Saunders, De Schisma Angl., pp. 178, 189.

for the maintenance of these "colleges" transmuted them into El Dorados.*

Scores of these "missionaries" now scoured England;† and worked on by these arts, the sowers of the wind soon reaped the whirlwind. This pestilent agitation bred a rebellion. Thousands broke into open war. The whole North surged in insurrection.‡ Communion tables were demolished; Bibles and service-books were torn in pieces; the mass was exultingly chanted in the cathedral of Durham; six thousand men-at-arms rallied under the earls of Northumberland and Westmoreland, writing the liberation of Mary of Scots and the re-establishment of Romanism in the island as legends on their banners.§

This outbreak was finally quelled; some of the fanatics who stirred it were beheaded; others escaped beyond the sea.‖ But it was a year of terror, and England shivered in the storm.

For the purpose of giving new life to the reactionists, the pontiff, in 1570, excommunicated Elizabeth.¶ But the beating of that Chinese gong startled no one. The *brutum fulmen* went unheeded. The European courts continued their correspondence with the anathematized queen; and the domestic papists, paralyzed by the fate of the malcon-

* Neale, vol. 1. Fuller, vol. 2, p. 490.

† Neale, vol. 1, p. 142; Burnet.

‡ Fuller, vol. 2, p. 484; Hopkins; Strype.

§ Punchard, vol. 2, pp. 465, 466.

‖ Hume, Fuller, Lingard, Hallam.

¶ Neale, vol. 1, p. 142; Strype, etc.

tents in the recent *émeute*, nursed their rage, and cursed with bated breath and whispered humbleness.

Strange to narrate, all through these anxious and frightened months the persecution of the Puritans was kept afoot.* Silly England consented to fight with one hand tied behind her back. While she suppressed the Romanist insurrection with her left hand, she used her right to thrust the stanchest adherents of the Reformation into Bridewell and Newgate prisons.† "Sink the island," cried Elizabeth, "but perish Puritanism." It was the ludicrous heroism of a petticoated Don Quixote.

* Neale, vol. 1, p. 112.

† Ibid., chap. 4.

CHAPTER XII.

"HOW NOT TO DO IT."

About 1570—before that, but more noticeably after—the governmental policy of England began to squint towards the fagot and the stake. Now for a dozen years the rigorous execution of the penal laws had made business for the civilians; the ecclesiastical courts had been thronged; thousands of honest men had been entangled in the meshes of the common and the canon law, and harassed in mind and broken in fortune* by the dilatory "circumlocution offices," whose motto was, "How not to do it." Yet neither the cunning lawyers of Temple Bar, nor the severity of Star-chamber decrees, had been able to wheedle or to coerce the dissidents into outward uniformity.

Indeed these measures, instead of bridging the chasm, widened it. Never before had the non-conformists of all sects been so numerous and so militant.† Until the recent Romanist insurrection, the papists had outwardly conformed; but now they too separated openly, defiantly, and they intrigued and scoffed.‡

Elizabeth sighed, and glanced towards Smithfield. As a feeler, she determined to execute a few

* Fuller, vol. 2, p. 497. Neale, vol. 1, p. 144.

† Ibid. Hopkins, Hist. of the Puritans.

‡ Ibid.

Anabaptists; if the country cried Amen to these *autos da fé*, then she might venture to strangle papists and to burn Puritans.* This move was cunning.

The Anabaptists, an innocent and evangelical sect, had long been the most hunted and hated of reformers. Not a nation in Europe but had anathematized them. Their distinctive tenet was the denial of baptism to infants.† They were indeed often charged with holding various dangerous doctrines; but their peculiar idea of baptism was of itself sufficient to bring upon them grievous punishment. The Anabaptists were among the earliest dissenters; the disciples of their creed were found among the Lollards as well as among the martyrs of the English Reformation.‡

Through two centuries search after search had been made for them, proclamation after proclamation had been launched against them. And even in the Elizabethan epoch they were so unpopular, that partisans of all schools of theology looked with grim complacency upon their judicial murder.§

Elizabeth then decided to initiate a *régime* of blood by kindling Anabaptist fires. Accordingly "of a congregation of Flemish refugees, meeting without Aldersgate Bars, London, and professing these principles, twenty-seven were imprisoned; four, bearing fagots at St. Paul's Cross, recanted,

* Collier. † Broadmead Records. Newell, p. 175.

‡ Fox, Acts, etc., book 1, chap. 10.

§ Perry, History of the Church of England, p. 11.

and obtained their release; eight were banished; two were burned at Smithfield."*

Instantly an ominous growl swept across the island. England shouted an imperative veto. The paradox was seen; and it was in relation to these unhappy victims of Protestant and royal persecution that old John Fox addressed his famous letter to Elizabeth, begging that "the piles and flames of Smithfield, so long ago extinguished, might not be revived."†

Headstrong as she was, the spinster queen had sense enough to see that she was foiled, and to acquiesce; but she at once set in increased motion the whole pitiless machinery for the enforcement of uniformity. The civil code was made more stringent, and the legislation against Romanism was especially stinging and acute.‡ Unquestionably a wiser policy might have been pursued even against the Vatican. But circumstances combined to palliate Elizabeth's extermination of the Jesuit and seminary priests, circumstances which did not shield her persecution of the reformers, always the cordial, loyal pillars of her menaced throne. The Romanist powers of Europe intrigued to gain a domestic party in Britain pledged to act against the government. The queen was denounced, nay, excommunicated by the pope. Therefore Elizabeth might, with some justice, see an implacable enemy in every papist, and do her utmost to root out a

* Newell, p. 176. † Ibid.

‡ Perry, p. 11. Neale, vol. 1, p. 143.

pernicious and plotting creed, a faith which was a juggle, a religion which was a midnight conspirator.

But the plain historic fact is, that Elizabeth's detestation of Puritanism even exceeded her hatred of popery. This crops out in her harangue to Malvesier, the French ambassador: "I will maintain the religion in which I was crowned and baptized; and I will suppress the papistical religion, that it shall not grow; but as for Puritanism, I will ROOT IT OUT, with the favorers thereof."*

The truth should seem to be that the exaggerated notions of authority and the love of pompous ceremony, which were among the most salient characteristics of the great queen, made her nearer akin than cousin to the pope; and she was in much closer sympathy with the priest-caste of Rome than with the democratic tendency which her sagacious instinct led her to detect in Puritanism.

In Elizabeth's eyes, the "unpardonable sin" was Puritanism. That, no services, no talents could extenuate; its adherents must be forced upon their knees to cry, I have sinned, and to hiccough, Church and state.

Even the martyrologist John Fox, one of the mildest and most lovable of men, was summoned by archbishop Parker to subscribe, "that the reputation of his piety might give the greater countenance to conformity." The old man produced the New Testament: "To this," said he, "I will subscribe." But when a subscription to the canons

* Malvesier's Letters, cited by Strype in Annals, vol. 2, p. 568.

was required of him, he refused it, saying, "I have nothing in the church save a prebend at Salisbury, and much good may it do you if you will take it from me."* "However," says Fuller, "such respect did the bishops—most, formerly, his fellow-exiles—bear to his age, parts, and pains, that he continued in his place till the day of his death;"† but even this illustrious Christian, shackled by his Puritanism, rose no higher in the church than a petty "prebend at Salisbury."

It was in 1570 that the controversy between the Conformists and the Puritans assumed a new phase. Hitherto it had been largely a quarrel over forms—the habits, the cross in baptism, and kneeling at the Lord's supper; now it broadened into more radical differences.‡

Thomas Cartwright, Margaret professor of divinity at Cambridge, "a courageous man, a popular preacher, a profound scholar, and master of an elegant Latin style," was the chief of this new assault.§

Cartwright "was in high esteem in the university, his lectures being frequented by vast crowds of scholars; and when he preached at St. Mary's, they were forced to take down the windows."‖

This champion of Puritanism inveighed against what he considered the blemishes of the Established church, and he enforced in his lectures these six

* Fuller, vol. 2, p. 475.
† Ibid.
‡ Neale, vol. 1, p. 144.
§ Fuller, vol. 2, p. 503.
‖ Neale, vol. 1, pp. 144, 145.

tenets: that the names and functions of archbishops and archdeacons ought to be abolished, as having no foundation in Scripture; that the offices of the lawful ministers of the church ought to be reduced to the apostolic institution—the bishops to preach and pray, the deacons to take charge of the poor; that there ought to be an equality of all ministers, each one to be chief in his own cure; that ministers should be chosen by the people, not created by civil authority; that ministers should be confined to their own parishes, not suffered to roam at large; that each church should be governed by its own minister and presbyters.*

This radical departure from the English ritual created a profound sensation. Cartwright's propositions were denounced as untrue and dangerous, while Cecil called upon the vice-chancellor of Cambridge to silence the innovator or to compel him to recant.†

From this bold preaching grew a multitude of letters, lectures, and pamphlets. Finally, Cartwright was expelled from the university, and driven beyond the sea by the malice of his foes.‡ While abroad he was chosen minister to the English merchants at Antwerp, and he carried on an epistolary correspondence with a number of noted divines in the Protestant universities of the Continent.§

But the excitement stirred by these events was

* Neale, vol. 1, pp. 144, 145. Newell, pp. 153, 154.

† Ibid.

‡ Strype; Brook, Life of Cartwright.

§ Ibid.

now momentarily eclipsed by a newer wonder. It was reported on the streets that the queen was about to consummate a Romanist marriage. First Anjou was said to be the chosen one; then the hawkers of the news asserted that Alençon was the person; but it was unanimously agreed that one of these two French princes had been selected as the husband of Elizabeth.*

The hubbub was unprecedented. England protested. Sir Philip Sidney wrote his royal mistress a spirited private remonstrance;† and the excitement was increased by the publication of a pamphlet in which the French princes were truly painted as the incarnation of the most odious vices, and in which the projected marriage was denounced as "an impious and sacrilegious union between a daughter of God and a son of the devil."‡

Elizabeth was terribly angered by this satire, and she caused its author, who was a brother-in-law of Cartwright, and a friend of the famous Spenser, one of the finest poets in English letters, to be tried in the Queen's Bench, and condemned to have his right hand smitten off by a butcher's knife and mallet.§ Page, the publisher, after suffering the same punishment, said firmly, pointing with his left hand to the amputated member on the scaffold, "There lies the hand of a true Englishman."‖

Frightened from her projected marriage by the

* Mackintosh, Hist. Eng., vol. 3, p. 279; Lingard, Froude.
† Lingard, vol. 4, p. 366. Strype, Life of Parker, bk. 4, ch. 2.
‡ Ibid. § Ibid. ‖ Ibid.; Newell, p. 156.

popular murmurs, Elizabeth relapsed into still gloomier fanaticism.

In 1572, the "Admonition to Parliament for the Reformation of Church Discipline" appeared. This was an echo of Cartwright's Cambridge lectures, and like its predecessors, it made a flutter in the dove-cote. Now again, as before, many pamphlets were bandied between the learned men of the respective parties; and Cartwright, who had just returned from the Continent, contended in this Olympian game of words with Whitgift, a learned and eloquent divine, who was the champion of the Conformist party.*

The question at issue was, "What is the fittest form of church government?"

The Puritans maintained that Parliament ought to establish by law a church discipline more agreeable to the Scripture model than the established one; and in order to show what form they should prefer, they appended to the volume which opened the controversy the letters of Beza and Gaultier to Leicester and bishop Parkhurst, letters which favored the continental order.†

The Established church men grounded their argument on the Erastian‡ principle that no form

* Fuller, vol. 2, p. 503. Brook, Life of Cartwright.

† Brook, Lives of the Puritans, vol. 2, pp. 185–190; Strype; Neale.

‡ Erastus was a German physician of the sixteenth century. His principle was that the church is to be recognized as simply a member of the general body called the state, and possessing no coercive power save through the arm of the civil magistrate. Newell, p. 158, note.

of church government is laid down in Scripture, but that the form of worship is left indifferent.*

The authors of the "Admonition" were flung into prison, where they lay for many months, and every effort was made by the government to seize their book, but in vain; neither could its successors be strangled in their birth, for they could not be found. Secret presses multiplied Puritan books, and these were so firmly retained, despite a royal proclamation against them, that the seeds of thought and protest were sown broadcast throughout the furrows of the time.†

The arbitrary action of the government made the tide set strongly against the bishops, for, aside from the merits of the case, in regard to which men might easily differ, the sentiment of fair-play, which lies at the bottom of every honest Saxon heart, was fatally offended. "If they did not fear discussion," said the impartial masses, "the bishops would not padlock free speech." Thus, notwithstanding the acute, learned, and very able defence of the English Establishment made by Whitgift, assisted by Parker and his *confréres*, the government lost *caste*, beaten more by its own besotted policy than by the arguments of its keen and earnest opponents.

At all events, it is certain that the universities, the metropolis, and the country at large, began to lean decidedly towards Puritanism. To this Strype bears sorrowing witness, informing us that, "not-

* Strype, Life of Parker; Newell.

† Strype, Annals, vol. 1, chap. 28.

withstanding the opposition the Puritans met with from the queen and her commissioners, by her repeated orders and commands, they yet got ground daily, and increased more and more, being favored by many in court and city."*

The Parliament had long been willing to attempt something in favor of the Puritans. One of the members, Strickland, "a grave and ancient man of great zeal," had, in 1571, offered a bill for a further reformation in the church which he had supported in two powerful speeches.† He was, however, rebuked in the open house for his impudence in venturing to meddle with the royal prerogative; and after the daily adjournment, Elizabeth cited the brave pleader before her council, and forbade him the Parliament house.‡ But this bold tyranny occasioned such a tumultuous debate, that the queen hastened to reverse her verdict.

Strickland was no sooner restored to his seat than he moved that "a confession of faith should be published and confirmed by Parliament, as it was in other Protestant countries."§ Another member, Norton, "a man wise, bold, and eloquent, stood up next," and supported Strickland's motion.||

A committee was appointed, and a list of articles was drawn up in substantial agreement with those already confirmed; but several of the old articles were omitted in the parliamentary rubric.

* Strype, Life of Parker, vol. 2, pp. 191, 192.

† D'Ewes' Journal, pp. 147, 156. Strype, Ann., vol. 2, p. 93.

‡ Ibid. Neale, vol. 1, p. 147. § Ibid.

|| D'Ewes' Journal, p. 148.

When the committee came to confer with the bishops, Parker asked why these had been stricken out. Sir Peter Wentworth, the great champion of civil and religious liberty in Elizabeth's reign, replied, "Because we have not yet examined how far they are agreeable to the word of God, having thus far confined ourselves chiefly to doctrines." The archbishop then remarked, "Surely you will refer yourselves wholly to us the bishops in these things." "No!" retorted Wentworth warmly; "no, by the faith I bear to God, we will pass nothing before we understand what it is, for to do so were to make you popes; make you popes who list, for we will make you none."*

These were brave words, and they show a vast improvement in the tone of English statesmanship since the lackey parliaments of Henry, Edward, and Mary assembled to record the whims of tyrant princes. As the French revolution was in the pages of Rousseau and Pascal long before it ran foaming through the streets of Paris, so the "great rebellion" scowled in these words of Peter Wentworth before it charged at Marston Moor and struck off a perjured prince's head.

But these bills did not amount to much, except as an indication of the growing spirit of the commons; for when they were presented to Elizabeth for her approval, the royal Jezebel "dashed" them, and they came to naught.†

* Neale, vol. 1, pp. 147, 148.

† Punchard, vol. 2, p. 470. D'Ewes; Strype, Life of Parker.

The Puritans next had recourse to the Convocation; but here they met with no sympathy, for this was the obsequious creature of the court.*

In the Parliament of 1572, the Puritans made another effort to win recognition from the state. But Elizabeth, after the passage of a reformatory bill, "strangled it with her own hands;" and then, deaf to the petition of the commons for redress, she prorogued the House without deigning to notice its prayer, flinging into the ears of the retiring members a severe reprimand for "their audacious, arrogant, and presumptuous folly, in thus, by superfluous speech, spending much time in meddling with affairs neither pertaining to them nor within the capacity of their understandings."†

But while the English Xantippe was thus scolding Parliament, she was scourging the Puritans with severer weapons than the tongue. Cartwright was arrested and thrown into prison as "a preacher of sedition."‡ There he lay and suffered for weary months, despite the intervention of Lord Burleigh and the prayer of the king of Scots.§ After being cuffed from jail to jail, browbeaten by mushroom prelates, and rated by ecclesiastical commissioners, he eventually retired to the island of Guernsey, where his later years were spent.

Cartwright's letters show that he never was a separatist, but that his aim as a Puritan was to

* Sparrow's Collections. Hopkins, Hist. Puritans. Froude.

† D'Ewes, Journal, p. 151; Brook.

‡ Brook, Life of Cartwright; Fuller. § Newell, p. 169.

adjust the discipline of the Established church to what he esteemed the word of God.* Yet for this honest endeavor his career was blocked, his usefulness was shackled, his fame was clouded, his constitution was broken by physical maltreatment, and his last years were imbittered by exile. Such was the garland which those unhappy times twined about the brow of enthusiasts for the truth.

At this very time, while she was persecuting the Puritans in England, Elizabeth was aiding the professors of the self-same tenets by her influence, money, and arms in Scotland, France, and the Netherlands.† And when in this same year of 1573, aghast England heard of the massacre of St. Bartholomew, the queen shrouded her court in mourning for the murdered Huguenots; then, decked out in "the trappings and the suits of woe," she turned to complete the butchery of the Puritans.

It is said that after the massacre of St. Bartholomew, the day was long remarkable for wet weather.‡

> "Bartholomew bemoans with rain
> The Gallic Atlas therein slain,"§

runs the old couplet. Perhaps the sky wept as much over England's hypocrisy as over the fanatical brutality of frenzied France.

* Newell, p. 69. † Perry, p. 13.

‡ Fuller, vol. 2, p. 505.

§ "Bartholomeus flet, quia Gallicus occubat Atlas."

CHAPTER XIII.

NOTES BY THE WAY.

"MAN," says Lamartine, "never fastens a chain about his brother's neck that God's own hand does not fix the yoke upon his own." Elizabeth, in attempting to girt the laws closer about the Puritans, almost choked conformity.

Matthew Parker, archbishop of Canterbury, was just dead, and evangelical England breathed freer. That prelate did not then, nor has he since, lacked panegyrists; but the main current of testimony tends to confirm the calm verdict of impartial history, that Parker was a haughty, worldly, and cruel churchman, more zealous to coerce honest consciences into the hypocrisy of apparent conformity, than active to garner souls into the heavenly kingdom.*

The liberalists esteemed the accession of Edmund Grindal to the primacy to be another triumph. He was the close friend of the leading Puritans within the church;† he had been an exile in the Marian age, and he was known to be a prelate of amiable temper and Christian principle.

So situated, and standing by the open grave of

* Hallam, Fuller, Newell, Strype, Neale, etc. Strype and Fuller can see no evil in Parker; but the others estimate his character more justly. See also Collier and Hume.

† Newell, p. 209.

"the most severe disciplinarian of Elizabeth's first hierarchy,"* the Puritans might moralize, "It is God's beneficent providence—death. When ideas have shaped themselves in a rigid mould, and become fossil, God takes off the weight of the dead men from their age, and leaves room for the new bud."

Strengthened then by the death of Parker in 1575, and by Grindal's piety, the devout men, both Puritans and Conformists, in the Established church, organized religious meetings which soon came to be called "Prophesyings;" a name suggested by Paul's words addressed to the Corinthian church: "Ye may all prophesy one by one, that all may learn, and all may be comforted."†

Strange to say, a Protestant princess objected even to these useful and harmless convocations. When they became popular, and were attended by numerous clergymen as well as distinguished laymen, Elizabeth, who was offended at the number of preachers who gathered on these occasions, and who "did not like that the laity should neglect their secular affairs by repairing so frequently to chapel," invoked the civil authorities to suppress these "unlawful assemblies."‡

Learning that the "Prophesyings" had received the countenance of the bishops, that archbishop Grindal himself strongly befriended them, and that

* Hallam, Cons. Hist., vol. 1, ch. 4.

† 1 Corinthians 14:31. Fuller, vol. 3, p. 6.

‡ Strype, Life of Grindal, book 2, chap. 2.

they "were much used now throughout most of the dioceses,"* the meddlesome and impudent spinster whose caprice governed England, sent for her new primate, and "rated him soundly." "S'death," cried she in this unique *concio ad clerum*, "*it is good for the church to have few preachers;* three or four will suffice for a county. I like not these exhortations; commend me to the reading of the homilies; 'tis enough. The number of preachers must be abridged; and I charge you, put down the 'Prophesyings.'"†

Grindal heard this mad tirade out; then quitting the royal presence, went home and wrote Elizabeth a long and able letter, in which he informed her of the usefulness and the necessity of preaching, declared that the "Prophesyings" were subservient to holy living, affirmed that whereas before the exercises there were not three able preachers in his diocese, now there were thirty fit to preach at Paul's Cross, and forty or fifty besides able to instruct their cures. Grindal concluded by assuring the queen that he could not, owing to the usefulness of the exercises, suppress them without offending God. "I say with Paul," added he, "I have no power to destroy, only to build up;" and with the same apostle, "I can do nothing against the truth, but for the truth."‡

This admirable rebuke from the first ecclesiastic in the kingdom so angered the petulant and vin-

* Strype, Annals, vol. 2, p. 133, and on.

† Strype, Grindal, book 2. ‡ Ibid., Appendix, No. 10.

dictive queen, that she ordered Grindal to be confined to his house, and had him sequestered from his archiepiscopal functions for six months by a Star-chamber decree.*

Thus peremptorily did Elizabeth act in a matter purely religious, walking beyond the outermost verge of her sacrilegious supremacy, and tieing the hands of the primate of England himself when, in the honest performance of his episcopal duties, he ventured to argue down her idle whims.

Although Burleigh and other statesmen endeavored to bend Grindal to obedience to the queen in this, the good prelate continued firm.† Then there was some talk of degrading him from his see; but this was finally abandoned, because Elizabeth, like Pilate, "feared the people." But Grindal "walked under a cloud" through the rest of his life. "Broken and feeble with grief," he became blind in 1582, whereon he resigned his primacy, surviving his lost honors but a few months.‡

Grindal's unselfish devotion has immortalized his memory; and it linked him by the kinship of suffering to the hearts of the Non-conformists, who were still more wickedly "meeted and peeled" under Elizabeth's Draconic code; and this too despite the fact that he, like Parker, abandoned in their case, after a few essays, the legitimate methods of persuasion for the severer logic of the laws.§ That "sweet Spenser" loved him is evinced by the

* Strype, Grindal, Appendix, No. 10; Neale, Newell.

† Newell, p. 213. ‡ Ibid., Strype, etc. § Newell, p. 209.

great poet's introduction of him under the anagram of his name, "*Algrind.*"

Upon the death of Grindal, says Hume, the queen determined "not to fall into the same error in her next choice; and she named Whitgift, a zealous churchman, who had already signalized his pen in controversy, and who, having in vain attempted to convince the Puritans by argument, was now resolved to open their eyes by power, and by the remorseless execution of the penal statutes. He informed her that the spiritual power lodged in the prelates was still insignificant; and as there was then no ecclesiastical commission in force, he engaged her to issue a new one, more arbitrary than any of the former, and conveying more unlimited authority."*

But while the new primate was thus forging his thunderbolts, vital piety, smitten through Grindal from the very throne, lay torpid. Sir Robert Cotton, referring to the times of the "Prophesyings," says, "In those days there was an emulation betwixt the clergy and the laity, and a strife whether of them should show themselves most affectionate to the gospel. Ministers haunted the houses of the worthiest men, where Jesuits now build their tabernacles, and poor country chapels were frequented by the best in the shire. The word of God was precious, prayer and preaching went hand in hand, until Archbishop Grindal's disgrace brought the flowing of these good graces to a still water."†

* Hume, Hist. of Eng., Reign of Elizabeth.

† Strype, Life of Grindal, book 2, chap. 9.

Indeed, the condition of Britain at this epoch was most scandalous. The rotten morals of the *saturnalia* had been vomited into England by sickened Rome. Formal hypocrisy was baptized religion. The earnest and devout men both in and out of the church were harassed and imprisoned. The Sabbath was openly blasphemed; it was a *gala* day, given up to riot, to gaming, to drunkenness.* Archbishop Parker was himself charged with "giving entertainments and feastings chiefly on the Lord's day."†

"Cabined, cribbed, confined" by the severity of the High Commission and the narrow terms of uniformity, the supply of preachers began to fail. The queen's wish was more than fulfilled; for whole counties, starving for the bread of life, were without a single minister.‡ And under the court *régime*, those provided with preachers were not much better off, "most of the old incumbents being either pluralists, non-residents, or disguised papists, fitter to sport with the timbrel and pipe than to take God's book into their hands." In the county of Cornwall there were a hundred and forty of these clerical drones, not one of whom could compose a sermon; robbed of their mass-book, they stood tongue-tied.§ A petition presented to the Parliament of 1579–80 says, that at least one half of the churches of Lon-

* Strype, Fuller, Hopkins, Neale, etc.

† Neale, vol. 1, p. 187.

‡ Ibid., p. 198. McCullough, British Empire, vol. 1, p. 399.

§ Ibid.

don were unfurnished with curates, and scarcely one in ten of those nominally provided possessed clergymen who conscientiously served their parishioners.*

"Yet at this very time," says Neale, "there was a rising generation of valuable preachers, ready and anxious for the ministry, if they might have been encouraged; for in a supplication of some of the students of Cambridge about this time, they acknowledge that there were plenty of able and well-furnished men among them, but that those could not get into livings upon equal conditions; while unlearned men, nay, the scum of the people, were preferred before them. So that in this great want of laborers, they stood idle in the market-place all the day, being urged by the bishops to pledge conformity, and to approve that, as agreeable to the word of God, which with no safety of conscience they could accord unto."†

Then beside these chafing neophytes stood the army of veteran ministers, deprived and silenced because they could not "take a false oath, and subscribe themselves slaves;" agonizing to preach, yet standing gagged by statutes, unable to utter a word, and slowly dying of despair.

Is it astonishing that morals and religion were at a low ebb in England? Even Strype, always the willing panegyrist of Elizabeth when truth did not tie his honest pen, draws this sombre picture of the

* Punchard, vol. 2, pp. 490, 491.

† Neale, vol. 1, pp. 198, 199.

situation: "The state of the church was now low and sadly neglected. The queen's own court was a harbor for epicures and atheists."*

No wonder then if Elizabeth and her inquisitorial satellites came, as Fuller confesses they did, to consider "all pious people as embraced under this nickname, 'Puritans,'"† and to hack indiscriminately right and left, pinching conformists as readily as dissidents.

Here again we summon Strype upon the witness-stand: "When it was ascertained that in several of the counties certain religiously disposed Conformists had contracted the habit of getting together on holy days, after dinner or supper, for conference and worship, the ecclesiastical commissioners cited the neighboring curates to explain why they did not forbid these 'unlawful assemblies.'" What they replied is not known; but on their return to their parishes, the *dangerous meetings* were suppressed.

The parties thus dealt with made this declaration: "We do not favor or maintain any of the opinions of the Anabaptists, Puritans, or Papists, but would be glad to learn our duty towards God, our prince, and magistrates, towards our neighbors and our families, in such sort as becomes good, faithful, and obedient subjects. The occasion of our assemblies on the holy days after supper was this: for that heretofore we have at divers times spent and consumed our holy days vainly, in drinking at the ale-

* In Life of Parker, vol. 2, p. 204.

† Fuller, vol. 2, p. 474.

house and playing at dice, cards, and other vain pastimes, for the which we have been often blamed by our pastor; so we thought it better to bestow our time in sober and godly reading the Scriptures, only for the purpose aforesaid and no other."*

Yet the government would not rescind its veto. "The rulers of church and state thought it a less evil for men to spend their time on holy days in drinking and gaming than in 'unauthorized' meetings for reading the Scriptures, prayer, and conference."†

This did not occur in Spain, among the mutterers of the mass; it did not take place in the Romanist Italy of the Borgias: these things happened in Protestant England; and in the reign, not of Mary, but of Elizabeth Tudor.

All great moral, all great political movements run easily, almost inevitably, into extremes, and breed fanaticism. In a community stirred and tossed by tumultuous excitement, it is always safe to prophesy that some minds will be unstrung and fanaticized. Men of vivid imagination, of speculative tendency, dreamers, will feel a strange exaltation, see visions, and seer-like, assume to lift the misty curtain of the future, and to foretell events.

Upon this fact, miscalled "Conservatives"—men who, had they lived at the time of the creation, would have cried with Cousin's lover of "the old ways," "Great God, what will become of Chaos?"—

* Strype, Life of Parker, vol. 2, pp. 381–385; Neale; Punchard.

† Punchard, vol. 2, p. 502.

base arguments against reform. But extravagants are not *caused* by progress; they are nature's protest against darkness. Extremists are men half awake, but whose eyes are not yet fully open, and they grope wildly in the dazzling sunshine.

Already the English Reformation had adopted a misshapen sect called the "FAMILISTS,"* "worse in their practices than in their opinions; for they grieved the Comforter, charging all their sins on God's Spirit for not effectually assisting them against themselves; counting themselves as innocent as the maid forced in the field, crying out, and having none to help her."†

Now, in the interstices of the controversy between the English Establishment and Puritanism, another hated sect cropped out; the "BROWNISTS"‡ began to grow. These sectaries accepted the articles of

* One Nicolas, born in Amsterdam, first vented this doctrine in his own country in 1550. His followers termed themselves the "Family of Love." See Fuller, vol. 2, p. 517, and on. Also Neale, Burnet, etc.

† Fuller, vol. 2, p. 519.

‡ "These people were called 'Brownists' from one Robert Brown, a preacher in the diocese of Norwich, descended of an ancient and honorable family, and nearly related to the lord-treasurer Cecil. He was educated at Corpus Christi college, Cambridge; and he preached sometimes in Bennet church, where the vehemence of his delivery gained him reputation. He was first a schoolmaster, then a lecturer at Islington; but being a fiery, hot-headed young man, he went about inveighing against the discipline and ceremonies of the church, and exhorting the people by no means to comply with them." Neale, vol. 1, pp. 204, and on. This conduct speedily brought Brown to the notice of the government. He was imprisoned; released through Burleigh's influence; sent home to his father; dismissed by him from the family; excommunicated; pardoned; given a church in Northamptonshire; and

faith of the English church, but they were narrow and rigid in their ideas of discipline.* Their own government was framed upon the apostolic model; and it was not this that gave them a bad name. They were severe bigots, and renounced communion with the Established church, which they denounced as no church, but a popish, anti-christian juggle, and with all other churches which did not exactly agree with their pattern.†

Their chief crime was *uncharitableness;* for they unchurched the whole Christian world on a question of *mere* form, Lutheran and Calvinist as well as the conforming churchmen. No one could be a follower of Christ unless he was a mutterer of their peculiar shibboleth.

Brownism was the counterpart of Whitgift's rigid uniformity. The lesson which the prelates taught these sectaries learned, "not wisely, but too well."

The principles of the "BROWNISTS" agreed in some respects with the *rationale* of Puritanism.‡ But with the impudent intolerance of that narrow sect the Puritans did not sympathize. They recognized the brotherhood of the Evangelicals; they fellowshipped Lutherans and Calvinists; they would gladly have fellowshipped the English Conformists, had not the bishops written "holier than thou"

after a life of vicissitudes, he finally died in jail, where he had been imprisoned for assaulting a constable. Pagett's Heresiography; Collier, Eccl. Hist., part 2, book 7; Strype, Annals, vol. 2, etc.

* Neale, vol. 1, pp. 205, 206. † Ibid.

‡ Ibid., Newell, Hopkins, Strype, etc.

across the forehead of the church. Even the "Separatists" did not deny that the English church was a *true* church, though they quarrelled with its ceremonial law.

The government, like a true inquisitor, listened to every idle story of its scouts; and when Elizabeth learned that the BROWNISTS held some of the tenets of Puritanism, she forgot that, since they subscribed to the Thirty-nine Articles, they also agreed in some things with the bishops; so, anxious to father on the dissenters all obnoxious *isms*, she termed the BROWNISTS Puritans, as she had already the "FAMILISTS," and anathematized them all through new statutes. Three men, convicted of scattering BROWNIST pamphlets through the kingdom, "were murdered under the forms of law;"* and complacent bishops culled objectionable passages from the tabooed books to prove the dangerous tendency of Puritanism.†

"The children of this world are, in their generation, wiser than the children of light."‡ "Rome understands, what no other church has ever understood, how to deal with enthusiasts. In some sects, particularly in infant sects, enthusiasm is permitted to be rampant. In other sects, especially in those long established and richly endowed, it is regarded with aversion. Rome neither submits to enthusiasm nor proscribes it; she *uses* it. She considers it as a great moving force, in itself neither good nor

* Newell, p. 192; Fuller, Hopkins, Neale, Strype, Collier, etc.

† Ibid.

‡ Luke 14:8.

bad, but which may be so directed as to produce great good or great evil. She knows that when religious feelings have obtained the complete empire of the mind, they impart a strange energy; that they raise men above the dominion of pain and pleasure; that obloquy becomes glory; that death itself is contemplated only as the beginning of a higher and happier life. She knows that a person in this state is no object of contempt. He may be vulgar, ignorant, visionary, extravagant; but he will do and suffer things which it is for her interest that somebody should do and suffer, yet from which calm and sober-minded men shrink. She accordingly enlists him in her service, assigns to him some forlorn hope, in which intrepidity and impetuosity are more wanted than judgment and self-command, and sends him forth with her benediction and applause.

"For a man thus minded there was no place within the pale of the Establishment. If he could not conform in every non-essential trifle, he must be gagged. If he desired to be a teacher, he must begin by being a schismatic. His choice was soon made. A congregation was formed. A plain building, with a desk and benches, was run up, and named Ebenezer or Bethel, and in a few weeks the church had lost by her narrowness a hundred families, not one of which entertained the least scruple about her articles, or possibly about her government, but who were driven to separate through affection for their pastor, or through disgust at his ill-usage.

"Far wiser is the Roman polity. Even for

female agency there is a place in her system. To devout women Rome assigns spiritual functions, dignities, and magistracies. In most Protestant countries, if a noble lady is moved by more than ordinary zeal for the propagation of religion, the chance is that, though she may disapprove of no one doctrine of the established church, she will end by giving her name to a new schism. If a pious and benevolent woman enters the cells of a prison to pray with the most unhappy and degraded of her sex, she does so without any authority from the church. No line of action is traced out for her; and it is well if the ordinary does not complain of her intrusion, and if the bishop does not shake his head at such irregular benevolence. At Rome, the countess of Huntingdon would have a place in the calendar as St. Selina, and Mrs. Fry would be foundress and first superior of the Blessed Order of Sisters of the jails.

"Place Ignatius Loyola at Oxford. He is certain to become the head of a formidable secession. Place John Wesley at Rome. He is sure to become the first general of a new society devoted to the interests and honor of the church. Place St. Theresa in London. Her restless enthusiasm ferments into madness, not untinctured with craft. She becomes a prophetess, the mother of the faithful, holds disputations with the devil, and issues sealed pardons to her adorers. Place Joanna Southcote at Rome. She founds an order of barefooted Carmelites, every one of whom is ready to suffer martyrdom for the church; a solemn service is consecrated to her memory; and her statue, placed over the holy water, strikes the eye of every stranger who enters St. Peter's."*

Now, whether we fully accept this philosophy or not, enough of it is true to prove this, that Protestantism cannot afford, in its conflict with Satan, to throw away as despicable any useful agencies; and that the church militant should be as cunning to save souls, as sinful human nature is to waste and destroy them.

* Macauley, Essay on Ranke's History of the Popes, Edinburg Review, October, 1840.

CHAPTER XIV.

THE LAST OF THE TUDORS.

THE lapse of time wrought no alleviation in the persecution of the Puritans. Rigid coercion was still the motto and the aspiration of the government.* One generation bequeathed to another the same fatal legacy of patient suffering for conscience' sake.

But England at large did not sympathize with the arbitrary measures of the court. A silent revolution was maturing. Many ministers, banished from the pulpit, were welcomed as domestic chaplains and private tutors into the families of the middle classes and the gentry. Here they were protected against oppression, and in this seclusion they found leisure to imbue the rising spirits of the epoch with their own hatred of tyranny, and passion for religious and political liberty.†

It was in these nurseries that the cradle of the "great rebellion" was rocked.

Yet, singularly enough, throughout the reign of Elizabeth there was not one Puritan *émeute*. Though banned and hunted, scourged and starved and burned, they never once were driven to rebel. Obeying their Master's requisition, when smitten upon one cheek, they turned the other also.‡

* Newell, p. 185; Hopkins, Strype. † Ibid.

‡ Matthew 5:39.

But if the Puritans were patient, the Romanists were not. No sooner was the cobweb of one plot swept down than they spun another. "They differed as hot and cold poison; the Jesuits more active and pragmatical, the seculars more slow and heavy, but both maintaining treacherous principles, destructive to the commonwealth."*

In 1586 the papists were peculiarly active. Elizabeth's recent execution of the queen of Scots had stirred the Vatican to venomous rage.† The Romanists of Europe determined to make one gigantic effort to strangle English Protestantism. Spain was selected as the avenger of the faith. This was fit. The crusades had been merely an episode in the history of other nations. Her whole existence had been a crusade. It was proper, therefore, that Spain should lead this assault. The "Invincible Armada" was launched.‡

"Now," says Fuller, "began that fatal year, generally foretold that it would be wonderful, as it proved no less. Whence the astrologers fetched their intelligence, whether from heaven or hell, from other stars, or from Lucifer alone, is uncertain. This is most certain, that their prediction, though hitting the mark, yet missed their meaning who both first reported and most believed it.

"Out came this invincible navy and army, perfectly appointed for both elements, water and land, to sail and march complete in all warlike equipage,

* Fuller, vol. 3, p. 152.

† Hume, Neale, Burnet.

‡ Ibid.

so that formerly, with far less provision, they had conquered another world. Mighty was the bulk of their ships, the sea seeming to groan under them, being a burden to it as they went, and to themselves as they returned, with all manner of artillery, prodigious in number and greatness, so that the report of their guns does still and ought ever to sound in the ears of the English, not to fright them with any terror, but to fill them with deserved thankfulness.

"It is said of Sennacherib, coming against Jerusalem with his numerous army, 'By the way that he came shall he return, and shall not come into this city, saith the Lord.'* As the latter part of this old prediction was verified here, no Spaniard setting foot on English ground under other notion than a prisoner, so God did not *them* the honor to return the same way; who coming by south-east, a way they knew, went back by south-west, a way they sought, chased by our ships past the forty-seventh degree of northern latitude, then and there left to be pursued after by cold and hunger.

"Thus having proved the English valor in conquering them, the Scotch constancy in not relieving them, the Irish cruelty in barbarously butchering them, the small reversion of this great navy which came home might be looked upon by religious eyes as relics, not for the adoration, but instruction of their nation hereafter, not to account any thing *invincible* which is less than *infinite*."†

* 2 Kings 19:33.

† Fuller, vol. 3, p. 97.

Camden and others have complained that, at this time, while England was under arms to defeat the Spaniard, the Puritans were factious, "dispersing pamphlets against the church and the prelates in the height of a common danger."* But it seems that these writings went merely to show that "the danger of the return of popery, of which all men were then apprehensive, arose largely from stopping the mouths of those ministers who were most zealous against it. It had been easy at that time to have distressed the government, but the Puritans on both sides of the Tweed were more afraid of the triumph of Rome than their adversaries. Those in Scotland entered into an association to assemble in arms, at what time and place their king should require, to assist the queen of England against the common foe,† while their brothers in London seized the opportunity to petition the queen to release their preachers, that the people might be better instructed in the duty of obedience to their civil governors, and not be left a prey to priests and Jesuits, who were traitors to her majesty and to the state. But Elizabeth returned no answer; she was content to jeopard the Reformation rather than relieve the Puritans.‡

Through these eventful years Sunday was much profaned, by the encouragement of plays and sports in the evening, and sometimes in the afternoon.

* "Ut externo bello sic etiam interno schismate hoc tempore laboravit Anglia," etc. Camden. † Hume, Lingard, etc.

‡ Neale, vol. 1, p. 259.

On one occasion a Puritan divine, in a sermon before the university of Cambridge, impeached the lawfulness of these games, on which he was cited before the vice-chancellor. Here the preacher maintained that the Sabbath ought to be observed by an abstinence from all worldly business, and spent in works of piety and charity, though he did not apprehend that Christians were bound to the strictness of the Jewish precepts.*

"The Parliament," says Neale, "had taken this matter into consideration, and passed a bill for the better and more reverent observance of the Sabbath, which the speaker of the Commons recommended to the queen in an elegant speech. But her majesty refused to sign it, under pretence of not suffering the Parliament to meddle with matters of religion, which she considered her sole prerogative. However, the thing appeared so reasonable, that without the sanction of a law the idea grew into esteem with all sober persons."†

A few years later the Sabbatarian controversy was again kindled. A Puritan pamphlet was published, in which it was urged that morality required the reservation of a seventh part of the time for worship; that Christians were bound to rest upon Sunday as much as the Jews were on the Mosaical Sabbath, the commandment of rest being moral and perpetual, and that therefore it was not lawful to follow studies or worldly business on that day, nor to use such recreations as were proper through the week.‡

* Neale, vol. 1, p. 249. † Ibid. ‡ Ibid., p. 298.

"This book had a wonderful spread among the people, and wrought a mighty reformation; so that the Lord's day, which used to be profaned by interludes, May-games, morrice-dances, and other gay sports, began to be kept more precisely. All the Puritans fell in with this rule, and distinguished themselves by spending that part of sacred time in public, family, and private acts of devotion, which the governing clergy exclaimed against as a restraint of rational liberty.

"Archbishop Whitgift called in all the copies of this pamphlet, by his letters and officers at synods and visitations, and forbade it to be reprinted. The Lord Chief-justice Popham did the same, both of them declaring that the Sabbath doctrine tallied neither with the doctrine of the church, nor with the laws and order of the kingdom; that it disturbed the peace of the commonwealth and of the church, tending to sedition in the one and to schism in the other;"* spite of all which the book was still read privately, and in greater demand than before the governmental raid upon it.†

The year 1591 was rendered memorable by the new phase which the controversy between Puritanism and the churchmen then put on. The occasion of this change of base was a disputation between two famous clergymen. Fuller has left so quaint an account of this matter, that we subjoin, but somewhat abridge it:

"Now began the heat and height of the sad

* Neale, vol. 1, p. 298.

† Ibid, p. 299.

contest between Richard Hooker, master, and Walter Travers, lecturer, of the Temple. We will be larger in the relating thereof, because we behold their actions, not as the deeds of private persons, but as the public champions of their party. Now as an army is but a champion diffused, so a champion may be said to be an army contracted. The prelatical party wrought to the height in and for Hooker; nor was the puritanical power less active in assisting Travers; both sides being glad that they had gotten two such eminent leaders, with whom they might engage with such credit to their cause.

"Hooker was born in Devonshire, bred in Oxford, one of a solid judgment and great reading; yea, such the depth of his learning, that his pen was a better bucket than his tongue to draw it out; a great defender, both by preaching and writing, of the church of England. Spotless was his conversation; and though some dirt was cast, none could stick on his reputation.

"Travers was brought up in Trinity college, Cambridge, where meeting with some discontents, he took occasion to travel beyond seas, and coming to Geneva, contracted familiarity with Beza and other foreign divines, with whom he by letters continued correspondence till his death. Then returned he, and commenced bachelor of divinity in Cambridge; and after that passed beyond sea again, and at Antwerp was ordained minister by the presbytery there. After some time spent in preaching with Cartwright unto the English factory of merchants at Antwerp, he at last came over into England, and for seven years together became lecturer in the Temple, refusing all presentative preferment, to decline subscription, and lived domestic chaplain in the house of the Lord-treasurer Cecil, being tutor for a time to Robert his son, afterwards earl of Salisbury. Although there was much heaving and shoving at him, as one disaffected to the discipline, yet God's goodness, his friend's greatness, and his own honesty, kept him, but with much difficulty, in his ministerial employment.

"Yea, so great grew the credit and reputation of Travers, that he and Cartwright were solemnly sent for to be divinity professors in the university of St. Andrew's, in Scotland. This proffer both refused, with return of their most affectionate thanks. In plain truth, they were loath to leave, and their friends were loath to be left by them, conceiving their pains might as well be bestowed in their native country; and Travers quietly continued lecturer at the Temple till Hooker became master thereof.

"Hooker's voice was low, stature little, gesture none at all, standing stone-still in the pulpit, as if the posture of his body were the emblem of his mind, immovable as his opinions. Where his eye was left fixed at the beginning, it was found fixed at the end of his sermon. In a word, the doctrine he delivered had nothing but itself to garnish it. His style was long and pithy, driving on a whole flock of clauses before he came to the close of a sentence. So that when the copiousness of his style met not with proportionable capacity in his auditors, it was unjustly censured as perplexed, tedious, and obscure. His sermons followed the inclination of his studies, and were for the most part on controversies and deep points of school-divinity.

"Travers' utterance was graceful, gestures plausible, matter profitable, method plain, and his style carried in it *indolem pietatis*, 'a genius of grace' flowing from his sanctified heart. Some say that the congregation in the Temple ebbed in the forenoon and flowed in the afternoon, and that the auditory of Travers was far the most numerous—the first occasion of emulation between them. But both were too wise to take exception at such trifles.

"Here might one on Sundays have seen almost as many writers as hearers. Not only young students, but even the gravest benchers, such as Sir Edward Coke and Sir James Altham then were, were not more exact in taking instructions from their clients, than in writing notes from the mouths of these preachers. The worst was, that though joined in affinity—their nearest kindred being joined together—Hooker and Travers acted on different principles, and clashed one against another; so that what Hooker delivered in the forenoon, Travers confuted in the afternoon. At the building of Solomon's temple, 'neither hammer nor axe nor tool of iron was heard therein;'* whereas, alas, in this Temple not only much knocking was heard, but, which was worse, the nails and pins which one master-builder drove in were driven out by the other. To pass by lesser differences between them about predestination, *Hooker maintained* that the church of Rome, though not a pure and perfect, yet is a true church; so that such as live and die therein, upon repentance of all sins of ignorance, may be saved. *Travers maintained* that the church of Rome was no true church; so that such as live and die therein, holding justification by works, cannot be said by the Scriptures to be saved.

"Thus much disturbance was caused; and here Archbishop Whitgift interposed his power, and silenced Travers from preaching either in the Temple or anywhere else. It was laid to his charge that he was no lawful ordained minister according to the church of England; that he preached here without license; that he had broken the order made in the seventh year of her majesty's reign, wherein it was provided that erroneous doctrine, if it came to be publicly taught, should not be publicly refuted, but that notice thereof should be given to the ordinary, to hear and determine such causes.

"As for Travers' silencing, many who were well pleased with the deed done, were offended at the manner of doing it; for all the congregation on a Sabbath in the afternoon were assembled, their attention prepared, the cloth, as I may say, and

* 1 Kings 6 : 7.

napkins were laid, yea, the guests were set, and their knives drawn for their spiritual repast, when suddenly, as Travers was going into the pulpit, a sorry fellow served him with a letter, prohibiting him to preach any more. In obedience to authority—the mild and constant submission whereunto won him respect with his adversaries—Travers calmly signified the same to the congregation, and requested them quietly to depart to their chambers. Thus was our good Zacharias struck dumb in the Temple, but not for infidelity. Meantime his auditory, pained that their pregnant expectation to hear him preach should prove so publicly abortive, and sent sermonless home, manifested a variety of passion, some grieving, some fuming, some murmuring; and the wisest sort, who held their tongues, shook their heads, as disliking the managing of the matter.

"Travers addressed himself by petition to the lords of the Privy-council, where his strength lay, as Hooker's in the Archbishop of Canterbury and the High Commission, grievously complaining that he was punished before he was heard, silenced—by him apprehended the heaviest penalty—before sent for, contrary to equity and reason: 'The law condemning none before it hear him, and know what he hath done.'*

* John 7:51. "To the exception against the lawfulness of his ministry, he pleaded that the communion of saints allows ordination legal in any Christian church. Orders herein are like degrees; and a doctor graduated in any university hath his title and place granted him in all Christendom. For want of license to

"The council-chamber was much divided about Travers' petition. All Whitgift's foes were *ipso facto* made Travers' favorers; besides, he had a large stock of friends on his own account. But Whitgift's finger moved more in church affairs than all the hands of all the privy-councillors besides; and he was content to suffer others to be believed—and perchance to believe themselves—great actors in church government, while he knew he could and did do all things himself therein.

"Thus Travers, notwithstanding the plenty of his potent friends, was overborne by the archbishop, and as he often complained, could never obtain to be brought to a fair hearing. But his grief hereat was something abated when Adam Loftus, archbishop of Dublin and chancellor of Ireland, his ancient colleague in Cambridge, invited him over to be provost of Trinity college in Dublin. Embracing the motion, over he went, accepting the place; and he continued some years therein, till discomposed by their civil wars, he returned into England, and lived here many years very obscurely—though in himself a shining light—as to the matter of outward appearance. Sometimes he did preach, rather when he durst than when he would; debarred from all cure of souls by his non-conformity. Yet had

preach, he pleaded that he was recommended to this place of the Temple by two letters of the bishop of London, the diocesan thereof. His anti-preaching in the afternoon, against what was delivered before, he excused by the example of Paul, who 'gave not place to Peter, no, not for an hour, that the truth of the gospel might continue among them.'" Gal. 2 : 5. Fuller, vol. 3, p. 130.

he Agur's wish, 'neither poverty nor riches,' though his *enough* seemed to be of shortest size. It matters not whether men's means be mounted, or their minds descend, so it be that both meet, as here in him, in a comfortable contentment."*

From this narrative it should seem that, even so early as the year 1591, the question at issue between Puritanism and the Establishment had radically changed. It was no longer a dispute about the accidentals of bishops; it began to broaden into a quarrel upon fundamentals.

"This also," says a recent churchman, "was the course which the argument took on the church side. The church theologians gradually changed their ground, so that there is a wide difference between the school of Whitgift and Hooker, and that of Bilson, Hall, and Laud. At first all that was contended for was, that episcopacy was permissible, and not against the Scriptures; that it was a church government ancient and allowable. This was held by Jewel, Whitgift, Cooper, and others; but these divines did not venture to urge its exclusive claims, or to connect the succession with the validity of the sacraments."†

In the reign of Elizabeth, remarks this same historian, "the real point at issue was not a question of conscience, but whether Puritans should be suffered to hold preferment in the church in open defiance of the requirements of the law."‡ He then

* Fuller, vol. 3, pp. 124–132.

† Perry, Hist. of Ch. of Eng., p. 19. ‡ Ibid., p. 17.

proceeds to say that "the Puritan clergy are fully chargeable with having shown a bitter and litigious spirit;" that, "taking as indulgent a view as possible of them, it cannot be denied that they were eminently provoking;" that "they fought factiously, and they fought unfairly;" and that "their steady obstinacy required and excused the severity of Whitgift."*

When this historian looked back across two hundred years to scrutinize the most momentous page of our English annals, he was either blinded by partiality, or else, under the influence of a dose of hellebore, he really dozed while he seemed to see.

No; his statement does not cover what lawyers call the *gist* of the great quarrel. The question at issue was, *whether or not conscientious non-conformity in things which the imposers held indifferent, but which the Puritans esteemed vitally injurious, should bar Christians from the right to worship God.*

It is easy to say that "ministers declining to conform might retire from the church."† But this latitude Elizabeth would not allow, as witness the history of her whole reign. All non-conformists, whether within or without the church, were harried with indiscriminate fierceness. The possibility of independence was not recognized. The government drove all men by statute into the bosom of the Establishment, and then compelled them by penal legislation to subscribe. Dissenters were

* Perry, pp. 16, 17, passim. † Ibid., p. 17.

outlawed. Every weapon that wit could devise and that ingenuity could shape was employed to coerce consciences. Men were gagged, starved, and burned into uniformity. So searching was the proscription, that a scholar might not obtain a license to teach school without previous subscription.* Therefore it was as dangerous for a papist to mutter mass, or for a separatist to exhort, as it was for a non-conforming churchman, standing within the temple, "to hint a fault, and hesitate dislike."

So idle is it to run a muck at the Puritans because they did not *all* secure peace, "when there was no peace," by becoming "come-outers" at the commencement.

Besides, in the infancy of the Establishment it embraced two sorts of reformers. One class clung tenaciously to the old ways in points of discipline, and pleaded usage and habit in their behalf. The other class loved the church just as dearly, but they yearned after what they esteemed a simpler and more scriptural pattern of church government. Surely there was here no occasion for gags and *autos da fé*. It was a case for arguments, not for executioners. The Establishment was still plastic, had not yet hardened into "the gristle and bone of manhood," if we may borrow Burke's phrase. While there was a chance that the reformers might succeed in moulding the nascent discipline into conformity to their convictions, they were neither "factious"

* Newell, p. 185; Hopkins; Neale, etc.

nor "unfair" in struggling earnestly to achieve a result which they honestly believed to be momentously important. But when the battle had gone hopelessly against them within the Establishment, then it was time to think of separation; and when convinced of this, they did come out and unite with the elder separatists, as we shall see.

It may be remarked *en passant*, that, had a little latitude been permitted at the outset, the gulf would have been bridged; no Curtius need have flung in his body in sad after-years in a vain attempt to fill up the chasm.

The historian upon whom we have been animadverting has himself penned these weighty words: "History can furnish no instance of ecclesiastical persons wielding temporal power usefully and profitably for their own character and the best interests of others. At any rate, the history of this period seems charged with solemn warning, and may be held, not unreasonably, to prove that, for a church to be in alliance with the state with safety and profit, it must submit to be intrusted with but a very limited amount of actual power; and that the full exercise of ecclesiastical discipline can never coexist without peril with the position of a church upheld and established by law."*

The later years of Elizabeth's reign were comparatively calm.† The queen, broken by age, wearied by care, sorrowing for her beheaded favorites,

* Perry, p. 66.

† Fuller, vol. 3, p. 152; Hume, Froude, Burnet.

had lost much of her old *hauteur;* she had no heart to persecute.* The Scottish king, who was heir to the crown, had been bred a Presbyterian, and this made the bishops cautious of acting with their pristine rancor against a party with whom the incoming monarch was identified.† The Puritans, tired, but watchful, "reposed themselves in a sad silence," believing that

> "They also serve who only stand and wait."

At length the event occurred which England sat breathlessly awaiting. On the 24th of March, 1603, the great queen lay dead. The proud mistress of the sea-girt island, the pincher of consciences, the trampler on the fundamental law of liberty—*Nemo tenetur scipsum prodere*—was herself summoned before the bar of the infinite Star-chamber Court. The muse of history closed and sealed the record of Elizabeth's reign.

* Burnet's Own Times. † Neale, vol. 1, p. 308.

CHAPTER XV.

THE PEDANT KING.

THE crown of England now passed from the house of Tudor by escheat, and it was grasped by the Stuarts, the Bourbons of British politics. James I. stooped to lift the sceptre from the grave of Elizabeth. He was the son of poor Mary Stuart, and the great-grandson of Margaret, eldest daughter of Henry VII., who had married the Scottish king in the preceding century.* On the failure of the male line, his hereditary title was of course clean, though the most eminent of the English constitutional historians argues elaborately that the Stuarts' claim was based less upon abstract right than on the tacit popular consent.†

James had reigned in Scotland from his infancy.‡ He brought with him into England a wife and three children. The eldest of these children did not live to reach his majority; the second, a daughter, married abroad; and the other was the famous Prince Charles, who was one day to lose his head under the revolutionary hatchet of the commonwealth.

The new king had been bred in the strictest

* Hume, vol. 2, p. 120. † Hallam, Con. Hist., chap. 6.

‡ Calderwood, True Hist. Church of Scotland, p. 256; Neale; Perry.

school of Presbyterianism, and he was steeped to the lips in oaths to maintain the Calvinistic principles.* He had subscribed the "Solemn League and Covenant;" and recently, standing in a general assembly at Edinburgh, with bonnet off and hands uplifted, he had "praised God that he was king of the Scottish church, the purest kirk in the world."†

On the accession of such a monarch, the Puritans could not but be jubilant. "Now," cried they, as they met in the market-place or congratulated each other on the side-walk, "now we may take Simeon's prayer upon our lips. We have a king who will at least ungag the pulpit and abate the rigor of the laws which ban our party."

But James' disposition had taken a strong contrary bias. "The more he knew of Puritanism, the less favor he bore it. He had remarked in the Scottish church a violent tendency towards republicanism, and a zealous attachment to civil liberty, principles nearly allied to that religious enthusiasm by which its members were actuated. In his capacity of monarch and in his *rôle* of theologian he had experienced the little complaisance which the Puritans were disposed to show him; while they controlled his commands, disputed his pet tenets, and to his face, before assembled Scotland, censured his government and his personal behavior. This was what his monarchical pride could never thor-

* Calderwood, True Hist. Church of Scotland, p. 256; Neale; Perry.

† Neale, vol 1, p. 318. Calderwood.

oughly digest,"* and he came to hate his reproving Nathan.

He was no sooner firmly seated on his new throne than, reflecting on these things, he decided to give the bishops the right hand of fellowship, and to flank Puritanism by deserting it.† This course was made easier by the chorus of gross adulation with which the bishops greeted him.‡ The vainest of men, his self-conceit was tickled by the most hyperbolical compliments. The most pedantic of kings, his weakness was pampered by the most lavish encomiums. James had the stomach of an ostrich for praise; no panegyric was too gross for him to swallow. In Scotland he had been curbed; in England he was given loose reign. Sychophancy, so new and so fascinating, quite won his heart.

Of course James had no honest religious principles. North of the Tweed he was a Presbyterian, because he dared be nothing else. What he termed *kingcraft*, the art of dissimulation, the science of appearance, the *finesse* of empty show, of which he was profound master, led him to frequent the kirk in Scotland, to become a rigid churchman in England, and it would have made him a mutterer of the mass at Rome.§ Indeed Sir Francis Walsingham, who had studied him closely, and who kept his ubiquitous spies at Holyrood, had come to the conclusion that "the king was either inclined to turn Pa-

* Hume, vol. 2, p. 123. † Perry, p. 28.
‡ Ibid., p. 30. § Macauley's Miscellaneous Essays.

pist or to be of no religion."* He was "an habitual swearer, a drunkard, and a liar," says Marsden;† and Hallam affirms that he "was all his life rather a bold liar than a good dissembler."‡

Such was his "sacred majesty" king James I., as he has been painted by the sober pen of history.

James was met in his progress to London by two petitions. One, entitled the *millenary* petition, because it was said to have been subscribed by a thousand hands, was presented by the Puritans.§ In it a reformation of certain ceremonies and alleged abuses was urged. The other bore the *imprimatur* of Oxford; and this pleaded for the maintenance of the *statu quo*.‖

When the king reached the metropolis, the plague was holding a ghastly *feté*; and the citizens were so terror-stricken that, on the occasion of the coronation, the streets "were almost desolate, and the pageants stood without spectators to gaze upon them."¶

But when these horrors had abated, and James had settled himself in Elizabeth's luxurious chair of state, he responded to the inimical petitions by a proclamation, in which he decreed a conference for the settlement of the matters in dispute.**

* Burnet's Own Times, p. 2.

† Marsden, Early Puritans, p. 367. See Shent's Ch. History, sec. 523.

‡ Hallam, Con. Hist., vol. 1, p. 291.

§ Neale, vol. 1, p. 320; Marsden, Newell.

‖ Perry, Neale, Heglin, etc.

¶ Calderwood; Strype's Whitgift.

** Cardwell, Documentary Annals, vol. 2. Strype, Life of Whitgift, p. 568.

Of this order was born the famous Conference of Hampton Court; and in January, 1604, the conflicting parties met in a drawing-room within the privy chamber of that historic palace,* the monument of Wolsey's despotism and humiliation.

The Establishment was represented by nine bishops, reinforced by the same number of lesser dignitaries; and of these, Whitgift and Bancroft were the leaders.†

Four ministers of the king's nomination‡ were the knight-errants of Puritanism in this sorry tilt; and Calderwood complains that "two of these were not sound," but were appointed "to spy and prevaricate."§

Raynolds, who was esteemed by his contemporaries the most learned man in England,‖ was the Atlas who bore upon his shoulders the Puritan cause. Wood, after an elaborate eulogy on this great divine's reading, memory, wit, judgment, industry, probity, and sanctity of life, closes the glowing record thus: "In a word, nothing can be spoken

* Fuller, vol. 3, pp. 172, 173. Burnet's Own Times.

† Ibid. The names of the church party were, Whitgift, archbishop of Canterbury; Bancroft, bishop of London; bishops Matthew, Bilson, Buffington, Rudd, Watson, Robinson, and Dove; and of lesser dignitaries, Boden, dean of Chester; the deans of the chapel-royal, St. Paul's, Salisbury, Gloucester, Worcester, and Windsor, and the archdeacon of Nottingham.

‡ These names were, Drs. John Raynolds and Thomas Sparks, professors of divinity at Oxford, and Drs. Chadderton and Knewstubs, professors of divinity at Cambridge.

§ Calderwood, p. 474.

‖ Newell, p. 223. Fuller.

against him, save only that he is a chief pillar of Puritanism, and a great favorer of non-conformity."*

The king, fancying himself possessed of a capacity which existed only in the imagination of his flatterers, and of a learning which was still more mythical, was now intent on glutting his vanity. "High on a throne of royal state," he was employed in dictating magisterially to an assembly of divines concerning points of faith and discipline.† The royal pedant,

"Like Cato, gave his little senate laws,
And sat attentive to his own applause;
While *statesmen* and *divines* each sentence raise,
And wonder with a foolish face of praise."

On the first day of the Conference, the Puritans were not admitted, the lords of the Privy-council forming the sole audience.‡ The whole session was devoted to satisfying his majesty upon several mooted points of discipline,§ and in *cramming* him, as the school phrase runs, for his next day's bout with non-conformity; for since James had been bred a Presbyterian, it was no Herculean task to let down the plummet and sound the shallow depths of his knowledge of the English ecclesiastical polity. At the last, the king expressed himself well satisfied on all points, and so ended the lesson.||

On the second day of the Conference—Sunday intervened between this session and the opening

* Wood, Hist. and Antiq. of the Univ. of Oxford, book 1, p. 301. † Hume, vol. 2, p. 123.

‡ Fuller, vol. 3, p. 172; Burnet, Strype. § Hume.

|| Lathbury, Prayer-book; Shent, Ch. Hist., etc.

one—the Puritans were ushered into the presence of the king. We quote Carlyle's description of what ensued:

"Awful, devout Puritanism, decent, dignified ceremonialism—both always of high moment in this world, but not of equally high—appeared here facing each other. The demands of the Puritans seem to modern times very limited indeed. They asked that there should be a new and correct translation of the Bible—granted. That there should be increased zeal in teaching it—omitted. That 'lay impropriations,' that is, tithes snatched from the old church by laymen, might be made to yield a seventh part towards maintaining ministers in dark regions which had none—refused. That the clergy in districts might be permitted to meet together and strengthen one another's hands, as in old times—indignantly refused. On the whole, if such a thing durst be hinted at, for the tone is almost inaudibly low and humble, that pious, straitened preachers, in terror of offending God by idolatry, and useful to human souls, might not be cast out of their parishes for genuflections, white surplices, and such like, but be allowed some Christian liberty in external things. These claims his majesty scouted to the winds, applauded by all bishops and dignitaries, lay and clerical."*

James loved to argue in the imperative mood. He was better at commands than at syllogisms. "I will have," said he, "one doctrine and one dis-

* Carlyle, Letters and Speeches of Cromwell, vol. 1, pp. 51, 52.

cipline, one religion, in substance and ceremony; and therefore I charge all never to speak more upon the point how far you are bound to obey, when the church hath ordained it."* He then avowed his maxim to be, "No BISHOP, NO KING."†

After some further theological skirmishing, James turned to Raynolds, and inquired whether he had any thing further to object. "No," said the overawed and browbeaten divine. Then rising from his chair, the monarch cried, "If this be all that you have to say for your party, I shall make them conform themselves, or I will harry them out of the land, or else do worse."‡

So fell the curtain on the second session.

On the third day, the friends of the Establishment were called into the Privy-chamber to enlighten the king upon the High Commission and the oath *ex officio*, both of which were held by the Puritans to be unconstitutional;§ as indeed the great lights of the English bar, Holt and Somers, Hale and Erskine, have since decided.

But since these relics of the Inquisition formed chief branches of the royal prerogative, James, who was only anxious for an excuse to clutch them, permitted himself to be convinced by the obsequious clergy.‖

When the king announced his determination to

* Fuller, vol. 3, p. 187. Barlow, p. 85. † Ibid.
‡ Ibid., Perry, Neale, Carlyle, etc.
§ Neale, vol. 1, p. 330, and on. Hallam, Con. Hist.
‖ Fuller, vol. 3; Perry, Strype.

retain these alien and atrocious tyrannies, Whitgift, in an ecstacy of servility, sobbed out, "Undoubtedly your majesty speaks by the special assistance of God's Spirit." And Bancroft outran the archbishop of Canterbury in this sycophantic scrub-race, by falling on his knees and adding, "I protest, my heart melteth with joy that Almighty God, of his singular mercy, hath given us such a king as, since Christ's time, hath not been."*

These speeches fitly closed the poorest and the meanest farce that has ever been enacted. Saxon servility here touched the muddiest bottom. The foremost divines in England, by position, stooped to pay this impious homage to a monarch who was known to be the most loquacious pedant, the basest coward, the most beastly drunkard, the most profane swearer, the filthiest conversationalist, the most licentious fop, the most cunning dissembler, and the most wholesale liar in the island;† of whom Bishop Burnet says, that "while hungry writers flattered him out of all measure at home, he was despised by all abroad as a pedant without true judgment, courage, or steadiness;"‡ and who was described by the sagacious Sully as "the wisest fool in Europe."§

Of the king's conduct at this mock Conference men of all parties speak in tones of like contempt.

* Barlow, Sum of Hampton Court Conference. From Barlow's account all others are taken. See Perry, p. 83; Fuller, vol. 3, p. 192.

† Colle's Detection; Holden, Court and Life of James, 1650; Kennet, Hist. Eng; Roumer, vol. 2; Harris, Hist. and Critical Acct. of the Life and Writings of James I.; etc.

‡ Burnet's Own Times, p. 8. § Sully, Memoirs, vol. 2.

At one moment he was a bully, at the next he was a buffoon, and then he changed into a bigot.* He was extravagantly elated at the figure he had made and the "victory" he had achieved over the Non-conformists. "I peppered them soundly," wrote he to a Scottish churchman.†

Who can wonder that a later generation scoffed and hissed at this picture of a narrow, pedantic, and blaspheming king, while all good men prayed God to save the church from the feeble knees and the itching palms of this bench of bishops?

The Conference gave little satisfaction. The bishops were internally conscious that they made no fine figure therein. "The Non-conformists complained that the king sent for their divines, not to have their scruples satisfied, but his pleasure propounded; not that he might know what they could *say*, but that they might know what he would *do*. Besides," adds honest Fuller, "it was said that the Conference was partially set forth by Dr. Barlow alone, who was their professed adversary, and to the great disadvantage of their divines. And when the Israelites go down to the Philistines to whet all their iron tools, no wonder if these set a sharp edge on their own and a blunt one on their enemies' weapons."‡

Several weeks after the *sine die* adjournment of the Conference, the king issued a proclamation, in which he ordered the rigid enforcement of the con-

* Newell, p. 229; Perry, Burnet, Calderwood, Strype, Shent, etc. † Ibid.; Strype; Whitgift, App., 239.

‡ Fuller, vol. 3, pp. 192, 193.

formity statutes, and took the initiatory steps towards "harrying the Puritans out of England."* At the same time he assumed the right to reshuffle and change some portions of the Liturgy upon his own *ipse dixit.* "It was a high strain of the prerogative," says Neale, "to alter a form of worship established by law merely by a royal proclamation, without consent of Parliament or convocation; for by the same power that his majesty altered one article in the Liturgy, he might set aside the whole; every sentence being equally established by act of Parliament. But this wise monarch made no scruple of dispensing with the laws. However, the force of all proclamations determined with the king's life; and since there was no act of Parliament to establish these amendments, it was argued very justly in the next reign, that this was not the Liturgy of the church of England, and that consequently it was not binding upon the clergy."†

Two weeks before the Conference at Hampton Court, Cartwright died.‡ He was one of the initiators of the Puritan controversy,§ and Fuller calls him the "brain of non-conformity."

Eight weeks later, Whitgift also went down to the grave.‖ We will not "torment him before his time." Some future Swift, some Douglas Jerrold, shall paint him with his immortal pen to the scornful detestation of the ages.

* Perry, p. 115, and others. † Neale, vol. 1, pp. 331, 332.
‡ Fuller, vol. 3, p. 171. Newell, p. 171.
§ Chap. 12, p. 167. ‖ Fuller, Perry, Strype.

CHAPTER XVI.

THE KING'S "FAITHFUL FRIENDS."

Bishop Bancroft, the *avant courier* of Laud, a prelate "most stiff and stern to press conformity,"* succeeded Whitgift in the see of Canterbury. Under his iron *régime* the differences between the two wings of the church became implacable. A wound not dangerous at the outset was poisoned by the remedies.† Men's consciences were racked with fresh zeal. The government "weeded men's lives, and made use, to their disgrace, of their infirmities." Each hour the throat of non-conformity was pressed more closely.

When Parliament assembled in 1604, James, in his opening harangue, offered "to meet the papists in the mid-way, excepting chiefly to the pontiff's assumed authority over princes;"‡ and he added that "the sect called Puritans was insufferable in any well-governed commonwealth."§ At the next session of Parliament, the royal Judas, in pursuit of his phantom of a union between Rome and the Establishment, grew still more vindictive, declaring the Romanists to be "*faithful subjects*," and this on the eve of the Gunpowder-plot; but expressing de-

* Fuller, vol. 3, p. 244.

† Bacon's Works, vol. 2, p. 544.

‡ Rapin, Hist. Eng., vol. 2, pp. 165, 166. Neale, vol. 2, p. 51.

§ Ibid.

testation of the Puritans, as worthy of fire for their opinions.*

At the same time a convocation, over which Bancroft presided, adopted the Book of Canons sanctioned by the king;† and in these it was maintained that all objectors to the Book of Common Prayer, the apostolical character of the Establishment, or the ordination of bishops, and all abettors of other churches independent of the legal one, were excommunicated, and abandoned to the wrath of God.‡

It puzzled the thinkers of that day to see in what respect these canons differed from the papal anathemas. Posterity has not solved this problem.

Grasping these thunderbolts, Bancroft commenced the battle. Fifteen hundred non-conforming clergymen were silenced, imprisoned, or exiled.§ "The clergy proceeded with a consistent disregard of the national liberties. The importation of foreign books was impeded; a severe ecclesiastical censorship was exercised over the press; frivolous acts were denounced as religious offences. A later convocation, in a series of canons, denied every doctrine of popular rights, asserting the superiority of the king to the Parliament and the laws, and admitting, in their zeal for absolute monarchy, no exception to the duty of passive obedience.

* Prince, p. 3. Bancroft, Hist. United States, vol. 1, p. 298.

† Constitution and Canons Eccl., Prince, p. 107.

‡ Sparrow's Collections, pp. 271–334. Constitutions and Canons, etc.

§ Newell, p. 231. Calderwood.

"But the oppressed party was neither intimidated nor weakened. The moderate men, who assented to external ceremonies as to things indifferent, were unwilling to enforce them by merciless cruelty; and they resisted, not the square cap and the surplice, but the *compulsory* imposition of them. Thus the opponents of the church became the guardians of popular liberty; the lines of the contending parties were distinctly drawn: the Established church and the monarchy on one side, were arrayed against the Puritan clergy and the people on the other."*

In this quarrel Parliament began to side openly with the Puritans; not because its members agreed *in toto* with the dissenting religious tenets, but because the church had injudiciously declared itself against the highest political aspirations of England. So the Commons resolutely favored the sect which was their natural ally in the struggle against civil despotism.†

This made James' anger blaze at white heat. The recent Parliaments had been so tenacious and vigorous in asserting the long buried, but now resuscitated rights guaranteed by *Magna Charta*, that the king one day exclaimed, "I had rather live like a hermit in the forest, than be a king over such a people as the pack of Puritans are that overrule the lower house."‡

* Newell, p. 231. Calderwood.

† Bancroft, Hist. of United States, vol. 1, p. 298.

‡ Hallam, Con. Hist., vol. 1, pp. 408-420.

Unfortunately on the side of the throne were the *éclat* of position, the omnipotence of wealth, the prestige of success, and the habit of submission, and these made the normal forces of society, justice, toleration, regulated liberty, long kick the beam.

But from the pack of odium which Puritanism, like Bunyan's Pilgrim, bore upon its shoulders, one parcel now slipped out. Custom, the mint-master of current words, had long confounded all dissenters under the one name, "Puritan." Now, however, the "Familists," "whose opinions were as senseless as their lives were sensual," in a petition to the king pointed out the radical differences between their sect and the Puritans, who were, as they knew, odious to him, hoping thus to curry favor with James. But "these Familists could not be so glad to leave the Puritans, as the Puritans were glad to be left by them."*

But the gabble of the "Familists," the murmurs of the Parliament, the cries of the Puritans for redress, and the pedantic clatter of the king were all brought to a sudden, though but momentary pause, by an "event which never took place."

England, tottering on the edge of a catastrophe, just cheated fate by a timely discovery. Death struck with its clammy fingers at the king and Parliament, and missed its aim by the miscarriage of a letter.

In 1605, "the Romanists, despairing either by flattery to woo, or force to wrest, any free and pub-

* Fuller, vol. 3, p. 210.

lic exercise of their religion from the state, entered into a conspiracy to blow up the Parliament-house with gunpowder."*

The very conception of such an idea is of itself the strongest argument that could be offered against the bigoted proscription of that illiberal age. The Romanist, like the Puritan, was hedged about with penalties and disabilities. The reformer submitted till patience ceased to be a virtue; then drawing an honest sword, smote off his shackles. The papist, true to the genius of his faith, plunged into a hidden life of cabal and intrigue, plot and conspiracy.

"The constant under-agitation of the body politic thus produced was in every way unfortunate: unfortunate for the Romanists, in furnishing a show of justice for the cruelties inflicted on them; for the government and the church, in keeping their bitter resentments aglow; for the Puritans, in giving the rulers an excuse for more arbitrary proceedings against them."†

At the very time that James was haranguing the Parliament on their behalf, his "*faithful subjects*" were conspiring to blow him into atoms.

"Treason without a Jesuit therein, is like a dry wall without either lime or mortar." So in this case, Gerrard, a whelp of that litter, was the cement to join the conspirators together with the sacrament of secrecy.‡

* Fuller, vol. 3, p. 212.
† Perry, pp. 64, 65.
‡ Fuller.

"At the outset," says Fuller, "an important scruple arose: how to part their friends from their foes in the Parliament, they having many in the house of alliance, yea, of the same—in conscience a nearer kindred—religion with themselves. Such an impartial destruction was uncharitable, yet an exact separation seemed impossible. Here a Jesuit, instead of untying, cut this knot asunder with this his sharp decision: that 'in such a case as this, it was lawful to kill friend and foe together.'*

"Be it remembered that, though these plotters intended at last with honor to own the action, when success had made all things secure, yet they proposed, when the blow was first given, and while the act was certain, but the success thereof doubtful, to father the fact on the Puritans. They thought their backs were broad enough to bear both the sin and the shame; and that this saddle, for the present, would finely fit their backs, whose discontent, as these plotters would pretend, unable otherwise to achieve their desired alteration in church government, had by this damnable treason effected the same. By transferring the fact on the innocent Puritans, they hoped not only to decline the odium of so hellish a design, but also, by the strangeness of the act and the unexpectedness of the actors, to amuse all men, and beget a universal distrust, that every man would grow jealous of himself. And

* The conspirators doubtless acted on the Jesuit doctrine that "the end justifies the means," and that "evil may be done that good may come."

while such amazement tied, in a manner, all hands, these plotters promised themselves the working out of their ends, partly by their home strength, and the rest by calling in the assistance of foreign princes.

"So they fell aworking in a vault beneath the Parliament-house. Dark the place, in the depth of the earth; dark the time, in the dead of the night; dark the design, the actors therein concealed by oath from others, and thereby combined among themselves. Oh, how easy is any work where high merit is conceived the wages thereof. In piercing through the wall nine feet thick, they imagined that thereby they hewed forth their way to heaven.

"But they digged more with their silver in an hour, than with their iron in many days; namely, when discovering a cellar hard by, they hired the same, and these pioneers saved much of their pains thereby. And now all things were carried so secretly, that there was no possibility of detection, seeing the actors themselves had solemnly sworn that they would not, and all others might as safely swear they could not make discovery thereof.

"But so it fell out, that the sitting of Parliament was put off from time to time; and accordingly their working in the vault, which attended the motion of Parliament, had several distinct intermissions and resumptions, as if God had given warning to these traitors, by the slow proceeding and oft adjourning of Parliament, meantime seriously to consider what they went about, and seasonably to desist from so damnable a design, as suspicious that at last that would be ruined which had been so long retarded. But no taking off their wheels will stay those chariots from drowning which God hath decreed shall be swallowed in the Red sea.*

"'Behold, here are fire and wood; but where is the lamb for the burnt-offering?' Alas, a whole flock of lambs were not far off, all appointed to the slaughter. The king, prince Henry, peers, bishops, judges, knights, burgesses, all destined to destruction. But thanks be to God, nothing was blown up but the treason, or brought to execution but the traitors.

"With a pen fetched from the feather of a fowl, a letter was written to the lord Monteagle in these words:

"'My Lord—Out of the love I bear to some of your friends, I have a care of your preservation; therefore I would advise you, as you tender your life, to devise some excuse to shift off your attendance at this Parliament, for God and man have concurred to punish the wickedness of these times. And think not slightingly of this advertisement, but retire yourself into your country, where you may await the event with safety; for though there be no appearance of any stir, yet I say they shall receive a terrible blow, this Parliament, and still not see who hurts them. This counsel is not to be contemned,

* Exodus 14:25

because it may do you good, and can do you no harm; for the danger is passed as soon as you burn this letter. And I hope God will give you grace to make good use of it, to whose holy protection I now commend you.'

"A strange letter from a strange hand, by a strange messenger, without date to it, name at it, and, I had almost said, sense in it; a letter which, even when it was opened, was still sealed, such the affected obscurity therein.

"The lord Monteagle, as loyalty advised him, communicated the letter to the earl of Salisbury, he to the king. His majesty, on a second perusal, expounded that the mystical 'blow' meant therein must be by gunpowder; and he gave orders for searching the rooms under the Parliament-house, on pretence of looking for lost hangings which were conveyed away.

"The first search, made about evening, discovered nothing but the cellar full of wood, and a man—Fawkes disguised—attending thereon. However, the sight of Fawkes so quickened the jealousy of Lord Monteagle, that this first slight search led to a second scouting, more closely and secretly performed.

"This was made at midnight into the vault under the Parliament-house. There 'the mystery of iniquity' was quickly discovered; a pile of fuel, faced over with billets, lined under with thirty-six barrels of powder, besides iron bars, to make the force of the explosion more effectual. Guy Fawkes was apprehended in the outer room, with a dark-lantern in his hand—the lively emblem of their design, whose dark side was turned to man, while the light part was exposed to God—and three matches, ready to give fire to the train."*

Fawkes confessed all; the conspirators were "solemnly arraigned, convicted, and condemned at London. So foul the fact, so fair the proof, they could say nothing for themselves." One of these caitiffs was Garnet, provincial of the English Jesuits, whom the pope afterwards canonized.†

Thus "murder will out," and "heaven defeated hell of its desired success."

* Fuller, vol. 3, pp. 212–219.

† Neale, vol. 1, p. 345. Fuller.

CHAPTER XVII.

THE BIRTH OF A NEW AND THE DEATH OF AN OLD EPOCH.

ENGLAND did not at once realize the ghastly horror which had so nearly robbed her of her king and legislature. But when the people became acquainted with the programme of the gunpowder-plotters, they uttered a vengeful cry. Parliament, echoing the opinion of the side-walk, was provoked to curb Romanism by the enactment of a rigid penal code.*

But this severity was soon relaxed. A courtier's hint was the key which unlocked a multitude of prison doors. One day Sir Dudley Carlton returned from Spain. Noticing that the king was accustomed to hunt unguarded, the ambassador button-holed him, and said, "My liege, if you use not more precaution, the Jesuits will assassinate you."† This air-drawn dagger terrified the royal coward. He disliked to give up hunting, so he ceased to persecute the papists. "I have the minutes of the council-book of the year 1606," says Burnet, "and they are full of orders for the discharge and transportation of incarcerated priests; sometimes ten a day were set free."‡

* Lingard, vol. 6, p. 68; Hume, Fox.

† Burnet's Own Times, p. 5.

‡ Ibid.

But these empty cells were not long aired. The Puritans replaced the Romanists. If the papists were trodden on, viper-like, they would hiss and sting. James thought it safer to spit upon the Reformation. This philosophy gave added venom to the crusade against Puritanism. Ere long a warm controversy sprang up among the Puritans as to the lawfulness and the policy of separation.* While this battle vexed the ranks of the non-conformists, the conforming clergy stood by as spectators of the combat. The larger portion of the Puritans decided still to adhere to the Establishment, influenced by the reflection that it was a true church, though they esteemed it corrupt in ceremony, and by the fact that the Separatists were even worse harried than themselves.†

Indeed the most rigid of the Separatists were already preparing to quit the island.‡ It was in 1607 that those pilgrims, whom God destined to be the fathers of religious America, took their sad farewell of dear, cruel England.

In the north of the island, scattered through the border towns of Yorkshire, and through the county hamlets of Nottingham and Lincoln, there lived in these years communities of stout yeomen "whose hearts the Lord had touched with heavenly zeal for his truth." They had "joined themselves by a covenant into a church estate in the fellowship of the

* Newell, Neale, Hume.

† Neale, vol. 1, p. 344; Newell, Fuller.

‡ Bancroft, Hist. of United States, vol. 1, p. 300.

gospel." Wedded to the Separatist tenets, these Puritans rejected "the offices and callings, the courts and canons" of the Establishment. Renouncing all ecclesiastical obedience to human authority, they planted themselves upon the Bible, under which they asserted for themselves an unlimited, never-ending right to make advances in the truth, and "to walk in all the ways which God had made known or should make known to them."*

The arbitrary government of James I. could ill brook the proclamation of such a gospel. So now, scourged, starved, and imprisoned at home, these congregations prepared to emigrate.†

The Netherlands were then the freest, most tolerant countries in Christendom. There also the Reformation had been shaped by the plastic hand of Calvin. Thus the exiles were attracted to the Low Countries. In Holland then they eventually settled, though they did not reach that haven without vicissitudes which would have chilled the ardor and affrighted the hearts of less dauntless heroes.

The continental career of the Pilgrims was no smooth gala festival. Strangers in a new land, with whose language they were mostly unacquainted, they made hard shift to live; and though they won the sympathy and secured the veneration of their honest entertainers, Holland was not "home." The busy crowds, shod in their wooden shoes, the guttural Belgic tongue, the quaintly gabled houses, the

* Bancroft, History of the United States, vol. 1, p. 300.

† Ibid.

flat banks of the canals which cobwebbed Holland, the dykes which shut out the sullen ocean, and which were defended by windmills whose long arms were dipped into the encroaching water to fling it back from the coasts usurped by the skill of man from the complaining sea—these bore no resemblance to the hills and vales of their lost island, and they could not compensate the exiles for the old, familiar landscape,

> "For the shieling wood and stream-girt,
> Where romance youth's summer sped;
> For the belfry by the gray kirk,
> In whose shadow slept their dead."

The Pilgrims tarried for a time in Amsterdam; thence they went to Leyden, that heroic town whose burghers had pawned it to the sea, to save it from the grip of the Spaniard and the pope.* There too they conquered all hearts by their piety, their patience, and their fortitude.

But despite the friendliness of their reception, "weighty reasons, often and seriously discussed, inclined the Pilgrims to look beyond Holland for a permanent abode. They had been bred to agricultural pursuits, and in the Netherlands they were forced to learn the mechanical trades. Brewster became a printer; Bradford learned the art of dyeing silk. The language of the Dutch never became pleasantly familiar. They lived but as men in exile. 'Their continual labors, with other crosses and

* Motley, Rise of the Dutch Republic, vol. 1.

sorrows, left them in danger to scatter or sink.'"* They yearned for a true and lasting home.

One day they decided that, since they might not return to England, where persecution frowned on them from the sands and cliffs, they would quit their Netherland firesides and settle in that shadowy and almost unknown NEW WORLD which Columbus had added to the Old.

This decision once made, the Pilgrims transmitted to England a request to be permitted to colonize America. "We are well weaned," wrote Robinson and Brewster, two of their most trusted teachers, "from the delicate milk of our mother country, and inured to the difficulties of a strange land. Our people are industrious and frugal. We are knit together as a body in a most sacred covenant of the Lord, of the violation whereof we make great conscience, and by virtue of which we hold ourselves straitly tied to all care of each other's good, and of the whole. It is not with us as with men whom small things can discourage."†

But nothing could be wrung from their surly king but an informal promise of neglect.‡ On this the exiles relied, exclaiming, "If there should afterwards be a purpose to wrong us, though we had a charter whose seal was as broad as the house-floor, there would be means enough found to reverse or recall it."§

At length all was ready. After innumerable discouragements, including one false start, when

* Bancroft, vol. 1, p. 303. † Ibid. ‡ Ibid. § Ibid.

they had been winnowed by the desertion of a portion of their friends whose hearts had failed them at the critical moment, the little company of one hundred and twenty souls, men, women, and children,* repaired to Delft-Haven. Here, since with the Pilgrims every undertaking began with God, they knelt by the side of the moaning sea, while Robinson invoked the heavenly benediction on his departing flock; after which that great teacher gave them a farewell which breathed a freedom of opinion and an independence of authority such as then was hardly known in the world.†

Then came the embarkation; the sails were spread, and "the Mayflower of a forlorn hope, freighted with the prospects of a future state, plunged across the unknown sea."

We may not pause to rehearse the touching story of the long, cold, and dangerous autumnal passage; of the landing on the inhospitable rocks at a dismal season; of their desertion by the ship which had brought them from Holland, and which seemed their only hold upon the world of fellow-men, a prey to the elements and to want, and fearfully ignorant of the power and temper of the savage tribes that filled the unexplored continent upon whose verge they stood.‡

"But all things wrought together for good. These trials of wandering and exile, of the ocean, the winter, the wilderness, and the savage foe, were

* Young's Narrative. Neale, Records of the Pilgrims, etc.

† Bancroft.

‡ Everett.

the final assurance of success. They kept away from the enterprise all patrician softness, all hereditary claim to preëminence. No effeminate nobility crowded into the austere ranks of the Pilgrims. No Carr, no Villiers desired to conduct this ill-provided band of outcast Puritans. No well-endowed clergy were desirous to quit their cathedrals to set up a splendid hierarchy in the frozen wilderness. No craving governors were anxious to be sent over to a cheerless El Dorado of ice and snow."*

But the gloomy presage did not daunt the conscientious exiles; through all they trusted God. When half their company lay dead on the chilly coast, and the rest seemed shivering towards the grave, they found strength to murmur, "Father, not our will, but thine be done."

And this unfaltering faith God owned, and he blessed their enterprise beyond their most sanguine hope or thought. "Successful indeed in its outset, it has been more and more successful at every subsequent point in the line of time. Accomplishing all they projected, what they projected is the least part that has come to pass. Forming a design in itself grand, bold, and even appalling in its requisite risks and sacrifices, the fulfilment of that design is the least thing which, in the steady progress of events, has flowed from their counsels and their efforts. Did they propose for themselves a refuge beyond the sea from the religious and political tyranny of Europe? They achieved not that alone,

* Everett, Orations and Speeches, vol. 1, p. 47.

but they have opened a wide asylum to all the victims of oppression throughout the world. Did they look for a retired spot, inoffensive from its obscurity, safe in its remoteness from the haunts of despots, where the little church of Leyden might enjoy freedom of conscience? Behold the mighty regions over which in peaceful conquest—*victoria sine clade*—they have borne the banners of the cross. Did they seek, under the common franchise of a trading-charter, to prosecute a frugal commerce in reimbursement of the expenses of their humble establishment? The fleets and navies of their descendants are on the farthest ocean, and the wealth of the Indies is now wafted on every tide to the coasts where, with hook and line, they painfully gathered up their frugal earnings. Did they in their brightest, most sanguine moments contemplate a thrifty, loyal, and prosperous colony, portioned off, like a younger son of the imperial family, to a humble and dutiful distance? Behold the spectacle of a powerful and independent republic, founded on the shores where some of those are but lately dead who saw the first-born of the Pilgrims."*

But while the Pilgrims were preparing to cross the sea, king James was full of his prerogative. He "apprehended that he could convince his subjects of its unlimited extent. For this purpose he turned preacher in the Star-chamber, and took this text: "Give the king thy judgments, O God, and thy righteousness to the king's son."†

* Everett, ut antea.

† Psalm 72 : 1.

"After dividing and subdividing, and giving the literal and the mystical meaning of his text, he applied it to the judges and courts of judicature, telling them that 'the king sitting in the throne of God, all judgments centre in him; and therefore, for inferior courts to determine difficult questions without consulting him, was to limit his power and encroach on his prerogative, which it was not lawful for the tongue of lawyer nor any subject to dispute.' As it is atheism and blasphemy to dispute what God can do, 'so,' said James, 'it is to take away that mystical reverence which belongs to him who sits in the throne of God.' Then addressing himself to his auditory, he advised them 'not to meddle with the king's prerogative or honor. Plead not,' he added, 'upon Puritanical principles, which make all things popular, but keep within the ancient limits.'"*

When Alexander sent word to the Lacedæmonians that he had made himself a god, they replied with easy nonchalance, "Be a god." But when king James set up for one, the Puritans, it seems, were not equally complaisant.

In 1618, twenty-four months after his plea for the prerogative, James, in order to repress the growth of Puritanism, by enlisting the natural depravity of the human heart against it, issued a declaration for the encouragement of Sunday sports, a declaration right in the teeth of a proclamation of an earlier date, and also counter to the Articles of

* Neale, vol. 1, p. 372.

the church ratified under the great seal, in which the morality of the day was affirmed. By this manifesto magistrates were directed not to disturb "any lawful recreations, such as dancing, either of men or women, archery, leaping, vaulting, Whitsun-ales, or May-games."*

"When this declaration was hawked abroad, it is not so hard to believe, as sad to recount, what grief and distraction was thereby occasioned in many honest men's hearts; the recreations specified being conceived impeditive to the observation of the Lord's day, yea, unsuitable and unbeseeming the essential duties thereof."†

The king had never been a stickler for purity of doctrine; he accepted what made for, and forbade what made against the maxims of absolutism. He was enamoured only of outward uniformity and clerical subserviency. His latest whim was to patronize the Arminian tenets. The most zealous advocates of that creed were now advanced to some of the best bishoprics in England. "These divines, apprehending that their principles were hardly consistent with the Thirty-nine Articles, fell in with the prerogative, and covered themselves under the wing of his majesty's pretensions to unlimited power. This gave rise to a new distinction at court between *church* and *state* Puritans. All were Puritans with king James who clutched the *Magna Charta* in opposition to his arbitrary government; these were Puritans in the state, as those were Puritans who

* Fuller, vol. 3, p. 270. Neale, vol. 1, p. 381. † Fuller.

had scruples about the ceremonies in the church. Ecclesiastical Puritanism was now reinforced by the Constitutionalists, and these united formed the great majority of the nation. To balance this potent party, James protected and countenanced the Arminians and the papists, who, in their turn, cried lustily for the prerogative, and hardened into a state faction against the fundamental laws and the sealed charters of the past."*

It was around these nucleus bodies that the satellites of either revolved.

And now the home record became as disgraceful as the foreign aspect was disastrous. The "Thirty Years' War" was desolating the Continent. Protestantism seemed at its last gasp. Gustavus Adolphus had not yet swooped with his Norsemen to the rescue; Richelieu had not yet commenced to spin his web of tortuous policy. The *Ultramontanists* were everywhere triumphant. Yet England looked on calmly and saw the Reformation choked. Even when the king's son-in-law lost the palatinate, while his daughter and her elector-husband were driven into Holland for a sanctuary, the British government merely muttered a verbal protest. The lazy indolence of the king, both as a father and a Protestant, was only broken by a demand for a subsidy, ostensibly to aid the good cause, but which the royal swindler dissipated in riot and licentiousness.†

But it is not necessary to go minutely into the history of the latter years of this imbecile pedant's

* Neale, vol. 1, p. 384.

† Hallam, Schiller.

disgraceful reign. James was consistent only in his hatred of the Puritans. Towards them the Nero, the Caligula of his character never changed. In all other respects he was a kaleidoscope, of which the shrewdest courtier could never "guess" the next combination.

He reduced England from a first-class to a second-rate power; his government was a prolonged plot; and so well known was his cowardice, that foreign nations always counted on it when settling their English policy. Thus Dionysio Lazari, who spent some years in Britain under James' rule, made a report to the Congregation for the Propagation of the Faith at Rome, in which, after specifying the means whereby Romanism might be advanced in England, he said that "he relied much on the plan of working upon the fears and suspicions of the king, who was timid, and who seemed indifferent to any religion."*

Macauley states that James, in order to effect his favorite project of marrying his son into one of the great continental houses, was ready to make immense concessions to Rome, and even to admit a modified primacy in the pope.†

He was always scheming to root out Scottish Presbyterianism, and to extend the English Establishment into the twin kingdom.‡ But this plot was foiled by the resolution of the Covenanters,

* Ranke, History of the Popes, vol. 2, p. 456.

† Macauley, Miscellaneous Essays.

‡ Wilson, Hist. of King James. Collier.

and the royal "god" found that his prerogative could not conjure this creation into existence.

Almost the only thing which posterity can find to laud in James' reign is the new translation of the Bible, which was then undertaken and completed; and even this was one of the scanty concessions which the evangelical party in the church wrung from the king at the Hampton Court conference. "The number of select and competent divines engaged in this great work," says Fuller, "was not too many, lest one such trouble another; and yet many, lest any thing might haply escape them. Neither courting praise for expedition, nor fearing reproach for slackness—seeing that in a business of moment none deserve blame for convenient slowness—they had expended almost three years in the work, not only examining the channels by the fountain, the translation with the original, which was necessary, but also comparing channels with channels, which was abundantly useful, in the Spanish, Italian, French, and Dutch languages. The Bible was published in 1611; and their learning, skilfulness, piety, discretion therein, have bound the church unto them in a debt of special remembrance and gratitude."*

It is also worthy of note, though James had little enough to do with it, that the first congregation of that sect, which afterwards won such wide fame and set on foot such mighty revolutions on either continent, the Independents, was gathered in England by a divine named Jacob, in James' age. Jacob, a

* Fuller, vol. 3, pp. 245-256.

spiritual son of that Robinson who led the Pilgrims at Leyden, formed his infant Congregational church in 1615.* Their chief principles were these: "the sufficiency of Scripture, leaving nothing to church practice or human tradition, these being but the iron feet and clay toes of that statue whose head and whole body ought to be pure scripture-gold; a refusal to make any present judgment binding on them in the future; the complete independence of the individual congregations."†

But to recur to James. He was a punctual attender on the *forms* of worship, and he affected to be something of a metaphysician. But he heard the exhortations of his clergy, and listened to the refinements of his court preacher, Andrews, the famous bishop of Winchester, precisely as, a little later, Louis XIV. sat, with his mistress by his side, and enjoyed the eloquent flights of Massillon and Bossuét.‡

But the tragi-comedy was well-nigh ended. In 1625 death cut short the pageant. James descended into the grave, and the court which Hallam estimates as the most immoral in English history,§ was robbed of its exemplar.

Away across the misty waters, on the rock at Plymouth, an epoch was commencing; in England an epoch lay dead in the coffin of king James.

* Neale, vol. 1, pp. 371, 372.
† Fuller, vol. 3, p. 462.
‡ Perry, p. 55.
§ Hallam, Con. Hist.

CHAPTER XVIII.

THE ENGLISH COMMONS.

ON the accession of Charles I., the times were pregnant with mighty changes. A revolution was maturing which God destined to be the eldest born of the Reformation. The people, weary and fretful, *felt*, rather than *saw* the approaching dissolution of the feudal idea. That haughty prerogative upon which the Tudors and the Stuarts leaned so heavily, was about to snap. To the maxims, the forms, the language of arbitrary monarchy, the English commons were soon to give the lie.

The tenets of unlimited power were an exotic in England; they were a recent importation from the Continent. In France, in Spain, in Italy, in Germany itself, the cradle of individualism, the liberties of subjects were held to exist only as subordinate rights, or rather, as concessions for which they were indebted to a despot's generosity.* "I am the state!" exclaimed arrogant imperialism.

In England these haughty pretensions were comparatively new. The middle class of islanders were not wont "to crook the pregnant hinges of the knee;" they were accustomed to make no Eastern *salaams*. *Magna Charta* had long been the Gibraltar of popular rights. But a new *régime* began

* Guizot, Hist. Eng. Rev., vol. 1, p. 7.

with the royalty of the Tudors. Henry VII. curbed the aristocracy of Britain, as Louis XI. broke the spirit of the feudalists in France. The iron barons of Runnymede melted into the courtier fops of a licentious and degenerate age.

The commons were long held too low to struggle against these innovations, but they cherished the memory of the old, free days all the more tenderly because the past was linked with epithets of contempt by the usurping court.

Gradually the people crept up to a higher level; the entrance of the lesser nobility and of the smaller landed proprietors into the House of Commons provided them with resolute and determined leaders. Thus it chanced that, "while the higher aristocracy crowded around the court, to make up for their spoliation of authority in borrowed dignities, as corrupting as they were precarious—and which, without giving them back their former fortunes, separated them more and more from the people—the gentry, the freeholders, the citizens, occupied mainly in improving their land, in extending their trade, in enlarging their minds through the keen competitions of active life, increased in riches and credit, and became daily more closely united, drawing the masses under their influence; in this way the yeomen, without show, without political design, almost unknown to themselves, took possession of the social forces of the island."*

Then came the Reformation. Men's minds were

* Guizot, ut antea.

emancipated. The people began to think and to question. The logical sequence of ecclesiastical freedom is civil liberty. Men who examined boldly the mysteries of *divine* power, might not long be shackled by *earthly* authority. Resistance to tyrants became obedience to God.

This inevitable tendency was invigorated by the triumphant civilization of the era. Commerce put its belt around the globe. The needle trembled to the pole, and timid mariners no longer hugged the mainland. "The career of maritime discovery had been pursued with daring intrepidity and with brilliant success. The voyages of Gosnold and Smith and Hudson, the enterprise of Raleigh and Delaware and Gorges, the compilations of Eden and Willes and Hakluyt had filled the commercial world with wonder."* London became immensely wealthy; and it was the Shylock to whom the king, the court, and most of the great nobles of the kingdom, always insolent and always needy, became debtors.†

The active brains and the industrious fingers of the people grasped so vast a portion of the public wealth, that it was found, on the opening of Parliament in 1628, that the House of Commons was three times as rich as the House of Lords.‡

Animated by this discovery, the yeomen next turned to examine how much the despotism of six decades had left them. They were surprised here also. Though for a long time strangers to resist-

* Bancroft. † Clarendon, Hist. of the Rebellion.
‡ Hume, vol. 2; Sanderson, Walker.

ance, the Commons had still the *means* of resistance in their hand. Parliament had not ceased to meet; sovereigns, finding it submissive, having often employed it as an instrument of their tyranny. Under Henry, Mary, and Elizabeth, juries had shown themselves complaisant and even servile, but they still existed. The towns had preserved their charters, the corporations their immunities. England did not lack free institutions half so much as the disposition and will to use them.* The forms were largely on the side of liberty; now, disgusted by the exercise of absolute power and enlightened by Christianity, the spirit and the purpose of the middle classes began to vivify these old, dead forms.

Such was the temper of England when Charles I. grasped his father's overgrown sceptre. There was much in the young king to placate resentment. He was orderly, chaste, sober, and religious so far as regarded the outward ceremonies of the faith, yet tinged with superstition and with bigotry.† "Sickened of the meanness, the talkative and familiar pedantry, the inert and pusillanimous politics of James, England looked forward to happiness and liberty under a king whom she could respect."‡

Neither Charles nor England knew how much they were estranged from each other.

The king's education had been unfortunate. He was taught to think that the maxims of absolutism

* Guizot, vol. 1, p. 11.

† Perinchief's Life of Charles I.; Womick's Memoirs; Clarendon.

‡ Guizot, vol. 1, p. 2.

knew no limit;* he imbibed an early and severe aversion to Puritanism both in church and state;† on his accession he adopted his father's favorite, the weak and vain Villiers; and though he had good natural abilities, yet he surrendered into the hands of minions the substance of that arbitrary power of which he was enamoured; "nor was he ever master of so much judgment in politics as to discern his own and the nation's true interest, or to take the advice of those who did."‡

He had a habit of duplicity.§ Like his father, he esteemed his promises as mere make-shifts, as expedients simply intended to tide over shallow spots; and when he had pawned his "royal word" to England, his design was to elude the public expectation.‖ He had not the art to please;¶ and with all his hypocrisy, he lacked what James I. called *kingcraft.*

Charles had recently returned from Spain, whither he had gone with the purpose of contracting a marriage with the Infanta. "He had been received at Madrid with great honors, and there he saw monarchy in all its splendor—majestic, supreme—exacting both from its attendants and from the people a devotedness and a respect almost re-

* Rapin, Hist. Eng., vol. 2, p. 570; Sidney's State Papers; Hume. † Rushworth, vol. 1; Neale, vol. 1, p. 401.

‡ Neale.

§ Newell, p. 249; King's Cabinet Opened, p. 4; Sidney's State Papers.

‖ Rushworth, Hume, Rapin; Harris, Life of Charles I.

¶ Hackett's Life of Bishop Williams, vol. 1, p. 210.

ligious; rarely contradicted, and always sure of carrying all before it, the sovereign, by his will alone, being above all opposition."* The Spanish match fell through, and Charles married Henrietta Maria of France, the daughter of Henri Quatre. "The impressions made on the English prince by this union were similar to those received in Spain, and henceforth the monarchies of Paris and Madrid became in his eyes a model of the natural and legitimate condition of a king."†

Of course such a prince could not read the portents of his time. Charles never comprehended his epoch; he was destined to lose his life in a mad tilt against the gravitation of his century.

In 1625 Parliament met. "It was almost a senate of kings that an absolute monarch called around his throne. Neither prince nor people, but least of all the latter, had as yet unravelled the principle or measured the strength of their claims; they met with the sincere hope and intention of settling any differences which might exist, when, in fact, their disunion was already consummated, for they all thought as sovereigns."‡

This radical disagreement was soon developed. Parliament instituted a boundless and searching examination of public affairs, and refused to grant the king the requisite subsidies to carry on the war which then raged with Spain, until he redressed the national grievances.§

* Guizot, Neale, Hume. † Ibid. ‡ Ibid.

§ Old Parl. Hist., vol. 6, p. 407.

Charles, indignant at the boldness of the Commons in standing upon terms with him, dissolved the Parliament.* His next step was clearly unconstitutional. He attempted to coerce a loan.† The success of this move was problematical; but with the sum thus "borrowed" an expedition was launched against Cadiz, which failed miserably, owing "to the ignorance of the admiral and the drunkenness of the troops."‡

Six months after the dissolution of the first parliament, the chagrined king, pinched for funds and with an empty exchequer, was obliged to convene the Commons and request a legitimate supply.§ In order to bar out of the new parliament the most active and obnoxious members of the old one, he had them named sheriffs of their respective counties, a nomination which disqualified them for a reëlection to the House.‖ Among the victims of this trick were Sir Edward Coke, and Sir Thomas Wentworth, then a popular orator with Puritanical predilections.¶

But notwithstanding the king's efforts to winnow out the stoutest champions of the people, this parliament proved more stubborn and decided than its predecessor. It not only withheld all subsidies, it impeached the duke of Buckingham.**

The king, incensed by this action, seized two of

* Old Parl. Hist., vol. 6, p. 407.

† Hume, vol. 2, p. 193; Neale, Guizot.

‡ Guizot, vol. 1, p. 22.

§ Hume, vol. 2, p. 193; Neale, Rushworth.

‖ Ibid.

¶ Neale.

** Hume, vol. 2, p. 194.

the managers of the impeachment and threw them into the Tower;* then turning to the Commons, he ominously hinted that unless they speedily furnished him with the required supplies, he should be obliged to try *new counsels*.† Lest the ambiguity of this phrase should puzzle the Commons, the vice-chamberlain informed the House that Charles meant, in case of further opposition, to abolish Parliament, and govern alone. "Let us be careful then," he added, "to preserve the king's good opinion of Parliament, lest we be stripped of our repute as a free people by our turbulency."

"These imprudent suggestions," says Hume, "rather gave warning than struck terror. The Commons thought that a precarious liberty, which was to be preserved by unlimited complaisance, was no liberty; and it was necessary, while yet in their power, to secure the Constitution by such invincible barriers, that no king or minister should ever for the future dare to speak such words to any parliament."‡

Instantly all business stopped. The House boldly proclaimed its *ultimatum*—the immediate release of its incarcerated members, or national bankruptcy. At last Charles yielded; the impeachers were set free;§ and incited by this example, the House of Lords demanded, as its *sine qua non*, the unconditional liberation of the earl of

* Hume, Rushworth, Clarendon, etc.
† Hume, vol. 2, p. 195. ‡ Ibid.
§ Ibid., Guizot, Neale, Perry.

Arundel, who had been recently confined in the Tower. To this also the enraged and beaten king assented.*

The Parliament then fell once more upon their grievances. The encroachments of Rome occasioned great anxiety. The queen, a "lady of a haughty spirit, and a great wit and beauty," was a Romanist; and trooping into England, ostensibly in her suite, came a swarm of papists.† Charles openly favored them, and influenced by his example, they "matched into the best families of the island."‡

The Arminian schism also troubled the Commons. Eventually a committee on religion was appointed, but it was soon gagged by the king, who informed the House that his supremacy had cognizance of religious differences.§ This fiat wrested these questions from the decision of the Parliament; but the debate, adjourned to the lobbies, still raged fiercely, until a royal proclamation commanded all to cease expressing an opinion on the controverted points.‖ "The Puritans thought that they might still write in defence of the received doctrine of the Thirty-nine Articles; but since the press was in the hands of their adversaries, some of their books were suppressed, some were mutilated, and others which got abroad were called in, while the authors and publishers were questioned in the

* Hume, vol. 2, p. 195; Guizot, Neale, Perry.

† Memoirs of Col. Hutchinson, by his Wife; Edinburgh ed., p. 85. ‡ Ibid. § Ibid. ‖ Neale, vol. 1, p. 410.

Star-chamber and High Commission courts, for engaging in a controversy prohibited by the government. Half a dozen bishops, called Arminians, undertook to decide on the truth or error of the writings of all the wise and great men of the nation, in doing which they were so partial that learning and industry were discouraged; men of gravity and great experience not being able to persuade themselves to submit their labors to be mangled and torn in pieces by a few younger divines who were both judges and parties in the affair. At length the booksellers, being nearly ruined, prepared a petition, in which they complained that the writings of the best authors were stifled in the press, while the books of their adversaries, papists and Arminians, were published and spread over the whole kingdom."* Rushworth records that, while the edge of the law was turned towards the Puritans to stop their mouths, their opponents were permitted to give uncontrolled liberty to their tongues and pens.

At this juncture, Charles, hopeless of wringing money from the Parliament, and determined not to accede to their just demands, prorogued both Houses,† and proceeded to follow the example of the Paris and Madrid monarchies.

* Neale, vol. 1, pp. 410, 411.

† Parl. Hist., vol. 2, p. 193. Whitelocke's Memorials of Eng. Affairs.

CHAPTER XIX.

THE "NEW COUNSELS."

THE heedless king had already trodden on the *magna charta;* he now took another step towards that ghastly Whitehall scaffold.

The "*new counsels*" which Charles had mentioned to the Parliament were now to be tried.* Another forced loan was decreed by a royal *ipse dixit:* commissioners were appointed to harvest this filched golden crop; and they were empowered to interrogate the refractory on the grounds of their refusal, to learn who had persuaded them to resist, by what discourse, and with what design.†

It has been truly said, that this was at once an attack upon the fortunes and the opinions of individuals. Even on the Continent, the most absolute government would have regarded such an expedient as high-handed, irregular, and unequal.‡ England now had a taste of what she might expect from an uncurbed prerogative. Gentlemen of birth and character, who refused to lend what sum the Council was pleased to demand of them, were taken from their residences and flung into distant jails.§ The

* Hume, vol. 2, p. 197.
† Parl. Hist., vol. 2; Neale, vol. 1; Whitelocke's Memorials.
‡ Hume. § Neale, vol. 1, p. 411; Rushworth, Carlyle.

poorer classes were saddled with soldiers who dragooned whole counties,* or else they were themselves pressed into the army. The seaports and maritime districts were commanded to supply and equip a specified number of armed vessels, this being the king's initial attempt to collect ship-money.† The city of London was rated at twenty ships. "Why," cried the astonished citizens, "that is a larger number than Elizabeth demanded to repel the Spanish Armada." The reply was, "The precedents of the past are obedience, not objections."‡

To justify this inquisitorial tyranny, the doctrine of passive obedience was everywhere preached.§ The court clergy made the island echo with their slavish pleas. One of these sermons was brought to Archbishop Abbot, the able and sincerely pious successor of Bancroft, to be licensed. The honest prelate read it with disgust, then threw it from him; he would not sully the Canterbury *imprimatur* by affixing it to so despicable a pamphlet. For this, Abbot was suspended from all his archiepiscopal functions, and banished to one of his country seats.‖ The archbishop's principles of liberty, together with his opposition to Buckingham, had always given him an ungracious reception at court, where he had the reputation of a Puritan; "for it is remarkable that this party made the privileges of the nation as

* Guizot. † Hume, Guizot, Rushworth.

‡ Whitelocke's Memorials, etc., p. 7.

§ Hume, Neale, Perry, Lathbury, Fuller, etc.

‖ Fuller, vol. 3, p. 349, and on; Guizot, Neale, Perry.

much a part of their religion as the church party did the prerogatives of the crown."* Though he was not formally impeached off the bench, Abbot, like Grindal, never regained his forfeited honors. His offence was too stupendous for pardon.

Notwithstanding its arbitrary course, the Council reaped but a lean harvest of guineas. The country held its pounds tightly; the metropolis equivocated, invented excuses, made pretences, and finally, when closely pressed, flatly refused to loan a shilling.†

The king, pressed and tormented for funds, yet too haughty to buy a supply by justice, passed from one usurpation to another, by the imprisonment of those from whom he could not "borrow." Nay, he insisted that the judges should decree it as a principle, that men arrested by his orders should not be permitted to find bail, which was a blow at one of the oldest, best-defined rights of Anglo-Saxon liberty.

This question was stirred by five gentlemen, who had been detained on the complaint of the royal Council, and who, at the court of King's-Bench, claimed to be set free on bail.‡

"The judges rejected the demand for bail, and remanded the prisoners to the Tower, but without establishing the principle the king had prescribed; for, already struck with a double fear, they neither dared show themselves servile nor just; and to save

* Hume, vol. 2, p. 198. † Ibid., p. 197.

‡ Hume, Guizot, Hutchinson, Memoirs, etc.

themselves from trouble, they refused their consent to despotism, and their aid to liberty."*

The king's exchequer had now gotten as low as the national expenses had mounted high. In this strait, says Neale, he had recourse to the Romanists, from whom he "got a good round sum by issuing a commission to the archbishop of York to compound with them for forfeitures which had accrued in the past, or which might fall due in future."† This expedient did indeed momentarily fill the royal coffers, while it gratified the inclination of the monarch to give indulgence to those religionists.‡ But this fatal policy drove many who were well-affected to the Establishment, but opposed to Romanism, into the Puritan camp,§ which now began to be esteemed the only Protestant rendezvous, as it had long been held to be the citadel of civil liberty.

The long unfed and hungry expenses of the king speedily ate up the new contents of the lean exchequer, and the court was again pinched by sharp want. Yet bankrupt and almost without an army, engaged already in a struggle with the house of Austria, standing at home on the verge of an abyss, while the irritation of the nation became daily more aggressive, baffled in his domestic programme and in his foreign policy, the crazy king flung down the gauntlet to Richelieu, and plunged chaotic England into the arena against France.‖

* Guizot, vol. 1, pp. 30, 31. † Neale, vol. 1, p. 411.
‡ Hume, vol. 2, p. 197. § Neale, Hume, Carlyle.
‖ Hume, vol. 2; Clarendon, vol. 1; Guizot, Carlyle, Perry.

This war was created by the intrigues of a licentious courtier. Villiers of Buckingham, desiring to return to Paris that he might prosecute an *amour* with Anne of Austria, begun when he went to escort Henrietta Maria to England, and for which he had been forbidden the kingdom by Louis XIII.,* prevailed on his royal master, who was his puppet, to undertake this mad crusade; and in order to give it a color of popularity, it was proclaimed that the object of the war was to succor the succumbing Huguenots.†

History scouts this pretext; for his majesty and his whole court had a mortal aversion to the Huguenots, who closely resembled the detested Puritans in discipline and worship, in religion and in politics.‡ "Buckingham had no religion at all; a portion of the king's counsellors were open Romanists; the rest believed that there was no salvation for Protestants outside the church of England; how then can it be credited that such a government, an absurd trinity of infidelity, papistry, and Arminianism, should wage war in defence of a religion which they held in the utmost contempt?"§

Of course nothing but disaster could await such hypocritical and senseless politics. A monarchy proud of its military prowess, learned one day that an expedition, conducted by Villiers in person, and intended to succor La Rochelle, which Richelieu

* Clarendon, Hume, Neale, etc. † Ibid.

‡ Hume, vol. 2, pp. 200, 201; Hist. of the Huguenots, Amer. Tract Society, 1866. § Neale, vol. 1, p. 414.

was slowly starving into submission, had failed miserably through the bungling incapacity of its chief, and that Buckingham was returning to England with a loss of two-thirds of his force, and totally discredited both as an admiral and as a general.*

Throughout the island "a multitude of families, beloved and respected by the people, were in mourning. The indignation became intense. The farmer left his fields, the apprentice quitted his shop, to inquire whether his master, a gentleman or citizen, had not lost a brother or a son; and they returned to their neighbors with an account of the disasters they had heard, of the trouble they had seen, cursing Buckingham and censuring the king."†

Losses of another kind still further imbittered the people, and especially the mercantile classes. The French navy endangered the safety and wrecked the prosperity of English commerce; their vessels rotted in port; their merchandise reposed in their warehouses; while the sailors, unemployed, talked of the recent defeat of the royal fleet, and of the causes of their own inaction. The gentry, the citizens, and the people became daily more closely united in one common feeling of resentment and disgust.‡

When Buckingham landed, even his hauteur was awed by the scoffs which smote him.§ But the unhappy king, anxious to screen his favorite, and compelled to settle a new programme, was per-

* Hume, vol. 2, p. 201.
† Guizot, vol. 1. pp. 31, 32.
‡ Ibid.
§ Clarendon, Neale, Guizot.

suaded to propitiate public opinion by giving out that Villiers had urged the convocation of the Parliament.* "Gain our hearts," said Sir Robert Colton, one of the mildest of the popular leaders, to the king, quoting the words of Burleigh to Elizabeth—"gain our hearts, and you will soon have our arms and purses."†

Charles, spurred by necessity, went now to the extreme of complaisance. The prisons were flung open; seventy-eight state-prisoners were released, twenty-seven of whom were elected to the new Parliament;‡ and in 1628, the jubilant Commons met at Westminster.§

Meanwhile the king had a relapse. In his speech at the opening session of Parliament, he threatened that, unless speedily relieved from his embarrassments, he would again resort to the "*new counsels*."‖ "A haughty solicitor, sinking under the weight of his faults and his misfortunes, he yet threatened to employ that independent and absolute monarchy which set him above all errors and reverses. So infatuated was he with his own supremacy, that it never entered into his mind that it could suffer any change; and full of arrogance, yet sincere, he thought it due to his honor and his rank to assume the tone and claim the rights of tyranny, even while borrowing the assistance of liberty."¶

* Parl. Hist., vol. 2, col. 218. † Ibid., col. 212-217.

‡ Rushworth, vol. 1, p. 473; Clarendon.

§ Hume, vol. 2, p. 202.

‖ Parl. Hist., vol. 2, col. 218; Guizot, Rushworth.

¶ Guizot, vol. 1, p. 34.

But the Commons were as proud and inflexible as the king was imperious. They were unmoved by the royal threats. "They were resolved solemnly to proclaim their liberties, to oblige the court to acknowledge them as primitive and independent, and to permit henceforth no *right* to pass for a *concession,* nor to allow any encroachment on the fundamental laws. Neither leaders nor followers were lacking for this grand design. The whole nation rallied round the Parliament. Within this sanctuary bold and clever men consulted how it should be accomplished. Sir Edward Coke,* the pride of magistracy, no less illustrious for his firmness than for his knowledge; Sir Thomas Wentworth, afterwards Lord Strafford, young, ardent, eloquent, born to command, and whose ambition was then satisfied with the admiration of his country;† Denzil Hollis, the youngest son of Lord Clare, in childhood the companion of Charles, but the sincere friend of liberty, and too proud to serve under a favorite;‡ Pym, a learned barrister, eminently skilled in the knowledge of the rights and customs of Parliament, cold, yet daring, and well knowing how to conduct himself with prudence as a leader of popular passions;§ and many others, destined, within a time much less than any of them could anticipate,

* "Born at Mileham, in Norfolk, 1549; he was then seventy-nine years of age."

† "Born at London, 1593; he was then thirty-five years of age."

‡ "Born at Hampton, 1597; he was then thirty-one years old."

§ "Born in Somersetshire, 1584; he was then forty-four years of age." Guizot.

to diverse fortunes and even opposite parties, were now united by the same principles and hopes. To this fearful coalition the court could only oppose the power of custom, the capricious temerity of Buckingham, and the haughty obstinacy of the king."*

Thus far the Commons had triumphed. "All unlawful projects to quench the thirst of the king's necessities," says Fuller, "had proved no better than sucking-bottles, soon emptied, and but cold the liquor they afforded. Nothing so natural as the milk of the breast; that is, subsidies granted by Parliament. But alas, to follow the metaphor, both the breasts, the two houses, were so sore with several grievances, that all money flowed from them with pain and difficulty; the rather because complaints were made of doctrines destructive to their propriety, lately preached and sanctioned at court."†

Five subsidies were voted the king; but the Commons refused to carry the bill through the house until the royal assent was obtained to a petition of rights which reaffirmed the essential clauses of *magna charta:* that no freeman should be detained in prison by the king and privy-council, without an expression of the cause of commitment for which by law he ought to be detained; that the *habeas corpus* should not be denied where the law allowed it; that no tax, loan, or benevolence should be imposed without the consent of Parliament;

* Guizot, vol. 1, pp. 34, 35. † Fuller, vol. 3, p. 352.

that no man should be forejudged of life or limb, or be exiled or destroyed, but by the judgment of his peers, according to the law of the land, or by act of Parliament.*

Charles was greatly elated when apprized of the vote of subsidies;† but when he learned of the conditions of the grant, his rage was boundless. A fierce struggle ensued. The king, borrowing the tone of Elizabeth, forbade Parliament to meddle in affairs of state.‡ But the firmness of the Commons eventually carried the day; and Charles, foiled again and trembling for the subsidies, assented to the bill of rights; and while he got his gold, the nation guaranteed its liberties.§

While the Commons were busied in diffusing printed copies of this law over England,|| the upper house was employed in reprimanding the preachers of passive obedience; and one Manwaring, "a man so criminous that he turned his titles into accusations," to quote Pym's strong phrase, was summoned before the bar of the House, and forced to make an humble submission, couched in words drawn up by the Lords.¶

Charles had hoped that the concession of the petition of rights would give him a respite; instead of which he was, within a few days, presented with two new remonstrances: one against Villiers, the

* Parl. Hist., vol. 2, col. 278. † Guizot, vol. 1, p. 36.

‡ Parl. Hist., col. 401.

§ Ibid., col. 409; Rushworth, vol. 1, p. 612.

|| Guizot, vol. 1, p. 45.

¶ Fuller, vol. 3, pp. 352–355; Perry, Neale, Carlyle, etc.

other against the arbitrary collection of the tonnage and poundage taxes.*

The king then lost patience, and hastening to Westminster Hall, he prorogued the Parliament.†

Two months later, in June, 1628, Buckingham was murdered.‡ The people, while deprecating the act, rejoiced in their deliverance. But this assassination threw the king back into tyranny. "He again bestowed his favor upon the adversaries of Parliament. Montague, whom the Commons had prosecuted, was promoted to the bishopric of Chichister; Manwaring, whom the House of Lords had condemned, was endowed with a rich benefice; Laud, already famous for enthusiastic devotion to the most arbitrary maxims of ecclesiastical and civil government, was translated to the see of London. Public acts corresponded with covert favors. The tonnage and poundage duty was rigorously collected, and the tribunals of exception continued to suspend the course of law. Silently entering upon another career of despotism, Charles had some reason to hope for success. He had detached from the Puritan party one of its most distinguished leaders and brilliant orators: Sir Thomas Wentworth

* Parl. Hist., vol. 2, col. 420, 431.

† Ibid., Rushworth, Hume, Clarendon.

‡ "In the hat of Felton, his murderer, a paper was found on which the last remonstrance of the House was quoted. Felton did not seek to escape, nor to defend himself, but only said that he looked on the duke as the enemy of the kingdom, and shook his head when questioned as to his accomplice. He died with composure." Guizot.

was made a peer, a privy-counsellor, and the king's chief minister; and now, surrounded by new friends, supported by a remodelled cabinet, abler, more serious, less unpopular than Buckingham's coterie had been, Charles awaited the second session of his third Parliament without fear or dread."*

In the winter of 1629, Parliament met according to prorogation, and they immediately opened their budget of grievances. They complained of the arbitrary action of the abnormal courts of High Commission and Star-chamber;† of the duplicity of the king in ordering his printer to alter the legal text of the bill of rights, and to substitute his first evasive answer for his final assent;‡ of the favor granted to false doctrines; of the bad distribution of dignities and employments; and generally, of the contempt shown for the liberties of the people.§

A committee on religion was appointed. Of this Oliver Cromwell, then in the lower house, was a leading member. There this extraordinary man made his first appearance in the stormy history of the age, stuttering and stamping through his maiden speech. After mentioning the recent promotion of Montague, who squinted towards Arminianism, and of Manwaring, who faced towards the Vatican, the future Colossus of the Revolution queried, "If these

* Guizot, vol. 1, pp. 47, 48.
† Parl. Hist., col. 438; Clarendon.
‡ Ibid., vol. 2, col. 435; Rushworth.
§ Rushworth, Parl. Hist., Clarendon.

be the paths to church preferment, whither are we drifting?"*

The king heard this, and gnawed his lip in silent anger; but shortly a violent scene in the House of Commons incensed him to madness.

Sir John Elliot proposed a new remonstrance against the collection of tonnage and poundage by the king. The speaker of the House, pleading an order from the king, refused to have it read, and quitted the chair. Instantly all was uproar. Several members seized the retiring speaker, forced him back into the chair, held him there, and then, with doors double-barred, passed an act declaring the levying of tonnage and poundage on the king's sole authority to be illegal, and branding all who should either pay or levy such taxes as guilty of high treason.†

In the mean time Charles, upon being acquainted with the uproar and its cause, ordered his guard to force the doors and disperse the members. But ere he could be obeyed, the Commons had adjourned for the day.‡

Thwarted in this, the king went to the House of Lords, and in a bitter speech, dissolved the Parliament *sine die*.

This done, he proceeded, in the face of the recently enacted bill of rights which he had solemnly subscribed, to arrest the most obnoxious

* Carlyle, Cromwell's Letters and Speeches, vol. 1.

† Parl. History, vol. 2, col. 487–491; Rushworth, Clarendon, Hume.

‡ Ibid.

members of the Commons, and to fling them into the Tower.* Here the popular champions were treated with equal rigor and contempt; and one of them, Sir John Elliot, died in this confinement,† a martyr to political liberty.

At Hampton Court and Whitehall high carnival was held. "Those who were papists in their hearts and those who were so openly—the servants and preachers of absolutism, men of intrigue and of pleasure, the indifferent to all creeds—already congratulated each other on this crowning triumph," and cried, "The people's guns are spiked."

But the rough and awkward stammerer of the house committee on religion did not take this courtier view; for Cromwell wrote home, "I fear me much that this battle is not yet begun."‡

* Parl. History, vol. 2, col. 487–491; Rushworth, Clarendon, Hume. The members arrested were Hollis, Hobart, Elliot, Hayman, Selden, Coriton, Long, Strode, and Valentine. See State Trials, vol. 3, pp. 235–335.

† Old Parl. Hist., vol. 8, p. 374; Neale, vol. 1, p. 425, etc.

‡ Carlyle, Cromwell's Letters, etc.

CHAPTER XX.

LAUD'S PRELACY.

WHEN Villiers was assassinated, his mantle fell upon the united shoulders of Strafford and Laud. These men became the brain of English absolutism. One affected the *rôle* of Richelieu, and domineered in politics; the other became the *Pontifex-maximus* of the church, and labored with the fervid zeal of a Loyola to consolidate and to broaden the domain of the Establishment.

Strafford carried with him into the king's camp the restless energy and the imperious will which had distinguished him in the House of Commons. Bold, fertile in expedients, tenacious of his purpose, he sought to *systematize* tyranny—to give to despotism the forms and the support of law. In this the timid arrogance of Charles baulked him, for the king was never provident for the future; satisfied with the possession of arbitrary power to-day, he never thought of guaranteeing it for the morrow. This *inertia* clogged all Strafford's exertions. "Full of energy, he bore the yoke of weakness, and his foresight was lost in the service of the blind."

Laud, born at Reading and educated at Oxford, where he resided until his fiftieth year,* had long

* Neale, vol. 1, p. 402.

been an enigma even to his friends. "I would I knew," wrote good bishop Hall to him on one occasion, "where to find you; to-day you are with the Romanists, to-morrow with us; our adversaries think you ours, and we think you theirs: your conscience finds you with both and neither. How long will you halt in this uncertainty?"*

Bred to the church, his ecclesiastical preferment had been marked. Severe in his conduct, simple in his life, rough in his manners, he was pushed forward by his own zealous and indefatigable ardor. He was *terribly in earnest,* and he was fanatically devoted to power. "To command and to punish was in his eyes to establish order, and order always seemed to him justice. In business he was tireless, but narrow, violent, and stern. At once incapable of balancing interests or respecting rights, he rashly persecuted liberties as abuses. Thwarting some by his probity, others by his blind animosity, he was as rude and irritable with courtiers as with citizens. He sought no friendship; he neither foresaw nor could bear any resistance; and he was constantly absorbed by some fixed notion which took possession of him with the violence, the passion, and the authority of a duty."†

The statesman and the priest never interfered with each other. Strafford worked out his problems by himself; Laud asked no advice, and would take none. Strafford endeavored to manipulate English politics into despotic precepts; Laud strug-

* Neale, vol. 1, p. 402. † Guizot, vol. 1, p. 61.

gled to emancipate the Establishment from its vassalage to the crown, and then to compel a universal conformity. Strafford was a hidden king; Laud was a hidden pope.

At the Reformation, the temporal sovereign had in some respects assumed towards the English church the relations before held by the pope.*

"Churchmen were soon aware of this defect in its constitution; but the perils to which it was exposed, and the high hand with which Henry VIII., and afterwards Elizabeth, carried matters, had given it no chance of redress. Attacked at once by the papists and the non-conformists, itself doubtful on many points, still wavering in its possessions and doctrines, the church feared to provoke the enmity of its new head, and devoted itself without restriction to the service of temporal power, acknowledging its own dependence, and yielding to the absolute supremacy of the throne, which could now alone save it from the environing perils.

"Towards the close of Elizabeth's reign, a few isolated symptoms announced rather higher pretensions on the part of the clergy. Bancroft maintained that episcopacy was not a human institution, but that it had been from apostolic times the government of the church, and that bishops held their rights, not from a temporal sovereign, but from God.† These claims were haughtily repressed by

* Guizot, vol. 1, p. 76.

† The sermon alluded to was preached on the 12th of January, 1588. Perry, Neale.

the despotism of the arrogant queen; but under James I. they were once more mooted. Zealous in proclaiming the *jus divinum* of the throne, the church began to plead loudly for the recognition of its own divinity; and those precepts which Bancroft had timidly insinuated were now openly avowed by the bench of bishops."*

When Charles and his Parliament began their quarrel, and the Commons deserted the throne, the Establishment, pointing to its own loyal record, hinted that its support through these dark hours could be won by the recognition of its claims. Charles, who was sincerely attached to the English church, was easily persuaded to cede, if not formally, at least essentially, his ecclesiastical supremacy to the episcopal authorities.† Then Laud, who held the see of London, began to think of increasing the external pomp of the church, and of subduing Puritanism to uniformity.

A cruel torture now began. If any Puritan chanced to hold a living, he was at once dismissed. If the non-conformist, gagged in the pulpit, turned to other pursuits, persecution dogged him and blocked each new avenue in which he essayed to tread. Starvation or conformity—this was the inexorable alternative.‡

"Puritan churches were seized, and the pomp

* Guizot, vol. 1, pp. 76, 77.

† Ibid., p. 79; Perry, Lathbury.

‡ Neale, Rushworth, Carlyle. See the account in Neale, vol. 1, p. 452, of a Mr. Workman.

of the Romanist worship was restored; though persecution kept away the congregation, a profuse magnificence adorned the walls. New churches were consecrated with splendid ceremony, and then the people were driven by force to attend them. Laud was fond of prescribing minutely the details of new ceremonies, sometimes borrowed from the Roman ritual, sometimes invented by his own ostentatious, yet narrow imagination. The least innovation, the least deviation of the non-conformists from the canons of the Liturgy was punished as a crime; while Laud innovated without consulting anybody, generally with the king's consent, but sometimes on his own authority. He changed the interior arrangements of the churches, the forms of worship, imperiously prescribing forms till then unknown, and even assumed to alter the Liturgy, which many parliaments had sanctioned; while the result, if not the aim of all these alterations, was to render the English church more conformable to that of Rome."*

The utmost partiality was shown to the Romanists. The press groaned beneath the load of pamphlets issued to prove the similarity between Rome and the Establishment;† and these were dedicated to Laud or to the king, and were not infrequently composed by theologians in exact agreement with the court.‡

* Guizot, vol. 1, pp. 83, 84.

† Whitelocke's Memorials, etc., p. 21; Guizot, Neale.

‡ Ibid.

At the same time the Puritans might not even defend the Thirty-nine Articles against the assaults of the Romanist publicists, or brush away the objections of the Paris Sorbonne.*

England at large anticipated the speedy recognition of the papal primacy;† so that when a daughter of the duke of Devonshire embraced the Roman faith, she replied to Laud, who had asked her the reasons for her change, "'T is chiefly because I hate to travel in a crowd; and as I perceive that your grace and many others are making haste to Rome, I wish to get there first, to escape being jostled."‡

The nearer the English church went to Rome, the tighter it choked Puritanism; and now the persecution grew so bitter and so searching, that many said good-by to England, and crossed the sea to join their exiled brothers on the Atlantic slope of the western continent.§ Bereaved of an asylum at home, whole families flocked every summer to the American colonies, swelling the New England settlements of Plymouth, Massachusetts Bay, Connecticut, and New Haven.‖ It has been estimated that four thousand planters quitted the island for the New World during the fierce *régime* of Laud, and that these carried with them five hundred pounds in gold, an immense sum for those days. Had Laud reigned twenty-four years, instead of twelve,

* Whitelocke's Memorials, etc., p. 21; Guizot, Neale.

† Guizot, vol. 1, p. 84; Neale.

‡ Whitelocke. Hume, vol. 2, p. 218.

§ Neale, vol. 1, p. 436.

‖ Ibid.

historians assert that England would have permanently lost one-fourth of her population, and would have been drained of a third of her wealth.*

The ebb and flow of this exodus, which carried off the soberest, most industrious, and most religious citizens of the island, was an excellent Nileometer, and showed the precise height of the tide of persecution.

But Laud found England too narrow; and if it had not been, he was too philanthropic to confine his exclusive attentions to one kingdom. Like Alexander, he pined for new worlds to conquer; and lo, when he lifted his eyes, he saw Scotland nodding in the arms of Presbyterianism. Instantly a frenzy seized him to clutch it, highland and lowland. As was usual with him, this frenzy at once assumed the garb of duty; so the restless prelate went to work. Like the Jesuits, he never scrupled as to *means* when the *end* was to his liking. So one day he opened the matter to the king, and then advised him to visit Scotland on pretext of being crowned at Edinburgh, and to carry with him a bevy of English bishops, that the coronation ceremony might be performed according to the English ritual.† To be sure, this was unlawful, since it was customary for the Scottish monarchs to be crowned under the Presbyterian code. But this did not trouble the elastic consciences of the king

* Neale, vol. 1, pp. 435–437.

† Hallam, Con. History. Calderwood, Hist. Ch. of Scotland; Neale.

and the prelate, for they both held the monarch to be irresponsible and enthroned above all law.

There were already some bishops in Scotland, and these, says Calderwood, "were become so awful with their grandeur and the king's assistance, that there was little resistance, howbeit great murmuring and malcontentment."*

On the 18th of June, 1633, Charles was crowned with much pomp at Edinburgh, "the ceremony being managed by his favorite bishop, who thrust away the bishop of Glasgow from his proper place in the pageant because he appeared without the embroidered habit of his order, which he scrupled to wear, as he was a moderate churchman."†

On the convocation of the Scottish parliament, the king assumed the tone of absolutism, dancing in this scene as Laud pulled the strings. The Houses were overawed and dragooned into silence; then two acts were declared passed, one acknowedging the royal prerogative, the other ratifying the attempted innovations of James I. When the affirmative vote on these bills was doubted, the king said that "the clerk's declarations must stand, unless any one would go to the bar of the House, and at the peril of his life accuse that underling of falsifying the record of Parliament."‡

Both Lords and Commons on the adjournment complained of this action as a breach of their privilege, affirming that parliaments were an absurd

* Calderwood, p. 614. † Neale, vol. 1, p. 454.
‡ Ibid., pp. 454, 455. Burnet's Own Times, pp. 11, 12.

pageantry, if the clerk might bend the vote, like a nose of wax, which way he pleased, and no scrutiny be allowed.

Meantime Charles, angry and sore, dissolved the Scotch Houses as he had the English, and quitted the country, having lost *caste* during his brief tarry on the north side of the Tweed, which proved fatal to him in a darker hour.*

But Laud had been partially successful: the introduction of the English liturgy had been more than mooted; a new bishopric had been created at Edinburgh; and his majesty's royal chapel in that ancient capital had been supplied with a service-book framed by himself, which he declared to be intended as a pattern for all cathedrals, chapels, and parish churches in that kingdom.†

On reaching London after this Scottish raid, the restless and ambitious prelate found a new honor awaiting him. Archbishop Abbot was just dead, and Laud was immediately advanced to the primate's seat in the see of Canterbury.‡ This spurred his zeal to still vaster efforts; and not the *tiara* of the pope, nor the red hat of a cardinal, but the triumphal crown of patriarch of three kingdoms glittered before his eyes and robbed him of all rest.

Laud now became the state. Charles *reigned;* Laud *governed.* His patronage was so vast that his *imprimatur* lifted whom he chose into civil or eccle-

* Rebellions in Scotland, 1638-1660. Calderwood, Neale.

† Ibid.

‡ Perry, Neale, Heylin.

siastical preferment.* His dependents swarmed in every essential office.† On his nod, complained the Commons, "pulpits prate that all we have is by the king's *jure divino;* and we see how willing time-servers be to change a good conscience for a good bishopric."‡

The whole kingdom was now overhauled. Innovations proceeded on a broader scale.§ Nothing was too great, nothing was too small for the Argus eyes of the new primate. He not only insisted that all English merchants resident on the Continent should employ no chaplains but such as used the English liturgy, and bullied foreign powers into enforcing this arbitrary *dictum,*‖ but "he pushed conformity to such an objectionable strictness, that the Dutch and Huguenot churches settled in England were bidden to choose between exile and the Establishment; and this notwithstanding immunity of worship had been guaranteed them by Elizabeth and by James I. If this did not actually amount to treachery, it had a very ugly look about it; and the wholesale reduction of a number of churches differing in confession and ritual from the English church, into its bosom, merely because the accident of their position gave the state power over them, was a stretch likely to scandalize even the well-disposed members of that church."¶

* Heylin, Life of Laud, p. 255. † Perry, p. 452.

‡ Speech of Sir F. Seymour. Rushworth, vol. 1, p. 499.

§ See Hume, chap. 52, a large portion of which is devoted to this subject. ‖ Rushworth, vol. 2. Heylin's Laud, p. 233.

¶ Perry, pp. 453, 454.

All England began to grumble. When men saw the rigor with which even the most insignificant observances were pressed, at the risk of civil war, upon the refractory nation, they began to think that a sane bench of bishops would never manifest such relentless and dangerous zeal without some momentous secret purpose; and the Puritans were firmly persuaded that Laud's scheme was to lead back the English by gradual steps to the religion of their ancestors.* "It must be confessed," says Hume, "that, though Laud deserved not the appellation of papist, the genius of his novelties was, in a modified degree, the genius of Rome: the same profound respect was exacted to the sacerdotal character, the same submission required to the creeds and to the decrees of synods and councils, the same pomp and ceremony was affected in worship, and the same superstitious regard was paid to days, postures, meats, and vestments. No wonder therefore that this prelate was everywhere among the Puritans regarded as the forerunner of antichrist."†

The result of this was momentously evil. The ghostly masquerading of Laud's puppet priests began to convulse the nation. Honest churchmen like Hall, sober Puritanism, and the constitutional party, commenced to rally the national conscience. England protested. Over the heads of the gamesters the heavens grew black; beneath the board on which they threw their dice heaved the volcano of 1640.

* Hume, vol. 2, p. 218. † Ibid., p. 219.

CHAPTER XXI.

THE TRIUMPH OF THE COURT.

THE king's campaign against the ancient liberties of England knew no cessation. No armistice was ever thought of. Officered by Strafford and Laud, the court swept on from triumph to triumph. A proclamation was issued making it penal to speak of assembling another Parliament.* Taxes were levied on the sole authority of the royal seal.† Tonnage and poundage was still collected; and in 1634, ship-money was levied on the whole kingdom.‡ "This was entirely arbitrary; by the same right any other tax might be imposed."§

It was against this despotic act that John Hampden, one of the brightest and grandest characters in history, the Phocion of his age, fleshed his maiden sword. Hampden owned an estate in Buckingham, on which he was rated at twenty shillings tax, the money to go towards building a navy. Convinced that in this the court invaded the domain of Parliament, the Bayard of the Revolution refused to pay his assessment. "He resolved, rather than submit to so illegal an imposition, to stand a legal prosecution, and to expose himself to all the indignation of the court."‖

* Rushworth, vol. 2, p. 3; Hume, Clarendon. † Ibid.
‡ Hume, vol. 2, p. 223, and on. § Ibid.
‖ Ibid., pp. 227, 228.

The case was argued during twelve days in the exchequer chamber, before all the judges of England; and the nation regarded with the utmost anxiety every circumstance of this celebrated trial. "The event was easily foreseen; but the principles and reasonings, and the behavior of the parties engaged in the trial, were much canvassed." Hampden was condemned by the judicial bench.* But liberty, though in chains, knew nothing but victory. The spirit of the masses was raised and fired. Hampden's name and fame spread though the island. Even the partisans of the court scarce ventured to avow the legality of their success.† Every day the populace grew more militant. The tyranny "of Charles was, if not the most cruel, at least the most unjust and despotic that England had ever endured. Without being able to allege, for excuse, any public necessity, without dazzling the people's minds by any great event—to satisfy obscure wants, to gratify a whim—he misunderstood and trespassed on the ancient rights, and opposed the present wishes of the country, setting at defiance both the laws and the opinion of the island; disregarding his own promises, he hazarded once and again every species of oppression, adopting the most violent resolutions, the most illegal measures; and all this, not to secure the triumph of a consistent and formidable system, but to maintain by daily expedients an authority never free from embarrassment.

* State Trials, vol. 3, col. 846–1254.

† May, Hist. Long Parl.; Guizot, etc.

Subtle counsellors were for ever rummaging among old records to discover a precedent for some forgotten iniquity, laboriously digging up the buried abuses of the past, and erecting them into the rights of the crown. Was the compliance of the judges at all doubted? The exceptional courts, set above the common law, were given usurped cognizance; and illegal magistrates became the accomplices of tyranny, when the legal judges refused to become its abettors."*

"Whom the gods would destroy, they first make mad." The court never paused in this insane tilt against the spirit of the age. Strafford continued to be severely insolent; Laud never slacked his hand. "The archbishop," says Hallam, "was intolerant not so much from bigotry as from systematic policy;"† but he was "more ambitious to undertake than politic to carry on."‡

The kingdom had long swarmed with pamphlets against the indecencies of the court and against the biting tyranny of Laud. Severe repressive measures had been taken. Still men wrote; and printers, tempted by the enormous profits sure to be made on the interdicted works, smuggled these obnoxious satires through the press. Tracts were scattered in the streets of every town and county hamlet; thousands were imported from Holland.§

* Guizot, vol. 1, p. 71.

† Hallam, Cons. Hist., vol. 1, p. 450.

‡ May, Hist. Long Parl., p. 19.

§ State Trials, vol. 3, col. 711.

One day—it was about the time of Hampden's trial—the royal council seized three of these offenders, Prynne, a lawyer, Barton, a theologian, and Bostwick, a physician. They were tried in the Star-chamber. Laud wished to have them indicted for high treason; but when told that it would be impossible to strain the law so as to convict them on that charge, it was decided to arraign them for felony.*

Trial, in Anglo-Saxon dialect, has a proud historic meaning. It includes indictment by impartial peers; a copy of such indictment, and a list of witnesses furnished the prisoner, with ample time to scrutinize both; liberty to choose, and time to get counsel; *mens sana in corpore sano*, to arrange a defence; and a judge and jury impartial as the lot of humanity will allow: honored bulwarks and safeguards, each one the trophy and result of a century's struggle.†

But now the accused were bidden to make an immediate defence; pen, ink, and paper were denied them; they were told that their pleadings must be signed by a counsellor, yet all access to their prison was barred for several days; when a lawyer was admitted, he refused to sign their papers through fear of compromising himself with the court; on requesting permission to write out and sign their own justification, they were denied the right, and told that unless a counsellor subscribed

* State Trials, vol. 3, col. 711.

† Phillips, Speeches, Lectures, etc., p. 286, Boston, 1863.

it, they would be sentenced as self-convicted criminals. "Your lordships," said Prynne, "ask for an impossibility; fear of your displeasure ties all hands." The court, unmoved and implacable, reiterated its declaration. Unable to comply, these English freemen, guilty of expressing their opinions through the press, were condemned to the pillory, to lose their ears, to pay a fine of five thousand pounds, and to perpetual imprisonment.*

When the day appointed for the execution of the sentence came, an immense crowd assembled. The executioner was ordering them away. "Let them remain," said Barton; "they must learn to suffer." The official did not insist, so the people remained. "My dear sir," said a woman to Barton, "this is the best sermon you ever preached." "I hope so," he answered; "and may God convert the hearers." One young man turned pale as he looked on. "My son," queried Barton, "why are you so pale? my heart is not weak; and if I needed more strength, God would not let me want it." The crowd drew nearer and nearer. Some one gave Bostwick a bunch of flowers; a bee lighted on it. "See this poor little bee," said he; "even on the pillory it comes and sips honey from the flowers; and why should not I enjoy here the honey of Jesus Christ?"

"Christians," cried Prynne, "if we had prized *our* liberty we should not be here; it is for the freedom of *you all* that we have exposed our own: keep it well, I implore you; remain firm; be true to God

* State Trials, vol. 3, col. 711–717.

and dear England; or else you and your children will fall into eternal servitude." The air rang with acclamations.*

The victims of this outrage, and of similar barbarities, were yeomen, with no especial talents to distinguish them, but filled and dignified by that faith which can move mountains; and they were now, by the folly of the government, clothed with the persuasive attributes of martyrdom. Nothing pleads so eloquently as suffering incurred for an idea. Many an insignificant idea has been persecuted into world-wide fame and influence; there is no instance of a truth *harried* into the grave.

Aside then from its wickedness, this crusade was an evidence of madness which should have *bastiled* its chiefs; for imprisonment is the strait-jacket of the morally insane.

It was in these times the distinguishing mark of a Puritan, to see him going to church twice a day on Sunday;† and in those districts where Puritanism predominated, the mere force of opinion kept down the legal recreations permitted on that day. Laud perceiving this, moved the king to publish still another declaration, encouraging those sports which sober, devout Puritanism eschewed. This Charles did; whereon the justices of the peace signed a petition in which they declared that these revels had not only introduced great profanation of the Sabbath, but riotous tippling, contempt of authority, quarrels, and murders; and they therefore

* Guizot, vol. 1, pp. 101, 102. † Neale, vol. 1, p. 313.

prayed that Sunday recreations might be suppressed as prejudicial to peace, sobriety, piety, and good government. To this the bishops were vehemently opposed, maintaining that the sports civilized their parishioners, and brought them more willingly to church.*

Singularly enough, we here observe the laity petitioning for the religious observance of the Sabbath, and the clergy pleading for its profanation.

The king sided with his primate, and a controversy which had slept for many years was now revived, and lent its voice to swell the general chorus of debate.†

Laud's presumption knew no bounds. He had long been accustomed to alter the Book of Common Prayer on his own authority;‡ now he assumed to fetch the business of Westminster Hall into the ecclesiastical courts; he held these courts in their own names, instead of, as before, in that of the king; he enlarged his own jurisdiction by claiming the right to visit the universities of Oxford and Cambridge *jure metropolitico;* and he incurred the penalty of a *præmunire* by framing new articles of visitation, to which the episcopal seal was alone affixed.§

If any within or without the church ventured to complain of these usurpations, deprivation gagged them, the courts of exception sentenced them, the

* Neale, vol. 1, p. 460; Perry, Harris. † Ibid.

‡ Lathbury, Book of Common Prayer; Perry, Guizot.

§ Neale, vol. 1, pp. 482, 483; Guizot, Hume.

pillory received them, and remorseless persecution dogged them ever after.*

Now again the Puritans began to quit the island. "The emigration was so rapid," says Perry, "that men whose views were far from Puritanical commenced to suspect that the gospel was passing westward: and about this time the devout Herbert wrote that much-noted couplet,

> "'Religion stands a tiptoe in the land,
> Ready to pass to the American strand.'"†

The court was alarmed; the king vetoed further emigration.‡ Conscientious men might no longer live honestly at home nor find peace in exile.

But liberty owes Charles I. its hearty thanks for this despotio act; for at that very time eight vessels lay anchored in the Thames, ready to sail for the New World; and on board of one of these were Hazlerig, Pym, Hampden, and Cromwell,§ the illustrious quartette of the Revolution.

History pauses and smiles grimly at this fact, and wonders whether the fated king would have shackled emigration if he had foreseen the ghastly future; and she asks herself, "How should I have writ the record, had these men quitted England?"

In order that he might be able to devote himself wholly to the coercion of his subjects, Charles had recently solicited a peace with Spain and

* Neale, vol. 1, pp. 482, 483; Guizot, Hume.

† Perry, p. 438. ‡ Rushworth, part 2, vol. 1, p. 409.

§ Neale, vol. 1, chap. 3. Reign of Charles I. Walpole, Catalogue of Royal and Noble Authors, vol. 1, p. 206.

France. This he procured from the house of Austria by disgraceful concessions, and from Richelieu by abandoning those whom he had inveigled into the war, and submitting to terms which the haughty cardinal dictated.*

"After such ill-conduct and disgrace," remarks one of the unhappy monarch's biographers, "we may well imagine that England was not much dreaded by its neighbors. This the king soon found; for the neutrality of his ports was violated both by the Spaniards and the Dutch; his subjects were insulted and wronged by them and by the French; nor did he ever receive any satisfaction for the affront put on him by the Dutch admiral in destroying the fleet of Spain in his harbor, contrary to his express command. Indeed the reputation of Britain had suffered so terribly, that pirates of all the neighboring nations took the liberty to infest the narrow seas; and the ships and coasts of the island were exposed to the rapine and barbarity of the Turk himself, who carried numbers into captivity. So feeble was the government, or so careless of the welfare of the people.†

Charles employed the leisure which he had purchased by disgrace in a blind attempt to coerce Scotland into exact conformity with the English ritual. What his father had wished for the sake of polity, he deemed indispensable on grounds of

* Sidney's State Papers, vol. 2, p. 612. D'Estrade, Letters and Negotiations, p. 29, 8vo, London, 1755.

† Harris, Life and Writings of Charles 1., vol. 2, pp. 162–180.

conscience. James had invaded Scotland with the power of a prince; Charles directed against it the implacable fury of a zealot.* In the execution of this design, fraud, violence, threats, corruption, every thing had been pressed. Despotism had even shown itself patient and supple; sometimes addressing itself to ecclesiastical ambition, sometimes to the interests of the small landed proprietors, offering to one high church dignities and honorable offices in the state, and to the others an easy redemption of their tithes; always advancing towards its goal, yet with cautious, slow, and subtle steps.†

Much had been already gained. The bishops had recovered their jurisdiction; new bishoprics were constantly created, and in these Laud installed his dependents. "One Forbes," says Burnet, "was made diocesan of the new bishopric at Edinburgh. His way of life and devotion was thought monastic, and his learning lay in antiquity; he studied to be a reconciler between Papist and Protestant, and he leaned rather towards Rome, as appears by his *Considerationes Modestæ*."‡ The archbishop of St. Andrew's held the great seal of Scotland.§ The bishop of Ross was made high-treasurer.‖ Out of fourteen prelates, nine had seats in the Privy-council, which they ruled.¶ The service-book was already

* Chambers, Rebellions in Scotland, 1638–1666, vol. 1, p. 55.
† Guizot, vol. 1, pp. 107, 108.
‡ Burnet's Own Times, p. 12. § Spottiswood.
‖ Maxwell, Guizot. ¶ Clarendon, vol. 1, pp. 148–150.

in use by the Scottish churchmen. Charles and Laud thought that the auspicious moment had come for completing their crafty work by imposing this *nucleus* church, with new canons and a Liturgy conformable to the English discipline, at once upon Scotland at large, without consulting either the Presbyterian clergy or the people.*

In 1636 the Book of Canons was promulgated. By it the whole system of Presbyterian church-government was at once laid prostrate.† But it was acquiesced in with a quietude ominous of an approaching storm. This was the herald of the service-book, which made its appearance some months later, prefaced by a charge from the king, in which all who rejected the innovating ritual were branded as rebels.‡

The Scottish Liturgy was not *totidem verbis* the same as the English; but though differing in some respects, it was the same in scope.§ The alterations were of two kinds: those intended to *ingratiate* the book, and those whose tendency was to make it *distasteful*.‖ Laud added some things to the Scotch ritual which he intended eventually to graft into the English Prayer-book; it being thought best, when making an alteration, to go at once to the full extent of what was intended to be the final creed of the twin kingdoms.

* Guizot, vol. 1, pp. 108, 109; Malcom; Laing, Hist. Scotland, vol. 3.

† Chambers, vol. 1, p. 58; Calderwood.

‡ Ibid. Hume, vol. 2.

§ Fuller, vol. 3, p. 396.

‖ Ibid.

But "the church of Scotland," says Fuller, "claimed not only to be independent and free as any church in Christendom—a sister, not a daughter, of England—but also had so high an opinion of its purity, that it participated more of Moses' platform on the mount than other congregations, being a reformed reformation; whose practice might be directing to others, and she sit to give, not take—write, not receive, copies from other churches; she desiring that all others were like unto her, save only in her afflictions."*

With trifling exceptions therefore, such as the Romanist noblemen and a portion of the northern Highlands, the whole inhabitants of Scotland, of whatever rank, may be described as at this time banded in one common cause against the forms which Charles was inaugurating. The people for conscience' sake—for to their untutored conception the whole ritual was a Papist rubric—and the higher classes from motives of interest; all were alike leagued in opposition to the innovations. The very officers of the state were not true to the service of their master, and Scotch Episcopacy itself entered into the feelings of the nation, if not with ostentatious activity, at least with secret good will.†

The Scotch, like their Puritan brothers of the south, had a horror of any thing which smacked of Rome; and since they were ruder and more unlettered than the Puritans, they carried their hatred

* Fuller, vol. 3, pp. 399, 400.

† Chambers, vol. 1, p. 61.

to a higher degree.* To them, whatever differed with their own simple discipline seemed surcharged with idolatry. It can easily be conceived then what an effect the pomp of Laud's prelacy was sure to have.

The king had commanded every clergyman throughout Scotland to buy two copies of the Service-book for the use of his parish; and the new ritual was to be introduced at Edinburgh on the approaching Easter; but the time was changed, so that the ceremony did not occur until Sunday, the 23d of July, 1637.†

On that day, in the midst of the service, the cathedral church of Edinburgh was mobbed, missiles were hurled at the officiating clergy, and the military were called in to clear the aisles.‡ "One old woman, who had endeavored to go out with the rest of the ejected Non-conformists, but without succeeding, took up her station in a remote corner of the cathedral, where, opening her Bible, she endeavored to shut out from her ears the sounds of the detested service-book which the bishop had recommenced intoning. As she was engaged in reading the sacred pages, a young man who sat behind her happened to pronounce the word *Amen* so audibly at the close of one of the prayers as to disturb her devotions. Quite enraged at the near presence of what she esteemed so vile an abomination, she start-

* Hume, vol. 2, p. 231.

† Burnet's Own Times, Spottiswood, Clarendon.

‡ Chambers, vol. 1, p. 64; Harris, Perry.

ed from her seat, gave the astounded offender a severe blow on the cheek, and thundered in his ears, 'Fause thief, is there nae ither part o' the kirk where ye may say your mass, but ye maun say 't at my lug?' The young man, says the pamphleteer who tells the story, being dashed with such an unexpected rencontre, lapsed into pensive silence as a token of his recantation."*

In the streets wild uproar reigned: and when the congregation was dismissed from the cathedral, the innovating churchmen were hooted and pelted, amid the cheers of the rioters.†

This Edinburgh mob, from which the better classes stood aloof, was at once a warning and a prophecy. But the crazy court heeded neither. The remonstrances of the Scotch were met by a proclamation to enforce the ritual.‡ Then highland and lowland began to heave in insurrection. The people loved their king, but they adored their religion. Resistance at once organized itself; with a fine instinct, Scotland recognized the fact that regulated liberty quadruples all social forces. Four *tables* were formed at Edinburgh; the nobility, the gentry, the ministry, and the burgesses had each one; and into their hands the whole authority was confided.§ This unique government, the offspring of an excited moment, worked as regularly and as

* Chambers, vol. 1, p. 65. † Ibid.

‡ Hume, vol. 2, p. 233; Hallam, Chambers, Clarendon.

§ Hume, volume 2, page 233; Calderwood, Clarendon, Rushworth.

orderly as it could had it been grouted in the habits of a dozen centuries.*

The English court witnessed these movements aghast. The king began to temporize. Negotiations ensued; but both sides were sour and suspicious, and diplomacy proved abortive.† Then war was resolved on. "These hounds," said Strafford, "must be whipped back to common-sense."‡

On their part, the Scotch remembered Bannockburn, and took heart. They "trusted in God and their good right." Thousands rushed to Edinburgh. The famous COVENANT was signed by which Popery was renounced; and all its subscribers were linked in a union to resist all innovations in religion, and to defend each other from all attacks whatsoever.§

"The people, without distinction of rank or condition, age or sex, flocked to the subscription of this paper; few disapproved of it, and still fewer dared openly condemn it. The king's ministers and counsellors were themselves seized by the general contagion; and none but rebels to God and traitors to their country, it was thought, could withdraw themselves from so salutary and so pious a combination."‖

In England also chaos seemed come again. In the cause of the Scotch the Puritans plainly saw

* Hume. † Chambers, vol. 1, pp. 72–128.

‡ Strafford's Letters, vol. 2, pp. 138, 156.

§ Chambers, Hume, Clarendon, Perry, Carlyle.

‖ Hume, vol. 2, p. 233.

their own.* A secret correspondence between the northern and the southern Non-conformists was speedily established;† the cold dislike of ages, the mutual contempt of Scot and Englishman, was melted into hearty brotherhood and cordial coöperation by the persuasive eloquence of a common danger and a common creed.

"Many," affirms Burnet, "who stoutly adhered in the sequel to the king's cause, were then much troubled by the whole conduct of affairs, as being neither wise, legal, nor just; and the violence with which Scotland did engage against the court may easily convince men that the provocation must have been very great to draw that loyal nation into such entire and vehement revolt."‡

But the king, like Strafford and like Laud, loved high, rough measures, though he had neither the skill to juggle success, nor the genius to command it in such *outré* government.§ His improvident folly was never more clearly shown than through these early scenes which formed the prologue to the fierce tragedy of civil war. The court had coldly, systematically provoked a war by attempting to revolutionize the polity of a proud, honest, irascible people; and when war came, England stood in undisguised sympathy with the insurgents; while the court, without money, without troops, without coöperation, gazed with stupid despair across the

* May, Hist. Long Parl., vol. 1, p. 96. † Ibid.

‡ Burnet's Own Times, p. 15.

§ Ibid., p. 17.

Tweed, and attempted to *chatter* down the angry, armed *émeute*.

Charles begged, borrowed, and stole from Jew and Gentile; but still the greedy maw of his expenses hungered for money. The little army which he had put in the field had no heart to fight in a cause which every one decried. In the hope that his presence would inspire enthusiasm, the king went to head the troops; and in the spirit of feudalism, he summoned his nobility to a rendezvous at York.* He thought this silly pageant would paralyze the armed bands of the Scots.

But this tournament of carpet-knights was disordered by intrigue, and it reeled in drunken license.† The army fraternized with the foe.‡ Richelieu fomented discord.§ The Dutch jeered from the Netherlands. The Spaniard ravaged the narrow seas. The rebellious Scotch hung triumphant upon the border.‖ Beneath the thin film of the court stood sullen discontent, arming itself at home. Frightened, broken, bankrupt, in despair, Charles hastened back to London; and astounded England heard one day that the bewildered king had been driven to the *dernier* resort of another Parliament.¶

* Clarendon, vol. 2, p. 281; May, Burnet.

† Guizot, vol. 1, p. 119; Rushworth.

‡ Whitelock, Memorials, etc., p. 31. Clarendon, vol. 1, pp. 217, 218.

§ Ibid.

‖ Burnet's Own Times; Hume.

¶ May, Hist. Long Parl. Parl. Hist., vol. 2.

CHAPTER XXII.

THE LONG PARLIAMENT.

In April, 1640, after an intermission of twelve years,* Parliament, assembled by the force of events, met once more at Westminster Hall. Its temper was gentle, but firm—*suaviter in modo, fortiter in re.*† Long banishment from their seats had neither quenched the hopes nor quelled the spirits of the national representatives. With almost laughable pertinacity, the lower house, after transacting the necessary routine business, proceeded at once to reappoint the old obnoxious committees on religion and grievances;‡ after which they invited the Lords to unite with them in a fast, "because the best way to attain unto a happy conclusion in public affairs was to beg the Divine assistance and direction by solemn humiliation."§

The court looked on with anxious attention; and Laud made a bold effort to neutralize the committees by proposing that they be formed of an equal number of clergy from the convocation, and Commons from the House, an innovation that found no favor.‖ Then Charles, angry at this rebuff, and

* The last parliament had met in 1628. See chap. 19, p. 265, seq.

† Perry, p. 598. Guizot, vol. 1, p. 126.

‡ Rushworth, vol. 3, p. 1133. Clarendon, vol. 1, p. 227.

§ Ibid.

‖ Parl. Hist., vol. 2, col. 560. Heylin, Life of Laud, p. 422.

impatient for subsidies, laid the Scotch war before the Commons, pleaded his necessities, and demanded a vote of money before listening to the debate on grievances,* which revived the precise state of affairs during the former parliament.

This point the wily Commons would not yield. Their only hold upon the king was through his empty exchequer; they could not trust his oft-broken promises; *his* wants supplied, they feared that *theirs* would go begging.

So the debate on grievances commenced. One member presented a petition from his constituents, complaining of the collection of ship-money, of illegal projects and monopolies, and of the Star-chamber and High Commission courts.† Another affirmed that "the commonwealth had been miserably massacred, that all property and liberty was shaken, that the church was distracted and its professors persecuted."‡ A third, Sir Benjamin Rudyard, the most eloquent orator then in the House, and a good friend to the Establishment,§ denounced the "many disorders that had been committed, by innovations in religion, violations of fundamental laws, and intrusions upon liberty."‖

Then Pym spoke. He denounced the illegal taxes, declaimed against the departures from the Constitution, inveighed against the encouragement

* Parl. Hist., vol. 2, col. 560.

† Rushworth, vol. 3, p. 1129.

‡ Ibid., p. 1130.

§ Ibid.

‖ Clarendon, vol. 1, p. 54. Rushworth, vol. 3, p. 1144.

of popery and those "innovations in religion which were calculated to translate Canterbury into Rome," and in an able, temperate speech, used these words: "Popish books published and used, the introduction of popish ceremonies, as altars, bowing towards the east, pictures, crucifixes, and the like, which of themselves are so many dry bones, when put together, make the man. We are not now content with the old ceremonies—I mean such as the constitution of the reformed church hath continued unto us—but we must introduce again many of those superstitious and infirm ceremonies which accompanied the most decrepid age of popery."*

The Commons had thus far ignored the Scottish war; indeed nothing but respect for the king restrained them from crying "Amen" to it.†

After no little parliamentary skirmishing, during which the two Houses collided, the king offered to give up his right to collect ship-money if the Commons would vote him twelve subsidies.‡ That amount was deemed exorbitant. "Then it is useless to deliberate," said Sir Henry Vane, "since the king will accept no other terms." The House was provoked; Charles was no less angry; and in an ill-starred moment he dissolved this Parliament, as he had all former ones.§

The country heard this news with astonishment. The wiser friends of the court trembled. The lib-

* Rushworth, vol. 3, p. 1133. † Guizot, vol. 1, p. 126.
‡ Rushworth, vol. 3, p. 1134. Parl. Hist., col. 563.
§ Parl. Hist., col. 563. Strafford's Letters.

eral party rejoiced; this last blunder in the game insured the king's checkmate. "What disturbs you?" queried St. John, the friend of Hampden and a popular leader in the House, when he met Clarendon a few hours after the dissolution of the Parliament. "That which disturbs more than one honest person," answered the courtier, "the imprudent prorogation of the Commons, who alone can remedy the present disorders." "Ah, well," said St. John, "before things grow better they must grow worse; this Parliament would never have applied the fitting remedy."*

This last action of the court had outraged public opinion. "The people were indignant at seeing their rights, their creed, their persons, their possessions, surrendered to the irresponsible will of the king and his council, while their ancestors had of old made war on and dictated laws to the sovereign. No philosophical theory, no learned distinction between royalty and democracy occupied their thought: the House of Commons engrossed their whole attention, as representing the normal forces of the state—the ancient coalition of the barons, as well as the nation at large: the Commons alone had of late defended the public liberties; it alone was esteemed capable of redeeming them. It was the lower house that was meant when Parliament was mentioned; and the lawfulness as well as the necessity of its political omnipotence became a maxim, and established itself in every mind."†

* Clarendon, vol. 1, p. 240. † Guizot, vol. 1, pp. 90, 91.

As regarded the church, the middle classes were largely Puritan; but very many of the country gentlemen had no systematic views either as respected its form or government; they had no hostility to episcopacy *per se*, but they hated the bishops as the peculiar aiders and upholders of tyranny.*

And these views would find expression. Spite of whipping, pillory, and prison—spite of edicts, proclamations, and search-warrants, "seditious books" might be purchased at every book-stall in London.† The Scottish charge that the bishops were papists in masquerade—an idea born of Laud's impolitic choice of clergymen who faced towards the Vatican to fill the northern bishoprics‡—was now echoed in England.§

Charles, under the influence of his queen, and impelled by his pecuniary embarrassments, had always adopted a conciliatory policy towards the Romanists. While the Puritans were gagged, cropped, and *bastilled*, papists were granted dispensations from the penal laws; they were allowed to compound for recusancy, and their contributions were solicited towards the necessities of the state.‖ The court had been largely Romanized; the wit and beauty of the queen made her a potent missionary; a papal nuncio had come into the island in 1637, bringing with him a vast store of trinkets and relics.¶ Walter Montagu and Toby Matthews,

* Guizot, vol. 1, pp. 90, 91.
† Perry, p. 561.
‡ Burnet's Own Times, p. 12.
§ Ibid.
‖ Perry, p. 546. Heylin's Laud.
¶ Heylin's Laud, p. 358.

two Jesuit proselytes, were actively intriguing for their newly adopted faith;* and in discussing the English prelates of that time, three only, Hall, Morton, and Darrant, were held by the holy pontiff to be obstinately opposed to the church of Rome.†

The people saw and pondered; many sober Protestants feared that they might live to see the open establishment of the Inquisition in the island.‡ In their eyes, Laud was the chief of this reaction. But the famous primate, while anxious to reconcile his order to Rome, and even willing to stretch a point "to reunite torn and divided Christendom,"§ was not willing to go further than halfway towards the Vatican; if he *made* concessions, he *expected* them.‖

But in revolutionary crises, great masses never stop to philosophize; they can only see the tendency of systems, and these they accept or reject as they make for or against their goal. Laud's theories very evidently ran counter to the current of the time; and the people came to hate this ghostly counsellor of despotism.

The publication, at this excited moment, of bishop Hall's treatise on the *jus divinum* of episcopacy, gave added vehemence to the swelling cho-

* Perry, p. 560.

† Heylin's Laud, p. 414, and on; also Perry, pp. 560, 561, note.

‡ Neale, vol. 1, ch. 4. Reign of Charles I. Hallam's Con. Hist., vol. 1, p. 470.

§ Laud's Works, vol. 6, p. 45, et seq.

‖ Perry, pp. 544–548.

rus of complaint. The good bishop's book was altered and "stiffened" by Laud; those passages in which Hall—one of the brightest names in English divinity, an ornament to any age, a clergyman whose evangelical catholicity has won him immortal fame—spoke of the pope as antichrist, or held too stoutly to the sanctity of the Sabbath, or admitted that a presbytery was of use where episcopacy could not be had, were either erased or eased;* and these alterations made the work all the more unpopular in England.

Meantime the court had resorted once more to the "*new counsels.*" Former usurpations were renewed. Taxation was levied.† Members of the Commons were imprisoned for words spoken in the sanctuary of Parliament.‡ The comedy called the "Scotch war" was at once the pretext and the sanction of this despotism. But in reality there was no war. The two nations refused to fight each other. When the armies stood face to face, they fraternized. Strafford's own presence in the camp had no effect;§ he could neither persuade, threaten, nor cajole the army into belligerency. When the English saw the written covenant floating on the Scottish standard, or heard the drum-beat summon the troops to sermon, or at sunrise heard the "hostile" camp ring with psalms and prayers, they lost

* Canterbury's Doom, pp. 273, 274. Perry, pp. 583, 584. Neale, vol. 1, p. 514.

† Parl. Hist., vol. 2, col. 584.

‡ Rushworth, pt. 2, vol. 2, p. 1196.

§ Guizot, vol. 1, p. 133. Strafford's Letters.

all heart. When accounts of the pious ardor and friendly disposition of the Scots towards themselves reached their ears, they were alternately softened and incensed; the soldiers, many of them Puritans pressed into reluctant service, cursed the impious war in which they were engaged; they were already vanquished without a battle when they entered the lists against their brothers and their God.*

Commander of an army which would not fire a shot; which massacred its officers if they were suspected of popery;† which scattered when the foe appeared; which stood with serene *sang froid* and saw the Scots parade in triumph from the banks of the Tyne to York—Strafford himself was conquered; and when Charles spoke of an armistice, the chagrined minister sullenly acquiesced.‡

The intense aversion to the war had already found vent in riot. London was placarded; Laud's archiepiscopal palace was sacked; its sore back galled with grievances, the nation reared, and bade fair to throw its booted and spurred riders. The popular excitement was heightened by the exaction of an oath from the clergy never to consent to any alteration in the government of the Established church.§ This raised a storm even among the conforming clergy,‖ for "it was deemed unreasonable,"

* Heylin, Life of Laud. Guizot.

† Rushworth, pt. 2, vol. 3, p. 1191.

‡ Burnet's Own Times.

§ Perry, Neale, Rushworth.

‖ Robert Sanderson wrote, from his parsonage at Boothby Pay-

says Fuller, "to demand such an oath, because some of the orders specified therein, as archdeacons, deans, archbishops, stand established only *jure humano sive ecclesiastico;* and no wise man ever denied but that by the same power they are alterable on just occasion."*

This oath was framed by the convocation which had been in session at the time of the recently prorogued Parliament; it concluded with an *et cœtera*, which provoked a smile of bitterness and mistrust;† beneath these words were supposed to lurk the pope and a whole college of cardinals.‡

This complication of disorders threw the king into deep melancholy. He spoke of assembling a grand council of the peers at York, a feudal convocation which had never met through four hundred years; but Charles half hoped that the peers, who

nell, "Finding, to my great grief, that great distaste is taken generally in the kingdom to the oath enjoined by the late canons, I hold it to be my bounden duty rather to hazard the reputation of my discretion, than not to give your grace some intimation thereof; and I am much afraid that multitudes of churchmen, not only of the preciser sort, but even such as are otherwise every way regular and conformable, will either utterly refuse to take the oath, or be drawn thereto by great effort with much difficulty and reluctancy. The peace of the church is apparently in danger to be more disquieted by this one occasion than by any thing which hath happened in our memories." Quoted in Perry, p. 617.

* Fuller, vol. 3, p. 410.

† This was the purport of the oath: "I swear never to give consent to any alteration in the government of this church, ruled as it is at present by archbishops, bishops, deacons, archdeacons, *etc.*" Sparrow's Collections, pp. 359, 360. Perry thinks that *et cœtera* was no snare, but a mistake. See Perry, p. 616.

‡ Perry, p. 618; Neale, Rushworth.

had in the past, when Parliament was weak, partaken of sovereign power, might now help him out of his "slough of despond."*

But ere the peers could be convened, the court was flooded with petitions for the convocation of another Parliament.† The king, timid and reluctant, yet succumbed.‡ Accordingly, when the peers met, they were merely entrusted with negotiations for a peace with Scotland, all other business being adjourned to the two Houses at Westminster-hall.§

On the 3d of November, 1640, the *Long Parliament*—as it was called from the length of its session—assembled at Westminster-hall. It was destined to be the most famous and the most powerful representative body which England has ever known. Little did its members foresee, as they took their seats on that chilly autumn morning, the prodigious revolutions in church and state which they were to set on foot. Chiefly country gentlemen, possessed of large fortune, of gravity, of wisdom, of profound culture, and passionately patriotic,‖ they were at the outset inclined to be satisfied with some few amendments in the national programme. But God led them on and on. Revolutions do not obey constables. The green withes of the law could not bind the Samson of 1641.

* Clarendon, vol. 1, p. 253.

† Rushworth, pt. 2, vol. 2, p. 1263.

‡ Clarendon, Hume.

§ Ibid., Rusnworth.

‖ Clarendon, Neale, Macauley, Carlyle, Newell, Rushworth.

Circumstances, grand, resistless, forced the Commons further than they thought or knew. They were true to the necessities of their struggle; and when the monarchy cried Veto to their acts, they launched the Commonwealth from the scaffold of the king.

They commenced soberly; but each word was emphasized by the remembrance that England stood behind it. Over the court fell a numb fear. Whitehall was shrouded in gloom. Charles never spoke of his haughty prerogative.

The Commons, now as always, presented a list of grievances. Petitions avouched them. Farmers, tradesmen, merchants, the professions, through their representatives, no longer sued for redress—they demanded it. It was enacted that no interval of more than three years should ever elapse in future between parliament and parliament; and this statute was made executive by the proviso that, if writs under the great seal were not issued at the stated periods, the returning officers should, without such writs, call together the constituent bodies for the choice of representatives.* The courts of exception—the Star-chamber, which was a political, the High Commission, which was an ecclesiastical usurpation—were abolished.† The Council of York, which had been armed, in defiance of law, by a pure act of prerogative, and which, under Strafford's presidency, had made the Great

* Macauley, Hist. of England. Hume.

† Parl. Hist. Clarendon.

Charter a dead letter north of the Trent,* was swept away. Puritan prisons were opened. Prynne, Bostwick, and Barton were brought out of durance and exile—they had been sent to the isle of Jersey—with great triumph; London welcomed them peaceably, but victoriously, with bays and rosemary in its hands and hats."† The royal council was dissolved; its members were impeached. Strafford was incarcerated; Laud was flung into the Tower‡—companions in misfortune as they had been in prosperity.

Tireless, quiet, fearfully in earnest, the Commons had adopted Wentworth's motto,§ and *thorough* was stamped on all their acts.

The trial of Strafford was hastened on. Deserted by the king, who had promised to protect him,‖ the hapless minister pronounced his immortal oration in defence of his clearly indefensible conduct, and concluded by the admonitory repetition of the Scripture words, "Put not your trust in princes."¶

The House then passed the Act of Attainder, and Strafford repaid his crimes by the forfeit of his life.

Laud's impeachment followed; he was less feared, but more hated, than his twin usurper. He was

* Clarendon. May's Long Parliament.

† Fuller, vol. 3, p. 412. Whitelocke's Memorials, etc., p. 36.

‡ Heylin's Laud; Clarendon, Macauley, Hume.

§ *Thorough* was the expressive name which Strafford had given in his correspondence to his policy. Strafford's Letters.

‖ Whitelocke, p. 36. Guizot, vol. 1, pp. 142, 143.

¶ State Trials, vol. 3, col. 1383.

not immediately executed, but remained in close confinement for several years; nor did he care to break the silence which appeared to swallow him up in the bowels of the gloomy Tower; he thought that oblivion for him was safety, and only asked to be forgotten.*

On the day of Strafford's attainder, the king gave his assent to a law which bound him not to adjourn, prorogue, or dissolve the existing Parliament without its own consent.† By this concession he signed his own death-warrant. This done, the two Houses, after ten months of arduous toil, adjourned for a short vacation.‡

Meantime, paralyzed at the aspect of the immense power and the resolute courage of the Commons, the court stood in gaping amazement. "The king concealed his uneasiness and sorrow in complete inaction; the judges, fearful for themselves, did not dare to protect a delinquent; the bishops, without attempting to prevent it, saw their innovations tumbling about their heads." The Puritan preachers returned, without any legal title, to the possession of their curacies and pulpits. The dissenting sects assembled with open doors. The press was unshackled; pamphlets of all kinds were freely circulated. Men said, "In this good time of Parliament, England may breathe and crown the happy epoch as a jubilee."§

* State Trials, vol. 3, col. 1383. Heylin's Laud; Guizot.

† Macauley, Hist. Eng., vol. 1, p. 76. May's Long Parliament. Parl. Hist.

‡ May's Long Parl.

§ Milton.

CHAPTER XXIII.

SWORDS ROUGH-GROUND.

In 1641, after a recess of six weeks, Parliament resumed its session, but it did not resume its unanimity. The court party had recovered from its lethargy. The parliamentary partisans of the government, though outnumbered, were still able and numerous; swept away by the excitement, they had at first succumbed, but no Lethe drugged their senses, and the intermission had allowed them to mature their policy, and to organize a stout fight for their idea.

The Puritan leaders, the statesmen of the lower house, though not prepared to proclaim the sovereignty of the Commons, did avow the independence of Parliament; and it was already in their minds to bereave the crown of its fatal prerogative by transferring the essential elements of government into the hands of the national representatives. Hampden, Pym, Vane, Hollis, Stapleton, knew that such a programme was an infraction of the existing laws; but they also knew that there was something more sacred than the *jus divinum* of kings, something more priceless than the chartered parchments of the past—LIBERTY; and aware that the Constitution, broad as it then was, did not insure that, they meant to guarantee it by more immutable enactments. They reverenced the past, but they reverenced the future still more. They recognized the value of law, but they knew that justice was still weightier. Fresh from the schools of Athens and Rome, they found at once the apology and the necessity for their unconstitutional action in Cicero's glorious Latin, "*Salus populi suprema lex.*"*

Under the apparent concord, a great schism was latent. Events soon developed the historic parties of the Roundheads and the Cavaliers.

On the first day of the new session, diversity of wishes and opinions was manifested. The Scottish Presbyterians, spreading through the country, had made many proselytes among the people, and even inoculated Parliament itself; so that when London sent up its famous prayer, known as the *root-and-branch petition*, for the entire abolition of episcopacy, it found ardent friends in the House.†

A little later, seven hundred ecclesiastics solicited the reform of the *temporal* authority of the bishops;‡ and this was followed in its turn by the arrival of nineteen petitions from several counties, signed by one hundred thousand names, recommending the maintenance of the Episcopal establishment.§

The Commons were divided in sentiment. The

* The safety of the people is the highest law.

† December 11, 1640. Rushworth, pt. 3, vol. 1, p. 93.

‡ Neale, vol. 1, chs. 6, 7. Clarendon. § Ibid.

more rigid Puritans urged the adoption of the *root-and-branch petition*, and they were supported by numbers of the country gentlemen, who had no especial dislike to the ritual, but in whose minds prelacy and tyranny, through the course of Laud, were synonymous terms.*

The moderates, headed by Lord Falkland, whom Clarendon esteemed the most extraordinary man of that extraordinary age,† refused to adopt so radical a policy, but they expressed their willingness to lop off all abuses.‡

The debate was violent and protracted. Eventually a bill was proposed barring ecclesiastics from all civil functions, and excluding the bishops from the House of Lords. On this the Commons compromised; but it was beaten in the upper house.§

The alliance between the two houses of Parliament was not at this time overcordial. The Lords, representing the hereditary interests, the vested rights, the aristocratic *caste* of the island, were timid by instinct and conservative by nature. They looked with suspicion upon any change, and bewailed innovation. If the Commons were the spurs of the revolution, the Lords were its checks.

The two Houses at this time represented different tendencies, the conservative and progressive: distinctions which are founded in diversity of temper, habit, education, intellect, and therefore present in all societies, and sure to exist so long as the

* Guizot, vol. 1, book 3.

† Clarendon, Memoirs.

‡ Parl. Hist., vol. 2, col. 794–814.

§ Ibid., col. 794.

human mind is drawn in opposite directions by the force of habit and by the charm of novelty. This difference is not confined to politics and religion; it is seen in literature, in art, in science, in surgery, in navigation, in mechanics, in agriculture, and even in mathematics. "Everywhere," observes Macauley, "there is a class of men who cling with fondness to whatever is ancient, and who, even when convinced by overpowering reasons that innovation would be beneficial, consent to it with many misgivings and forebodings. There is always another class of men sanguine, bold in speculation, always pressing forward, quick to discern the imperfections of whatever exists, and disposed to think lightly of the risks and inconveniences which attend improvements. Both are necessary; but of both the best specimens are found not far from the common frontier."*

Stuart Mill thinks that conservatism is necessarily stupid, but holds that, since two-thirds of the constituents of every society are also stupid, it may plume itself on always being sure to have the largest party.†

But even the conservatism of the House of Lords grew radical under the pressure of events. Thus far the revolution had been moral. News came that Ireland was heaving in rebellion. Half civilized, crowded down into vassalage by their conquerors, bigoted Romanists, the aboriginal

* Macauley, Hist. Eng., vol. 1, pp. 76, 77.

† Speech in the House of Commons, June 18, 1866.

tribes had risen against the colonists, and a war which was a massacre desolated the green island. National and theological hatred gave the outbreak increased ferocity, and the butchery of Protestants rivalled in horror the Paris St. Bartholomew.*

"A horrible suspicion, unjust indeed, but not altogether unnatural, seized the Parliament. The queen was an avowed Romanist; the king was not regarded by the Puritans, whom he had mercilessly persecuted, as a sincere Protestant; and so notorious was his duplicity, that there was no treachery of which he was not believed capable. It was soon whispered that this awful holocaust of Rome in Erin was part of a vast work of darkness which had been planned at Whitehall."†

Then passion broke loose; a remonstrance, enumerating the faults of the king's administration from the date of his accession, and covering both civil and religious grievances, was introduced. This was addressed, not to the king, but to the people, and it was couched in haughty language. After a rancorous debate, it was adopted by a small majority.‡

Meantime riot raged in the streets. The pulpit bewailed the dangers which menaced religion from the desperate attempts of papists and malignants; frantic multitudes crowded to Westminster, and in-

* Hume, vol. 2, pp. 268–273.

† Macauley, History of England, vol. 1, p. 82.

‡ Parl. History. May's Long Parliament.

sulted the prelates and the Cavaliers on the route to and from Parliament.*

The Romans had a custom that, once a year, a solemn festival should be held, in which their slaves had full-liberty to ease their minds by saying of their masters what they pleased. In England the *saturnalia* seemed now resurrected. But the prelates, less complacent than the ancients, were displeased with the "plain speech" of the plebeians; so one day they sent up to the Lords a *protestation*, in which they stated that, though they had an undoubted right to sit in the upper house, they were restrained therefrom by the affronts of the unruly multitude. Since therefore they could not safely take their seats, they protested against all legislation during their absence.†

The protestation was signed by twelve bishops, and heartily approved by the king.‡

This ill-timed and silly act compromised both king and prelates. "As soon as it was presented to the Lords," says Hume, "that House desired a conference with the Commons, whom they informed of this ill-starred paper. The opportunity was seized with joy and triumph. An impeachment for high-treason was immediately issued against the prelates, as endeavoring to subvert the fundamental laws by invalidating the authority of legislation. They were, on the first demand, sequestrated from Parliament, and committed to custody. No man

* Hume, vol. 2, pp. 278, 279

† Ibid.; Fuller, Lathbury.

‡ Hume, Macauley.

in either house ventured to speak a word in their vindication, so much was every one displeased at the egregious imprudence of which they had been guilty. One person alone said that he did not believe them guilty of high-treason, but that they were stark mad, and he therefore desired that they might be sent to Bedlam."*

But the king's treachery soon made this "Ossa like a wart." Bereaved of Strafford and deprived of Laud, Charles had expressed his wish to govern in harmony with the Commons, and in order to that, had proposed to call into his cabinet constitutional loyalists like Falkland, Hyde, and Colepepper, all of whom were distinguished by the share which they had taken in the reformation of abuses, yet whose attachment to the existing forms was decided and sincere.†

Had this been done, the revolution might even then have been averted. A strong party backed the constitutionalists; custom was on their side; and had the king been honest, the headsman's axe would have been left to rust. But he hated his new advisers; "they were by no means men after his own heart. They were lovers of liberty, and they were attached to the existing *régime* only because they thought that a few reforms would insure liberty. They had joined in condemning his tyranny, in abridging his power, and in punishing his instruments. They were even indeed prepared to defend by strictly legal means his strictly legal preroga-

* Hume, vol. 2, p. 277.

† Guizot, vol. 1, p. 157. Clarendon, vol. 2, p. 73.

tives; but they would have recoiled with horror from the thought of renewing Laud's usurpations or reviving Strafford's projects of "*thorough*." They were therefore, in the king's estimation, traitors who differed only in the degree of their seditious malignity from Pym and Hampden."*

His project then of calling the constitutionalist chiefs into his council was an empty *ruse*, a shallow trick to gain time. One day, without prior consultation with his friends, he sent the attorney-general to impeach Hampden, Pym, Hollis, and other Puritan leaders of the Commons, at the bar of the House of Lords; and his insanity carried him so far that he even invaded the sanctuary of Westminster Hall by marching at the head of his guard to seize them in person.†

Abashed and dismayed, the Cavaliers stood silent. The opposition leaders escaped arrest,‡ but this attempt taught them that their necks were now staked on success. London was stirred to portentous rage.§ England at large began to arm. The Puritan clergy inspired their disciples to a manful defence of the "good old cause." The colors of the Parliament were on every hat.‖ Whitehall itself was surrounded by a cordon of offended yeomen.¶ And the king, fearing his own arrest, quitted his capital, and skulked like a malefactor to the provincial town of York.**

* Macauley, vol. 1, p. 84.

† May's Long Parl.; Clarendon, Burnet. ‡ Ibid.

§ Guizot, Clarendon. ‖ Ibid. ¶ Ibid.

** Harris, Life of Charles I.; Clarendon, Carlyle.

What followed falls properly into the department of civil history; but in those times political and religious affairs were so closely married that it is impossible to divorce them. If we would get a clear insight into English Protestantism in the seventeenth century, we must also understand the politics of the age. And indeed it has been well said, that in the great rebellion it was not so much the civil as the religious grievances of England that gathered adherents to the Parliament. It was PURITANISM watching with jealousy the tendencies towards the hated system of Rome, and clinging to the Bible and to purity of faith and form, which vivified and dignified the struggle.

At length, in 1642, after tedious negotiations, succeeded by crimination and recrimination, the sword was unsheathed, and the disputed questions were left to the decision of that stern arbitrator, war.

Englishmen were summoned to choose sides in this death-dance. To republican eyes the Parliament was so self-evidently right in every essential respect, that men often find it hard to believe that honest, even if mistaken Cavaliers could have fought under the banners of the king. But the England of 1642 was not the United States of 1866. The constitutionalists, many of whom were possessed of marked virtues and abilities, forced to choose between two dangers, and honestly wedded to the monarchy, esteemed it their duty rather to rally to the aid of a prince whose past conduct they condemned, and whose word inspired them with little confidence, than to suffer the subversion of the royal polity. The Romanists were royalists because the queen was of their faith, and also because they knew that Charles granted them a much more liberal toleration than the Puritans would concede. "On the same side were the great body of the clergy, both the universities, and all those laymen who were strongly attached to episcopal government and to the English ritual. These respectable classes found themselves in the company of some allies much less decorous than themselves. Puritan austerity drove to the king's faction all who made pleasure their business, who affected gallantry, splendor of dress, or taste in the higher arts. With these went all who lived by amusing the leisure of others, from the painter and the comic poet down to the rope-dancer and the Merry Andrew; for these artists knew that they might thrive under a superb and luxurious despotism, but must starve under the rigid rule of the precisians."*

The whole royalist party is not chargeable with "the profligacy and baseness of the horse-boys, the gamblers, and the bravos, whom the hope of plunder attracted from all the dens of Whitefriars to the standard of the king; nor were the Cavaliers the instruments which despots in other countries have employed, with the mutes who throng their ante-chambers, and the janizaries who mount guard

* Macauley, Hist. of Eng., vol. 1, p. 79.

at their gates. They were not mere machines for destruction, dressed up in uniforms, caned into skill, intoxicated into valor, defending without love, destroying without hatred. There was a freedom in their subserviency, a nobleness in their very degradation. They were indeed misled, but often by no base or selfish motive. Compassion, misconceptions of romantic honor, the prejudices of childhood, and the venerable names of history, threw over them a spell potent as that of Duessa; and like the Red-cross knight, they thought that they were doing battle for some injured beauty, while they defended a false and loathsome sorceress. In truth they scarcely entered into the merits of the political question; they had not themselves been pinched or harried, and they knew nothing and cared less for those who had. It was not for a treacherous king or an intolerant church that they fought, but for the old banner which had waved in so many battles over the heads of their fathers, and for the altars at which they had received the hands of their brides. Though nothing could be more erroneous than their political opinions, they possessed, in a fairer degree than their adversaries, those qualities which are the grace of private life; with many of the vices of the round-table, they had also many of its virtues—courtesy, generosity, tenderness, and respect for woman."*

The parliamentary muster was in strong contrast with the king's glittering array. Under the

* Macauley, Essay on Milton.

banner of the Commons stood incarnated Puritanism, reinforced by the small freeholders, the merchants, the shop-keepers, the municipal corporations; by those members of the Established church who still adhered to the Cavinistic doctrines which forty years before had been generally held by the prelates and the clergy, but who had no affection for the Genevan discipline; and by a formidable minority of the aristocracy.

But the *Puritans* were at once the main stay and the inspiration of the popular cause; and they were attracted towards the Parliament by its preponderating religious earnestness. Officered by Pym, the Papinian of England; by Hampden, a statesman and a soldier *sans peur et sans reproche;* by Harry Vane—

> "Vane, young in years, but in sage counsel old;"

by Fairfax,

> "Whose name in arms through Europe rings,
> Filling each mouth with envy or with praise,
> And all her jealous monarchs with amaze,
> And rumors loud that daunt remotest kings;"

by Cromwell, the

> "Chief of men, who through a cloud
> Not of war only, but distractions rude,
> Guided by faith and matchless fortitude;"

and by Milton, the mouth-piece and the trenchant pen of "the good old cause"—officered by such chiefs, militant Puritanism, linking hands with civil liberty, could not but receive the benediction of the God of battle.

CHAPTER XXIV.

THE GOOD FIGHT FOR TOLERATION.

THE early months of 1642 were spent by both king and Parliament in active preparation for their death-grip. The two athletes lavished their cunning upon their training before venturing to face each other in the arena.

Charles, traversing the northern and western counties, recruited an army by plausible harangues, by spendthrift promises, by the woful aspect of his ruffled regality; and the enthusiastic Cavaliers, pawning their jewels, mortgaging their estates, melting their silver chargers and christening-bowls, hastened to enlist.*

Nor was the Parliament less active: severe and methodical taxation coined gold; a militia force was organized; the train-bands of the cities were armed, and the provident statesmen of the Commons collected all the elements of their scattered strength.† The importance of effecting an alliance with Scotland was soon felt and seen. The northern kingdom was, in some sense, the inaugurator of the strife, since the *bellum Episcopale* had struck the tocsin of armed resistance. Scotland, from the Orkneys to the Tweed, was obstinately and intolerantly tied in

* Macauley, Hist. Eng., vol. 1, p. 88. Neale, vol. 2, p. 19.
† Hume, May's Long Parl., etc.

the Covenant. The Presbyterian clergy ruled there as absolutely as the bishops did in England under Laud.* Not only so, but the Presbyterians had gained firm foothold in the Parliament itself; and now, when a league was proposed, it was urged as a *sine qua non*, that episcopacy should be formally abolished.† "Marvellous art and industry," remarks Clarendon, "were employed in engineering this bill. A majority of the Commons were really against it, and it was hardly submitted to by the House of Peers; yet it passed without one negative vote; and bonfires and bell-peals ratified the act in London."‡ "It may seem strange," comments Neale, "that Parliament should abolish the existing Establishment before they had agreed upon another; but the Scots would not declare for them till they had done it. Had the two houses been inclined to Presbytery, as some have maintained, it had been easy to have adopted the Scots' model at once; but as the bill for extirpating episcopacy was not to take place till above a year forward, it was apparent that they were willing it should not take place at all, if in that time they could come to an accommodation with the king; and if the breach should then remain, they proposed to consult with an assembly of divines what form to erect in its stead. Thus the old ritual lay prostrate for eighteen years,

* Chambers, in his history of the rebellions in Scotland, tells some strange stories of the despotic authority of the Presbyterian clergy. See vol. 1, pp. 43-46, Introduction.

† Parl. Hist. May's Long Parl.

‡ Clarendon, vol. 1, p. 279.

although never legally abolished for want of the royal assent; and therefore at the Restoration it took place again, without any new law to restore it: the Presbyterians, who were then in the saddle, not understanding this, did not provide against it, as they might have done."*

An anecdote illustrates the lack of zeal which characterized the loyalists in the House of Commons. On this very occasion, when the life or death of the church of England was in earnest debate, the Cavaliers, weary and hungry, quitted Westminster Hall to carouse in an adjoining coffee-house. During their absence, the bill was passed, which caused Lord Falkland to remark, that "the enemies of the church hated it worse than the devil, while its very best friends did not like it so well as their dinner."†

Meanwhile war had actually commenced. Edgehill was soaked in fraternal gore. Twelve months of checkered conflict passed, and the king, triumphant in the north and west, was the decided gainer. Already England had lost the flower of her sons. The "brave Lord Brooke," one of the brightest ornaments of the Puritan party, the Sydney of the war, was slain.‡ Falkland, the Bayard of the royalist party, had fought his last battle.§ Hampden had fallen, as became him, vainly endeavoring, by his heroic example, to inspire his followers with courage to face the fiery cavalry of Rupert.‖

* Neale, vol. 2, pp. 18, 19.

† Clarendon.

‡ March 2, 1643.

§ September 20, 1643.

‖ June 24, 1643.

"Nothing is here for tears; nothing to wail
Or knock the breast; no weakness, no contempt,
Dispraise or blame; nothing but well and fair."

Agitated by these losses and reverses, Parliament sent a commission, headed by Vane, whose eloquence, address, capacity, and tolerant breadth of statesmanship made him the fitting successor of Hampden, to Edinburgh, to solicit a closer union. These negotiations were successful. The "Solemn League and Covenant" was signed by the Scottish convention of states and by the general assembly, and the next morning the commissioners departed for London, to obtain the assent of England to the nascent confederacy.*

This famous paper consisted of six articles, pledging those who took it to mutual brotherhood; to the preservation of Presbyterianism in Scotland; to the extirpation of popery, prelacy, "and whatsoever was contrary to sound doctrine and the power of godliness; and to the maintenance of the liberties of both kingdoms."†

There was much debate over the *form* of the Covenant, even before it was signed in Scotland. Vane desired a *civil league;* the Scotch pressed for a *religious covenant.* Vane, a devotee of toleration, knew that the Covenanters claimed that divine right on which the bishops grounded Episcopacy as the prerogative of Presbyterianism, and he dreaded lest

* Burnet, Mem. of the Hamiltons. Baillie, Letters, vol. 1, p. 381.

† Chambers, vol. 1, pp. 231–253. Burnet, Mem. of the Hamiltons.

the synod should replace the prelates, and in their turn press conformity, as happened in the sequel.

But the Scotch were stubborn; home necessities pressed; so the utmost concession that Vane's skilful diplomacy could wring was, that the paper should be called a *league*, to meet the views of those who did not approve of its religious aspect, and a *covenant* for the satisfaction of such as chiefly valued its ecclesiastical character.*

But during the pendency of this debate, that celebrated convocation was called which history recognizes as *The Westminster Assembly of Divines.*

Against the formal protest of the king,† Parliament ordained, on its own authority, a convention of "learned and godly divines and others, to be consulted with by the Parliament, for settling the government and liturgy of the church of England."‡

Ten lords, twenty commoners, and one hundred and twenty-one clergymen were summoned by name to attend, and equal liberty in voting and debating was conceded.§ The two houses appointed themselves the court of *dernier ressort.*‖

On the 1st of July, 1643, sixty-nine divines, accompanied by the parliamentary delegation, assembled in that magnificent chapel which Henry VII. had reared at Westminster, and one of the finest specimens of mediæval church architecture in Eng-

* Hume, vol. 2, p. 305; Neale, vol. 2, p. 67; Chambers, ut antea.

† Clarendon, Burnet.

‡ Parl. Hist., vol. 3, col. 173; Rushworth, part 3, vol. 3, p. 475.

§ Ibid.

‖ Parl. Hist., vol. 3, col. 173.

land. But to the grave worthies in black—for in imitation of the foreign Protestants, the clergy had discarded their canonical habits*—this "haunt of prelacy" was veiled with gloomy associations. As they glanced around, they thought of Laud, of the Star-chamber, of the High Commission, of cropped ears, slit noses, and confiscated goods. The vaulted roof, clinging from the clustered pillars in the walls like branches of lofty trees interlaced, forming a rich canopy of leaves, had no charms for them. If the building was "a poem in stone," it related a sad story; "and the fretwork, elaborately spread over the cold walls and roof, became no unapt symbol of that ingeniously wrought system of perverted religion elaborated in Rome, which overreached society through the middle ages, and which has been fitly termed 'a petrifaction of Christianity.' Now, when pacing those dim aisles, perhaps they felt a struggle in their breasts between emotions of taste and the sentiments of faith; and the charms of artistic beauty were weakened, if not dispelled, by the remembrance of the ecclesiastical despotism which, by means like these, among others, for so many centuries held captive the minds of their forefathers."†

Still they entered this

——— "Studious cloister pale,"

and considered mooted and knotty points of theology under

* Neale, vol. 2, p. 63.
† Stoughton, Spiritual Heroes, pp. 144, 145.

——— "the high embowered roof,
With antique pillars massy proof,
And storied windows, richly dight,
Casting a dim, religious light."

Hallam describes the Westminster Assembly as "equal in learning, good sense, and other merits, to any lower house of convocation that ever made a figure in England."* And Baxter says, "The divines there assembled were men eminent in learning, godliness, ministerial abilities, and fidelity; and being not worthy to be one of them myself, I may the more freely speak the truth, even in the face of malice and envy, that so far as I am able to judge, by the information of all history of that kind, the Christian world since the days of the apostles had never a synod of more excellent divines than this and the Synod of Dort."†

Milton's opinion was not so favorable. He thought the convocation the hand on the dial, moving and pointing as directed by the clock of Presbyterianism; and he could never forgive it the attempt to enact that creed into the national religion instead of decreeing toleration.‡

When the doctrinal debates began, three parties were developed. The majority were *Presbyterians*, men who believed that elders, clerical and lay, were the only divinely appointed rulers of the church; and that synods, general and provincial, were the only ecclesiastical courts of divine appointment.§

* Hallam, Cons. Hist., vol. 1, p. 609.

† Baxter's Life and Times, p. 193. ‡ Milton, Prose Works.

§ Chambers, Neale, Newell, Clarendon, Baxter.

Next in number and authority were the *Erastians*,* who held that the precise form of church government was not appointed in Scripture, but was left entirely to the magistracy, with whom alone resided the power to inflict punishment for offences;† and such eminent men as Selden, Whitelocke, and Oliver St. John were the chiefs of this party.‡

Last came the *Independents*, a small party, just rising into reputation, the fathers of modern Congregationalism, the brothers of the exiled Pilgrims of Plymouth rock. They conceived that every Christian congregation had, under Christ, supreme jurisdiction in things spiritual over its own pastor and its own members; they rejected the interposition of the magistrate in religious affairs; they held that the individual churches were destitute of temporal sanction; in their eyes, appeals to the provincial and national synods were scarcely less unscriptural than appeals to the court of Arches or to the Vatican: holding to the democracy of Christianity, they esteemed popery, prelacy, and Presbyterianism to be merely three forms of one great apostasy.§

In politics they were, to use the phrase of their time, root-and-branch men; or, to use the kindred phrase of our age, radicals. Not content with limiting the power of the monarch, they were desirous to erect a commonwealth on the ruins of the old English polity.||

* Chap. 12, p. 170, note.

† Hume, Newell, etc.

‡ Newell, p. 269.

§ Macauley, Hist. Eng., vol. 1, p. 90; Hume, vol. 2, pp. 314, 315.

|| Macauley, p. 91.

Among the Independents were found the only friends which toleration then could count. All of that party were not true to their principles or logical in their applications, as events amply demonstrated when they controlled the commonwealth; but their philosophers, their orators, their statesmen were enamoured of the completest intellectual liberty. 'T is the rare credit of the party. Vane was the parliamentary advocate of this grand fundamental truth, the hardest to learn, and the most necessary. Cromwell was its champion in the field; Milton was its knight-errant in the domain of letters.

In September, 1643, the commissioners returned from Scotland with the *Solemn League and Covenant.* The Parliament immediately referred it to the Westminster divines,* who were then discussing the doctrinal Articles of the church of England. By this time the few Episcopal divines who had appeared had seceded, leaving to their opponents a clear field.† All other questions were at once adjourned, and the Assembly opened a debate upon the Articles of Confederation. The Independents disliked several of the clauses of the Covenant; but the imperious necessities of the state overbore all opposition, and the document was shortly voted by the Assembly and by both houses of Parliament, article by article, "each person standing uncovered, with right hand uplifted. A prayer concluded the

* Baillie's Letters; Burnet, Parl. Hist.
† Burnet, Neale, Clarendon.

solemnity; after which the Commons went up into the chancel, and subscribed their names in one roll of parchment, whither they were followed by the Assembly, who subscribed theirs in another, in both which the Covenant was fairly transcribed."*

An oath to support the union was enforced in Scotland by the severest penalties;† and in England it was required of all over eighteen years of age, the punishment for non-compliance being citation before the House of Commons and disfranchisement.‡

This done, the Assembly dispatched letters to the Protestant churches in France, in Switzerland, and in the Netherlands, reciting their recent action, and requesting the sympathy of their coreligionists.§ And this was followed by a counter-appeal to foreign Protestantism by the king.‖

From this time the dissolution of the Establishment may be dated; or if not the dissolution, then the trance; for it slept without awaking through eighteen years. There were no ecclesiastical courts, no visitations, no habits, no ceremonies, not even the Prayer-book itself. The Assembly of divines, sitting, as had the old convocations, during the entire session of Parliament, passed all church business through their hands; the parishes elected their ministers, the Assembly examined and approved

* Neale, vol. 2, p. 68.

† Chambers, vol. 1, chap. 12. Baillie's Letters.

‡ Clarendon, Hume, Neale, Burnet.

§ Neale, vol. 2, pp. 72, 73.

‖ Ibid.

them, and Parliament confirmed them in their benefices. It was to Westminster that petitioners for sequestered livings also resorted.*

But though the Westminster Assembly continued its sessions until the establishment of the Commonwealth, in its last years it dwindled away in point of numbers, sank in public estimation, and declined in reputation and influence.† The opening months of its existence were its busiest. In 1646 the Confession of Faith was completed; the doctrinal part of which the Parliament adopted, rejecting the discipline. At that time also the Larger Catechism, for exposition in the pulpit, and the Shorter Catechism, for the instruction of children, were prepared.‡

But the famous debate on toleration took place within thirty days after the subscription of the Covenant.

The Presbyterians, usurping the discarded prerogatives of the Episcopal bench, shackled the press, interfered with the civil rights of the people, and pressed conformity with their creed;§ so that England had first a *single* pope, at Rome, then a *bench* of popes, the bishops, and finally an *Assembly* of popes, at Westminster.

Besides, the absurdity was seen of men who had just been baiting down the prelates as persecutors, now, in their own prosperity, proving the hollow-

* Neale, vol. 2, pp. 74, 75. † Stoughton, p. 183.

‡ Whitelocke, Memorials, etc.

§ Hume, Clarendon, Neale, Guizot, etc.

ness of their former protests by enacting the same *rôle*. Vane protested, Cromwell stormed, Milton argued and satirized by turns,* addressing to the Parliament the noblest plea for an unshackled press ever penned or uttered, and addressing to the people his caustic comment,

"*New presbyter* is but *old priest* WRIT LARGE."

There were but five Independents in the Assembly;† but these were men of rare ability and active eloquence; so that, reinforced by the scholarship, the genius, and the zeal of their party outside of Westminster, they contrived to make themselves felt and heard.

"The divines had at first met in Westminster chapel. The coolness of that spacious edifice was pleasant in the summer months; but when the winter cold came on, the Assembly adjourned to the Jerusalem chamber, whose plain architecture was more in harmony with the Puritans than the florid gothic of the chapel they had left. This, according to the old chronicler Fabian, supported by Shakspeare, was the death-scene of Henry IV.

"Romance and poetry have thus thrown their rainbow hues over the room; but far nobler associations are linked with it when it is remembered as the spot where the advocates of religious liberty stood and fought one of their earliest battles. The

* Prose Works. See also Milton's Life, Am. Tract Soc., 1866.

† Their names were, Nye, Burroughs, Bridge, Greenhill, and Carter. Newell, p. 269. Nye and Burroughs were the Luther and the Melancthon of the little band.

dying Harry, prevented from accomplishing his wished-for crusade to Palestine, is a picture of no mean interest; but it pales before the scene of those five brave ones who contended for the claims of God and the rights of man, and carried on a moral crusade against those who had usurped the holy land of conscience."*

The two parties joined battle on the *jus divinum* of Presbyterianism. When the Assembly decided yes, the Independents protested.† But the debate grew still sharper when the Assembly proposed to enforce by civil penalties their rigid code. "No," said the Independents, "by God's command the magistrate is discharged to put the least discourtesy on any man, Turk, Jew, Papist, Socinian, or whatever, for his religion."‡

This was something "new under the sun." Men had pleaded and died for *their own faith;* but these heroes leaped beyond them. Braver than Cranmer, broader than Cartwright, they were not satisfied with freedom for themselves; they demanded it for the human race.

Nor was this the offspring of indifference. They were not doubting Thomases or careless Gallios. They hated error, they abhorred sin; but they made a distinction which their brother Puritans did not. "Let even the erring ones in these happy days remain untouched by law, unharmed by civil

* Stoughton. † Ibid., p. 175, et seq.

‡ Quoted from a pamphlet by John Goodwin, a famous Independent, to whom Baillie refers in his Letters.

penalties," they pleaded. "What," asked the Presbyterians, "will you then tolerate error, adopt schism, and banquet Romanism?" "No, brothers," was the reply, "we are foes to error as much as you; most intolerant are we of all that invades Christ's empire to disturb its peace; but in conquering error, we must not employ any weapons which God has forbidden; and 'the weapons of our warfare are not carnal.'"*

Though outvoted and shouted down in the Assembly, the champions of toleration became popular in the street and in the Commons. The decision of the divines on the *jus divinum* of Presbyterianism was modified by Parliament, which also refused to alienate the *power of the keys* in ecclesiastical offences.† Thus barred by the authoritative veto of "the powers that be" from enforcing their principles by the sword, the Presbyterians never succeeded in nationalizing their ecclesiasticism. Nor did they forgive the party which had balked them of success, and which ere long supplanted them in power.‡

* This whole debate is admirably summarized by Stoughton, pp. 160-183.

† Hallam, Neale, Burnet, Hume.

‡ Newell, p. 270; Whitelocke, Memorials, etc; Neale, vol. 2.

CHAPTER XXV.

THOROUGH.

FROM the year 1644 forward, to the establishment of the Commonwealth, events jostled and elbowed each other. Change succeeded change, growth succeeded growth. In civil wars, that party which is buoyed up by enthusiasm and has a purpose, is sure to control the present and to mould the future. The men who sit, like the figure on our coin, with their heads turned back, are pressed by revolutionary gravitation into the grave of the past. Live growths rive dead matter.

The English rebellion of 1641 illustrates this. Every day the *Thorough* party gained in influence and *prestige.* There were many changes in the Parliament. Old leaders were dead, or shelved. Bedford was an apostate; Pym had been borne with princely honors to a grave among the Plantagenets. Vane, ardent, resolute, uncompromising, began to shape the time in a republican model.*

So in the army. Essex and his lieutenants, mere holiday warriors, *dilettante* soldiers, were pushed from their camp-stools; Cromwell and Ireton marshalled Britain to a higher struggle; and as the nation was more in earnest, so its leaders

* Macauley, Hist. of England, vol. 1, p. 91.

at the council-board and in the field were seen to be.

Cromwell's rise was as remarkable as it was rapid. "Bred to peaceful occupations, he had, at more than forty years of age, accepted a colonel's commission in the parliamentary army. No sooner had he become a soldier, than he discovered, with the keen eye of genius, what Essex and men like Essex, with all their experience, were unable to perceive. He saw precisely where the strength of the royalists lay, and by what means alone that strength could be overpowered. He saw that it was necessary to reconstruct the army of the Parliament. At the outset their ranks had been filled with hirelings whom want and idleness had induced to enlist—the usual element of the rank and file of armies. Hampden's regiment had been considered one of the best, yet he described it as a mere rabble of tapsters and serving-men out of place.

"The Cavaliers were gentlemen, high-spirited, ardent, accustomed to the use of arms, to bold riding, and to perilous sport—the image of war. Mounted on their favorite horses, and commanding little bands composed of their younger brothers, their game-keepers, their huntsmen, they were perfectly qualified for guerilla warfare. The steadiness, the prompt obedience, the mechanical precision of movement, which are characteristic of the regular soldier, these gallant volunteers never attained. But they were at first opposed to enemies as undisciplined as themselves, and far less active, athletic, and daring. For a time therefore the Cavaliers were successful in almost every encounter.

"Cromwell changed all this. He saw that an army might be built out of materials less showy indeed, but more solid than those of which the dashing squadrons of the king were composed. It was necessary to look for recruits who were not mere mercenaries, for recruits of decent station and grave character, fearing God and zealous for liberty. With such men he filled his own regiment; and while he subjected them to a discipline more rigid than had ever before been known in England, he administered to their intellectual and moral nature stimulants of fearful potency."*

Time passed; the Parliament gradually entrusted more and more power to their great captain. The army was remodelled and made over into the image of the "Ironsides" squadron. Fairfax, a brave soldier, became the nominal commander-in-chief of the popular forces; but Cromwell's were the keener eye, the cooler brain, and stouter arm which virtually presided at the helm.

Then the Parliament swept on from success to success. The reconstructed army moved to victory with the precision of machines, while burning with the wild fanaticism of crusaders. Every soldier had a double life. In camp he was a field-preacher perhaps, or a politician. If the first, he would lead the devotions of the men, and admonish a back-

* Macauley, ut antea.

sliding major or colonel. If the second, he would head a club, elect delegates, and pass resolutions. But in the heat of battle he became a simple soldier, obedient, inflexible, rigid.

It was this double life, this rare union of political and religious enthusiasm, with perfect organization and subordination, which gave Cromwell's army its irresistibility. It was at once a church and a camp, an incarnate sermon and a warlike thunderbolt.

And it never met an enemy which could withstand its onset. "In England, Scotland, Ireland, Flanders, the Puritan warriors, often surrounded by difficulties, sometimes contending against threefold odds, not only never failed to conquer, but never failed to destroy whatever force opposed them. They at length came to regard the day of battle as a day of certain triumph, and marched against the most renowned battalions of Europe with disdainful confidence. Turenne was startled by the shout of stern exultation with which his English allies advanced to the combat, and expressed the delight of a true soldier when he learned that it was ever the custom of Cromwell's pikemen to rejoice greatly when they beheld the enemy; and the banished Cavaliers felt an emotion of national pride when they saw a brigade of their Puritan countrymen, outnumbered by foes and abandoned by allies, drive before it in headlong rout the finest infantry of Spain, and force a passage into a counterscarp which had just been pronounced impregnable by the ablest marshals of France."*

Baxter confirms this account, and, since he was with the army, his testimony is conclusive: "Many, yea, the generality of those people throughout England who went by the name of Puritans, who followed sermons, prayed in their families, read books of devotion, and were strict observers of the Sabbath, being avowed enemies to swearing, drunkenness, and all profaneness, adhered to the Parliament, and filled up their armies afterwards, because they heard the king's soldiers with horrid oaths abuse the name of God, and saw them living in debauchery, while the Parliament soldiers flocked to sermons, talked of religion, prayed and sung psalms together on guards. And all sober men of my acquaintance who opposed the Parliament, used to say, 'The king has the best cause, but the Parliament has the best men.' "†

Under Cromwell's *régime* the war did not long hang doubtful. Marston Moor shattered the royal strength; Naseby gave the king's cause its *coup de grace*. In the winter of 1646 the last fortress of the Cavaliers succumbed.‡

But while peace was being conquered in the field, momentous events were occurring at the capital and in the Parliament.

In 1645, Laud was executed, the penalty of his impeachment and conviction of high-treason. Pos-

* Macauley, ut antea. † Baxter's Life and Times.

‡ Carlyle, Hume, Clarendon, etc.

terity cries "Amen" to this sentence, but it absolves the primate from the stigma of Romanism. "However," remarks Fuller, "most apparent it is, by several passages in his life, that he endeavored to take up many controversies between us and the church of Rome, so as to compromise the difference, and to bring us to a vicinity, if not contiguity therewith; an impossible design, if granted lawful, as some, every way his equals, did adjudge. For composition is impossible with such who will not agree, except all they sue for and all the charges of their suit be to the utmost farthing awarded unto them. Our reconciliation with Rome is clogged with the same impossibilities: she may *be gone to*, but will never *be met with;* such her pride or peevishness as not to stir a step to obviate any of a different religion. Rome will never unpope itself so far as to part with its pretended supremacy and infallibility, which cuts off all possibility of Protestants' treaty with her."*

Parliament through these years was very busy. Some of its acts were good, some bad, some mixed. Rigid Presbyterianism was in the saddle, so that many of the ordinances now put forth squinted towards the settlement of the church down into the "fixed ways" of that discipline.† To recite even the chief of those acts which wear the countenance of an ecclesiastical tendency, would swell these pages into volumes. Indeed Sir Simons D'Ewes affirms that the religious laws of the Long Parlia-

* Fuller, vol. 3, p. 475. † Baxter, Guizot, Neale, etc.

ment exceed in number and bulk all the statutes made before that time since the Conquest.*

Very early in the contest Parliament repealed the anti-sabbatarian legislation of the past, and enacted a law compelling the decent observance of the day.† "Sunday," says Neale, "was observed with remarkable strictness, the churches being crowded with numerous attentive hearers three or four times a day; the officers of the peace patrolled the streets, and shut up all ale-houses; there was no travelling on the road nor walking in the fields, except in cases of necessity. Religious exercises were set up in private families, as reading the Scriptures, prayer, repetition of sermons, and singing of psalms, which was so universal that one might walk through the city of London on the evening of the Lord's day without seeing an idle person, or hearing any thing but the voice of prayer or praise from churches and private houses."‡

In 1646 the Parliament abolished the offices and titles of bishops and archbishops throughout England and Wales, and appropriated their revenues to the discharge of the national debt.§ This reduced very many excellent clergymen from affluence to beggary, bishops Usher, Morton, and Hall being among the sufferers; and though the two Houses voted them very considerable pensions, in lieu of their lands thus sequestered, due care was

* D'Ewes; cited in Fuller, vol. 3, p. 490.

† Parl. Hist.; Whitelocke, Clarendon.

‡ Neale, vol. 2, p. 23.

§ Parl. Hist.; Newell, etc.

not taken to secure prompt payment; nor would several of the deprived prelates so far countenance the votes of Parliament as to apply for this proffered aid.*

Indeed the clergy on both sides suffered terribly from the calamities incident to the times. Where the king encamped, the Cavaliers, incensed against the Puritan preachers as the trumpeters of the rebellion, searched out their residences, plundering, harassing, and imprisoning with indiscriminate zeal. Where the Parliament hung out its banners, even the iron discipline of Cromwell could not check the insults and spoliation which awaited the Episcopal clergy and their sympathizers, whom the Roundheads termed "malignants." No servant-girl complained of their rough gallantry. Not an ounce of plate was taken from the shops of the goldsmiths. But a Pelagian sermon, or a window in which the Virgin and child were painted, stirred riot and provoked a raid.†

Another source of suffering and sorrow was the large number of sequestered clergymen, men deprived of their livings ostensibly on account of their scandalous lives—avouched often by the oaths of witnesses proved insufficient or malicious—but really because Presbyterianism hungered for their benefices.‡ But Parliament had the grace to award a fifth part of the revenues of the sequestered livings to the ejected clergymen for the maintenance

* Neale, vol. 2, p. 49.

† Ibid.; Macauley, Carlyle.

‡ Ibid.

of their families,* "which was a Christian act," says Fuller, "and one which I should have been glad to have seen imitated at the Restoration. But moderate men bemoaned these severities, for as much corruption was let out by these ejectments, many scandalous ministers being deservedly punished, so at the same time the veins of the English church were also emptied of much good blood."†

In the mean time Charles, fairly expelled from England by the prowess of Cromwell, had crossed the Tweed, and surrendered his person into the hands of the Scotch. Here he was held in honorable captivity, while the Parliament was apprized of the event.‡

The king began at once to intrigue: he employed every wile known to his jesuitical diplomacy to detach the Covenanters from the English alliance; he endeavored to cajole the Scots into the conclusion of a private treaty. But his efforts were vain.§ He closely scrutinized the behavior of the Presbyterian ministers towards himself, knowing well their omnipotent influence in Scotland. He did not get much consolation from them. One preacher reproached him to his face with his misgovernment, and on concluding his sermon read this psalm:

> "Why dost thou, tyrant, boast thyself,
> Thy wicked deeds to praise?"

* Neale, vol. 2, pp. 49, 95; Newell, Fuller, Clarendon.

† Fuller's Worthies.

‡ Hume, vol. 2, p. 334.

§ Neale, vol. 2, p. 205.

The king rose and called for that other psalm which begins thus:

> "Have mercy, Lord, on me, I pray,
> For men would me devour."

The good-natured audience, in pity to fallen majesty, showed for once greater deference to the king than to the minister, and sang the hymn which Charles requested.*

Posts hurried to and fro between London and Scotland, when news came that the king had taken asylum in the north; negotiation ensued, and eventually Charles was delivered to the Parliament.†

Complaisant Presbyterianism rubbed its hands. The king was its prisoner; the best livings in England yielded it support; Parliament was its mouthpiece. But one thing remained—its indissoluble marriage with the civil authority;‡ and all was prepared for this, when lo, Cromwell entered and forbade the bans.

The army was wedded to the Independent tenets.§ It had long fretted at the evident gravitation of the Parliament towards intolerant Presbyterianism. It had growled when it was proposed to nationalize *any* creed. It favored the toleration of all evangelical sects.

Now, in opposition to the Parliament at Westminster, a military parliament was held in the camp; the army was represented in this upon re-

* Hume, ut antea. † Hume, Clarendon, Burnet.

‡ Neale, vol. 2, p. 208.

§ Walker, Hist. of Independency, pt. 2; Carlyle.

publican principles. The king was seized by Cromwell's order. That great soldier was elected *generalissimo,* and the troops started for London. Diplomacy failed to stay their march; and despite the protest of the Parliament and the belligerent attitude of Scotland, Cromwell entered the metropolis, quartered his regiments in Whitehall and the Meuse, and placed the government beneath his warriors' heels.*

This military *coup de état* broke the back of the haughty Presbyterian majority in the Commons. They still possessed the *forms* of authority, but they knew that from that moment the army was the real arbiter of the island.

* Hume, vol. 2, chs. 58, 59, passim; Harris' Cromwell, etc.

CHAPTER XXVI.

THE SCAFFOLD AT WHITEHALL.

CHARLES I. digged his own grave by perfidy. He was given at least two opportunities to regain the lost sceptre, once by Cromwell, once by Parliament. His political Jesuitism balked every plan for an accommodation. To such an extent had insincerity now tainted his whole nature, that his most devoted friends could not refrain from complaining to each other, with bitter grief and shame, of his crooked politics.

Immediately after his seizure by the army, Cromwell had several interviews with Charles. The king attempted with the great captain what he tried successively with every section of the victorious Roundheads, to undermine him by cajolery and by machinations. The officers offered to guarantee Charles the throne, with liberty of conscience in Episcopacy, provided he would consent to toleration, and govern by the law;* and this liberal proposition the crazy king defeated by intrigue. In the very midst of this effort at reconciliation, a secret correspondence between the king and the queen was discovered, in which Chárles freely opened his false heart. It was clearly shown that though publicly recognizing the houses at Westminster as

* Carlyle's Cromwell's Letters and Speeches, volume 1; Neale, Harris, Macauley.

a legal Parliament, he had at the same time made a private minute in council, declaring the recognition null; that though publicly disclaiming all thought of calling in foreign aid against his people, he had privately solicited aid from France, from Denmark, and from Lorraine; that though publicly denying that he employed Papists, he bade his friends enlist every Papist who would serve; that though publicly taking the sacrament at Oxford, as a pledge that he never would connive at Popery, he privately assured his wife that he intended to tolerate Popery in England, and that he actually authorized Lord Glamorgan to promise that Popery should be established in Ireland; and that though now plausibly treating with the army, he was really plotting Cromwell's overthrow, and cementing a private treaty with the Scots.*

In anger and disgust, the long-headed soldier quitted the presence of the perjured monarch, fully convinced that either Charles must die or that midnight stabbers would deprive both himself and the newly acquired public liberty of existence.†

Cromwell told his royal prisoner that he would no longer be responsible for his safety. Charles took the hint. Mounting his charger at midnight, in 1647, he stole from Hampton Court, and hurrying across the country, sought an asylum, but found a prison, in the Isle of Wight.‡

* Macauley, Hist. of Eng.; Neale, Harris, Hume, Clarendon.

† Carlyle's Cromwell's Letters, etc.

‡ Harris, Life of Charles I.; Neale.

At London the Presbyterians, overawed by the army, made no open move; but couriers were dispatched into Scotland with letters couched in words of bitter complaint. Unbounded liberty of conscience, which the Covenanters held in the utmost abhorrence, was enforced, they said; and the Covenant itself was pronounced in the house, by a member of the Commons, to be "an almanac out of date."*

Scottish Presbyterianism, influenced by these appeals from the coerced members, who formed the parliamentary majority in England, and in execution of the treaty entered into with the king, began to arm for the delivery of the subdued Parliament and for the reinstatement of the royal captive.†

Instantly the army quitted the capital, and marched to meet the Scots.‡ Then the Parliament regained courage; it commenced negotiations with Charles; politicians with their diplomacy, theologians with their syllogisms, invaded the Isle of Wight.§ Now again Charles' obstinacy defeated every scheme. Strangely impressed with his own importance,‖ he would make no decided concessions, but seemed desirous to await the course of events. The Parliament, on their part, though anxious to conclude a pacification ere the army should again return to domineer, still would assent to no plan

* Hume, vol. 2, p. 348.

† Chambers, Rebellions in Scotland; Parl. Hist.; Carlyle.

‡ Hume, vol. 2, p. 348. § Ibid., p. 350.

‖ Neale, vol. 2, p. 238.

which did not include the denial of toleration and the establishment of Presbyterianism.*

These negotiations were still pending when the army, triumphant everywhere, returned to London, and the dawdlers at the Isle of Wight learned too late that they had lost the golden moment. The Independents were provoked at the bad faith of the Parliament in negotiating with the king in their absence, and they began to threaten.† Parliament meantime attempted, in the face of the army, to close a treaty with the king;‡ whereupon Cromwell seized the most prominent members of the Presbyterian majority *en route* to Westminster, excluded one hundred and sixty of the Commons from their seats, threw the legislative authority into the hands of threescore Independents, and thus "*purged* the house."§

Then came the final scene. The king was seized, brought to London, and the "*rump* Parliament," as it was nicknamed, voted his impeachment. The Lords said, No; their house was closed.‖ The people were declared to be the source of all just power. Of this idea was born a popular tribunal, before which Charles Stuart was arraigned, tried, convicted, and sentenced as a tyrant, *hostis humani generis.*¶ In front of the banqueting-hall of his own palace at Whitehall, the unhappy monarch lost his head.

* Hume, vol. 2, p. 351. † Ibid., p. 354. ‡ Ibid.

§ Ibid., p. 354; Parl. Hist.

‖ Macauley, Hist. England, vol. 1, p. 99.

¶ Carlyle, Hume, Harris, Clarendon. etc.

Liberty, dipping her finger in his blood, countersigned the verdict; then turning to dazed Europe, she wrote upon the frontlet of the nascent Commonwealth her simple motto: "Resistance to tyrants is obedience to God."

Various were the comments. The Cavaliers,

> "Whose phrase of sorrow
> Conjured the wandering stars, and made them stand
> Like wonder-wounded hearers,"

embalmed the dead king's memory in their heart of hearts. Charles became that most dangerous of things, a sentiment. The Presbyterians, some on account of their exclusion from the Commons, anxious mainly to make a point against the hated Independents, became

> "The painting of a sorrow;
> A face without a heart,"

and clamored loudly in their turn against the "murder" of the king. The Cromwellians alone were unmoved. They pleaded necessity, appealed to the record, and said sternly, *Sic semper tyrannis.*

The government was at once new-modelled. A Commonwealth was inaugurated. The oaths of supremacy and allegiance were abolished. All civil officers were tendered an *engagement* which bound them to be true and faithful to the *de facto* authorities.* The representative system was ably reformed;† and as many of the ousted Commons as would

* Neale, vol. 2, p. 315; Carlyle, Harris.

† Clarendon. The manner in which this was done extorts the warm praise of this old royalist historian.

sign the *engagement* were returned to the Parliament.* A constitution as perfect as any then known was framed. The executive authority was vested in a Council of State; and England, emancipated from thraldom to a king, assumed the garb of republicanism, and declared the Commonwealth to be the lawful heir of the dead monarch.

Consummate wisdom swayed the national counsels, and success awaited democratic politics. Vane,

"Than whom a better senator ne'er held
The helm of Rome, when gowns, not arms, repelled
The fierce Epirot and the Afran bold,
Keen both to settle peace and to unfold
The drift of hollow states, hard to be spelled,"

became the leader of the Commons. Milton,

"Dear son of memory, great heir of fame,"

was chosen secretary of state; while above all loomed Cromwell.

But a mere proclamation did not settle the new Commonwealth. Conspiracies were formed. The army mutinied.† These half-born *émeutes* were at once strangled; and then, behold, another hostile movement threatened to mar all. The Independents were equally odious to the Romanists and to the Presbyterians. The Romanist head-quarters were in Ireland; the Presbyterian camp was in Scotland. Both, on the death of the king, transferred their allegiance to his eldest son Charles II.‡

* Neale, vol. 2, p. 315; Guizot; Godwin, Hist. Commonwealth.

† Macauley; Guizot, Cromwell and Commonwealth; Godwin, etc.

‡ Guizot's Cromwell and the Commonwealth.; Commons' Jour.

With an energy which never flagged, the Puritan statesmen met and baffled this danger. Cromwell was sent into Ireland to reduce that turbulent province to submission. He took with him fourteen thousand "Ironsides." This army had the appearance of a camp-meeting. The day before embarkation was observed as a day of fasting and prayer; Cromwell himself expounded some parts of Scripture pertinent to the occasion. Then the expedition sailed; not an oath was heard, and the soldiers spent their leisure hours in reading their Bibles, in singing psalms, and in religious conferences.*

"Entirely amazing to us in these material days, all this," observes Carlyle with characteristic quaintness. "These are the longest heads and the stoutest hearts in England, and this is the thing they do; this is the way they, for their part, begin dispatch of business. The looker-on may, if he be an earnest man, gaze with very many thoughts for which there is no word. Does it look like madness? Madness lies close by, as madness does to the highest wisdom of man's life always; but this is not mad. This stern element, it is the mother of the lightnings and the splendors."†

Nothing could stay such men. Ireland, which had never been subdued during the five centuries of slaughter which had elapsed since the landing of

* Guizot, Cromwell and the Commonwealth; Commons' Journal; Whitelocke's Memorials.

† Carlyle's Cromwell's Letters and Speeches, vol. 1, p. 337.

the first Norman settlers, was now subjugated by these warlike saints in less than a twelvemonth. Cromwell "resolved to put an end to that conflict of races and creeds which had so long distracted the island. Accordingly he gave loose reign to the fierce enthusiasm of his followers, waged war resembling that which Israel waged on the Canaanites, smote the idolaters with the edge of the sword," and supplied the void which death had made by pouring in Anglo-Saxon colonists of the Protestant faith. "Strange to say, under this iron rule the conquered country began to wear an outward face of prosperity. Districts which had recently been as wild as those where the first white settlers of Connecticut were contending with the red men, were in a brief space transformed into the likeness of Kent and Norfolk. New buildings, new plantations, new roads, were everywhere seen. The rent of Irish estates rose fast, and soon English land-owners began to complain that they were met in every market by the products of the sister island, and to clamor for protecting laws."*

Having thus performed this mission, cruelly, wickedly, but effectually, Cromwell crossed the Irish sea, marched to London, reported to the Council of State, and then without pause swept into Scotland. "The young king was there. He had consented to profess himself a Presbyterian, and

* Macauley, Hist. of Eng., vol. 1, p. 101. This summary of the great English rhetorician is amply substantiated by all other authoritative writers.

to subscribe to the Covenant; and in return for these concessions, the austere Puritans who bore sway at Edinburgh had permitted him to hold, under their inspection and control, a melancholy court in the long deserted halls of Holyrood. This mock royalty was of short duration. In two great battles, Dunbar and Worcester, Cromwell annihilated the military force of Scotland. Charles, narrowly escaping capture, skulked across the sea. The ancient kingdom of the Stuarts was reduced, for the first time, to profound submission. Of that independence so manfully defended against the ablest and the mightiest of the Plantagenets, no vestige was left. The English Parliament made laws for Scotland; English judges held assizes there. Even that stubborn church, which had held its own against so many assailants, now scarce dared to utter an audible murmur."*

England wearied into peace, Ireland subjugated into peace, Scotland harried into peace, the army everywhere successful, Cromwell the hero of the island—such was the political situation at the close of 1651.

* Macauley, ut antea.

CHAPTER XXVII.

THE COMMONWEALTH.

UNDER the Commonwealth toleration was broader than it had ever before been in the island. The Covenant oath was discarded; no other civil qualification was required than the *engagement:* this opened the doors of political office; it also was sufficient to obtain any vacant benefice.* Many of the Episcopal divines now made their submission to the *statu quo.* Thus they gained a foothold, a half-recognition; for though they might not read the Liturgy in form, they were permitted to frame their prayers as near it as they chose. Many Episcopal assemblies were connived at, where the Prayer-book itself was used. But when these clergymen were discovered to be plotters against the state, this liberty was suspended. Still it is said that the Episcopalians would not have been denied open toleration if they had consented to give security for their acquiescent behavior.†

The sectaries were very numerous; and contemporaneous writers placed the Independents at the head of these, not as having the larger number of disciples, but because they were the most influential, and on account of their tolerant principles,

* Godwin, Hist. of the Commonwealth; Whitelocke.
† Neale, vol. 2, p. 349.

since they insisted upon granting perfect freedom of conscience to all who agreed in the fundamentals of religion, and stood ready to fellowship every evangelical sect.*

The Baptists also were a rising sect. In the early years of the civil war they had forty-seven congregations in England.† Although the hand of authority had fallen heavy upon them through a hundred years, they were worthy, industrious, devout, and peaceable citizens, mostly of the middle and lower classes; but they could point to several of the ablest and most learned ministers in Britain as their coreligionists and champions.‡

It was under the Commonwealth that the society of Friends first acquired public fame.§ In 1648, George Fox, their most celebrated teacher, began to preach. He was of humble birth, and being attracted towards sober thoughts, he devoted himself to religion.‖ His chief tenet was, that "people should receive the inner teaching of the Spirit of Christ, and make that a rule."¶ He taught that

* Neale, vol. 2, p. 211, et seq.; Baxter's Life and Times; Whitelocke.

† Haynes, Hist. of the Baptist Denomination; Orchard, Hist. of Foreign Baptists; Neale, vol. 2. Mr. Cornwall of Emmanuel college, and Mr. Toombs, educated at Oxford, were accounted their most learned men at this time. "Their confession consisted of fifty-two articles, and was strictly Calvinistic in the doctrinal part, and according to the Independent discipline." Neale, vol. 2, p. 111.

‡ Ibid.

§ Neale, vol. 2, pp. 332–334; Sewel, Hist. of the Quakers.

‖ Wagstaff, Hist. of Society of Friends; Sewel.

¶ Ibid.

every thing depended upon the anointing of the Spirit, and that God, who made the world, did not dwell in temples made with hands. Those peculiarities of language, dress, and manner which now distinguish this sect, bear the seal of his *imprimatur*, and owe their origin to him.

Misunderstood and ill-reported, the *Quakers*—as they were termed because they trembled when they spoke*—were long cruelly oppressed. Their refusal to recognize any title and to take any oath, seemed to the magistrates of the time to be wanton whims of disrespect. Outrage, in this case as in all others, bred fanaticism, and many of the Quakers went to absurd extremes. But when it was understood that their peculiar ideas were conscientiously held, they were treated with less rigor, and society welcomed in them some of its best and most philanthropic members.†

The Presbyterians were the most numerous of the sects, and they were the descendants of the bishops in their opposition to free conscience.‡ It was against them that the army arrayed itself, that Vane inveighed, that Cromwell thundered, and that Milton wrote those celebrated lines, addressed to the great regicide:

> "Much remains
> To conquer still; peace hath her victories
> No less renowned than war; new foes arise,
> Threatening to bind our souls in secular chains:

* Neale, vol. 2, pp. 332, 333.

† Baxter's Life and Times; Neale.

‡ Neale, vol. 2, p. 365.

Help us to save free conscience from the paw
Of hireling wolves, whose gospel is their maw."*

This intolerant spirit was largely suppressed by the Council of State; but the Presbyterians were fretful, and much more troublesome than the Episcopalian or the Romanist parties all through these years.† They had played a desperate game for church aggrandizement, and almost won it, and lost it; and writhing in exile from Westminster, they never could feel reconciled to the result.

"An act had passed in 1649 for the propagation of the gospel in Wales, and commissioners were appointed for ejecting ignorant and scandalous clergymen, and replacing them by fitter preachers. Pursuant to this law, it is said that within three years there were one hundred and fifty good preachers in the thirteen Welsh counties, most of whom spoke three or four times a week. In every market-place there was placed one, and in most large towns two school-masters, able, learned, and university men; the tithes were all employed as directed by the Parliament, that is, in the maintenance of godly ministers, in the payment of taxes and officers, in the remuneration of school-masters, and in the payment of their fifths to the wives and children of sequestered clergymen."‡

The whole island was kept in excellent order.§

* Milton, Poetical Works, sonnet on "Cromwell."

† Neale; Milton, Prose Works; Godwin, Hist. of the Commonwealth.

‡ Neale, vol. 2, p. 350.

§ Godwin, Hist. of Commonwealth; Whitelocke; Commons' Journal.

The troops were held in exact discipline; money was plenty; the exchequer, always heretofore bare and hungry, was now fat and full; the civil list was well paid;* commerce spread its wings on every sea; justice was carefully and promptly administered;† vice was suppressed and punished; "there was a great appearance of devotion; the Sabbath was strictly kept; none might walk the streets in time of divine service; tipplers were scourged from the public-houses; Sunday evenings were spent in catechizing the children, in singing psalms, and in other acts of family devotion, insomuch that an acquaintance with the principles of religion and the gift of prayer increased prodigiously among the common people."‡

It is also among the trophies of the Commonwealth that it ungagged the press. Grown wiser than the bishops, and braver than the Presbyterian Parliament, the Council of State made no effort to check polemics. Royalist pamphlets of the most seductive and seditious kind were openly printed and widely circulated; and the state disdained to notice these in any other way than by confuting them. To the old warfare of swords succeeded a nobler warfare of intellects; brains, not muscle, met in the arena and grappled for the victory. In these contests, Milton was the great champion of the Commonwealth; and his sublime and austere genius

* Carlyle; Forster's Statesmen of the Commonwealth.

† Hume, vol. 2; Forster, etc.

‡ Neale, vol. 2, p. 347, 348.

enabled him to bear off a trophy where any other would have balked. His political pamphlets, and especially his first and second defence of the people of England against the hireling assault of the continental pedant Salmasius, in which he upholds the principles as well as the actions of the revolution, are models of argumentative declamation, and before them the most gorgeous passages of Burke sink into insignificance.*

The diplomatic record of the Commonwealth is as admirable as its domestic management. Never before had England been so influential, so irresistible.† Richelieu, in dying, bade his successor steer clear of "those rough-shod Puritans;"‡ Spain and France made haste to recognize the new-launched government;§ the Dutch Republic quailed before the thunder of Blake's guns; Europe at large treated the island with unprecedented consideration, and left its card upon the marble table of the Council of State with deferential awe.

But notwithstanding the blaze of glory in which its policy was sheeted, the government was not popular at home. It was an essentially revolutionary junto; when peace came, the conditions of its existence began to fail. The feverish, morbid energy which had hitherto exhausted itself in the subjugation of obstacles, was now forced to seek a new

* Concerning Milton's success in these literary combats there is but one opinion. See his various lives; also Guizot, Godwin, Forster, Clarendon, Carlyle, Macauley, etc.

† Godwin, Hist. Commonwealth; Hume, Neale, Forster, etc.

‡ Guizot, Forster. § Guizot's Cromwell, etc., vol. 1, ch. 3.

vent, and it began to harass the people. Stretches of authority which are necessary in times of civil commotion, and which martial law sanctions, under a pacification become abuses and strut as tyranny. All hawkers and public singers were suppressed; and whenever any one was found exercising either of these callings, he was seized and taken to a house of correction to be whipped as a common rogue.* The publication of proceedings and debates before the high courts of justice was stringently prohibited.† In contravention of the laws and traditions of the country, the House of Commons, in repeated instances, constituted itself a judicial bureau, and condemned offenders, whom it could not hope to reach in any other way, to exile, to heavy fines, to the pillory, and to prolonged imprisonment without a trial.‡

For such extra-judicial action, with its concomitant vexations, wide-spread and rankling, no vigor, no talent of administration could compensate in the popular estimation. It was thought that the best governments were the most unobtrusive; that beneath the ægis of their laws society stood sheltered, while authority itself kept out of sight, and was felt only through its benefactions.

Besides, the Commonwealth professed to base itself upon the people; their will was its only title-

* Commons' Journal, vol. 6, pp. 276, 298.

† Ibid.; Whitelocke, p. 340.

‡ Ibid. Guizot, in Cromwell and the Commonwealth, has admirably analyzed this passage in English history, and to his rationale we refer all curious readers. See vol. 1, pp. 69, et seq.

deed. It was not, like the monarchy it had tried and beheaded, covered with the hoar of age, linked through a thousand associations with men's memory of the past, grouted in the habits and the statutes of a thousand years. No; it was the negative of these; and remembering the old Latin law, *obsta principiis*, it should have created for itself a higher sanction than antique custom, and *guarded against the beginning* of discontent by anchoring itself in the hearts of all Englishmen.

This the "Rump" parliament not only failed to do, but worse, it had the hardihood to alienate its only supporter, Cromwell, by breaking a lance against the army. Conqueror and master, it beheld arising in its midst a conqueror and a master against whom it was incapable of defending itself. The new-born Commonwealth felt that Cromwell domineered over it; at every crisis of peril or alarm it had recourse to him, and when the crisis passed, it grew terrified at the credit and renown which he had acquired by saving it. And Cromwell, on his side, while lavish in his demonstrations of the most humble devotedness to the Commonwealth, gave continual expression to his dissatisfaction with many features of the governmental policy.*

Each one began to seek for a pretext to destroy the other. Cromwell found one first.

At the close of their session in 1652, the Commons, instead of dissolving and giving way to a new parliament, voted to go over the legal time, and

* Guizot, vol. 1, p. 71; D'Aubigné's Protectorate.

they elected another council of state out of their own body.* A little later, in preparation for a war with Holland, they began to augment the fleet out of the land forces, a proceeding which tended to disarm Cromwell by depriving him of his devoted soldiers.† The astute general saw the danger, and as usual, acted with prompt vigor. The army declined to serve in the navy, and immediately sent up a petition in favor of reform and a dissolution of Parliament.‡ The Parliament, angry at what it termed the "insolence" of its servants, passed an act making it treason to petition for their dissolution.§ Then the storm burst. Cromwell summoned a council of officers at Whitehall; all agreed that the Commons should be forced to give way; and in the spring of 1653 the great soldier entered Westminster Hall, expelled the Commons from their seats before the guns of a file of musketeers, and seizing the archives, locked and double-barred the doors of the representative chamber. Thence he proceeded to the Council of State, and stamping them out of existence, freed England from the curse of a Venetian oligarchy.‖

Although the Cavaliers, the Presbyterians, and the Levellers, acting from very different motives, loaded Cromwell with invectives and formed conspiracies against his person, his action received the

* Commons' Journal, vol. 6; Ludlow's Memoirs. † Ibid.

‡ Hutchinson's Memoirs; Ludlow's Mem.; Whitelocke, etc.

§ Macauley, Guizot, Whitelocke, Southey's Life of Cromwell.

‖ Commons' Journal; Forster's Statesmen of the Commonwealth.

hearty sympathy of the masses, and this—since in that revolutionary epoch all legal safeguards were trodden down—is his sufficient warrant.

A new state was at once settled; that parliament which has passed into history as *Barebone's Parliament*—so called from one of its most active members—was convened, and Cromwell, as chief executive, was clothed with the powers of a Dutch stadtholder. Five months passed unmarked by events of any ecclesiastical importance. Then Cromwell, finding that his legislature questioned the authority under which they met, and that he was in danger of being deprived of the restricted power which was absolutely necessary to his personal safety and to the general welfare, dismissed "Praise God Barebones" and his followers, as he had the "Long" and the "Rump" parliaments.* Once more the government was new modelled, a form which squinted towards monarchy was elaborated,† and under this Cromwell, assisted by a council, assumed supreme authority, under the title of "Lord Protector of the Commonwealth of England, Scotland, and Ireland."‡

This constitutes what is called Cromwell's "usurpation." Perhaps it is rightly named; but we apprehend that it would be difficult to show in what respect he was a greater offender than the authorities whom he superseded. Undoubtedly he trans-

* Ludlow's Memoirs; Guizot; Hutchinson's Memoirs.

† Guizot, vol. 2, pp. 35-123; Hume; D'Aubigné's Protectorate.

‡ Ibid.; T. Cromwell, Life and Times of Oliver Cromwell.

gressed the constitutional law of England; and so did the Long Parliament; so also did the Commonwealth. The apology for all, is that Latin which justified the first appeal to arms—*salus populi suprema lex.*

If it be pleaded that parliaments came from the people and represented their opinion, the ready response is, that this mantle wraps Cromwell's administration also in its folds; for the peaceful acquiescence of three kingdoms made his acts theirs. We think, with Macauley, that "a good constitution is infinitely better than the best despot." We also suspect, with him, "that at the time of which we speak the violence of religious and political enmities rendered a normal, constitutional settlement next to impossible," the choice lying not between Cromwell and strict republicanism, but between Cromwell and the Stuarts. The student of history, on a fair comparison of the events of the Protectorate with the thirty years which succeeded the Restoration, cannot choose but cry "Amen" to the "usurpation" of Oliver Cromwell.

On the day following Cromwell's dissolution of the Parliament, a crowd collected at the door of the House of Commons, to read an immense placard which had been placed there during the night by some witty Cavalier, who sought to avenge his ruined cause by a squib; it bore this inscription:

"THIS HOUSE TO LET UNFURNISHED."*

* Ludlow's Memoirs, p. 194; cited in Guizot's Cromwell, vol. 1, pp. 357, 358.

CHAPTER XXVIII.

THE PROTECTORATE.

Now, take it all in all, commenced the most remarkable administration which Europe had ever seen. A well-to-do yeoman, aided by his own genius and passionate energy, had ascended by rapid steps from the floor of Parliament to the royal platform of a hundred kings. Clothed in the purple of the ousted Stuarts, he affirmed that his assumption of the government was not so much the effect of his own ambition as of a bold resolution not to permit the nation to fall back into anarchy and blood. He added, "Here I sit, sword in hand, and I am not to be jostled out of the saddle by seditious murmurs, by votes, or by resolutions."

Ere long the marvellous statesmanship of the puritanical Protector placated England into quietude, and made the Continent his vassal.

Cromwell first turned his attention to domestic affairs. Three parties in the state were his open enemies: the Royalists, the Presbyterians, and the Levellers.* The royalists were irreconcilable; they plotted to assassinate him, and were always on the *qui vive* for an *émeute*. The Presbyterians "were in principle for the king and the covenant; after the battle of Worcester they were terrified into com-

* Neale, vol. 2, pp. 370–374; Guizot, Hume.

pliance with the Commonwealth. But when Cromwell broke that government in pieces, his surprising advancement filled them with new fears, for they considered him not only a usurper, but a sectarian who would countenance the free exercise of religion, provided only that men would live peaceably under his government; and though he assured them that he would continue religion on the footing of the existing Establishment, nothing would satisfy them so long as their discipline was disarmed of its coercive power."*

The levellers were split into two parties; one of them was enamoured of radical democracy, and as its chiefs were deists who cared little for religion, Cromwell nicknamed them the *heathen*. The other was composed of fifth monarchy men; these were heated enthusiasts, who lived in expectation of the speedy personal reign of Christ. They were fierce to pull down all churches, to destroy the clergy, and "to leave religion free, without either encouragement or restraint."†

These three parties hated each other as bitterly as they detested the Protector; and Cromwell, with infinite tact, played one off against the other, and thus, in these mutual bickerings, dulled the keen edge of that resentment which might have cut his authority if turned unitedly against himself.‡

His chief supporters were the Independents,

* Neale, vol. 2, pp. 370, 371.

† Ibid.; Godwin, Hist. Commonwealth; Forster's Statesmen, etc.

‡ Ibid.

who looked upon him as the head of their party, because he was averse to church power and for universal toleration; the city of London, whose merchants craved peace and a stable government as the chief necessity of successful trade; and the army, whose pride and affection knew no bounds.*

"The Protector's wisdom," says Neale, "appeared in nothing more than in his unwearied endeavors to make all religious parties easy. He indulged the army in its enthusiastic raptures, and sometimes joined in the prayers and sermons of the camp. He countenanced the Presbyterians by assuring them that he would maintain the public ministry. He supported the Independents by making them his chaplains, by preferring them to considerable livings in the church and universities, and by uniting them in one commission with the Presbyterians as triers of all such as desired to be admitted to benefices."†

A civil establishment of religion of a peculiar kind was now in existence. Christianity was not left solely to the voluntary principle for support, but a part of the old revenues of the church, and also grants of public money, were appropriated to this use. Yet this establishment was unique, and differed essentially from any that had preceded it, and from that which came in with the Restoration. The purpose of the Presbyterians had been and still was, to twist the English Establishment into a

* Neale, vol. 2, pp. 370, 371; Godwin, Hist. Commonwealth; Forster's Statesmen, etc.

† Neale, vol. 2, p. 364.

form similar to that of the Scottish church, in which all religionists except themselves should be excluded from the protection and pecuniary support of the state. This the influence of the more liberal parties had always held in check; and now, under the Protectorate, all Protestants holding evangelical sentiments were invited to nestle under the wing of the Establishment.*

"An agreement in the fundamental truths of Christianity, together with the possession of personal piety and adequate ministerial gifts, were the only requisites demanded of those who sought to enjoy ecclesiastical benefices. Triers were appointed by the government to ascertain the qualifications of clergymen; and though ridicule in abundance has been poured upon the proceedings of these men, it has been proved that, on the whole, they discharged their duty with rectitude and prudence. Baxter, whose independence and integrity of judgment in such matters is universally conceded, acknowledges that these commissioners did abundance of good to the church.† No doubt there were instances in which conscientious high churchmen were roughly dealt with—and clergymen who thus suffered wrong for the sake of principle are deserving of honor—yet, for the most part by far, those who were excluded by the triers had, by their scandalous lives, proved themselves totally unfit for the holy office which they had assumed."‡

* Stoughton, Spiritual Heroes, p. 250, et seq.

† Ibid. ‡ Ibid.; Neale, vol. 2, pp. 365, 366.

Cromwell personally drew around him men of different denominations, and divided among them his favors. We have seen that, though the Presbyterians formed the greater number of those who were supported by the state, ministers of other sects were admitted to share in its emoluments. The same liberality prevailed at court. Though the Protector was most attached to the Independents, he also employed Presbyterians in his service. Manton prayed at his inauguration, Baxter preached in his chapel, and Calamy was admitted to his councils. Moderate Episcopalians and Baptists might be found in the pulpits of parish churches; and in some parts of England there were county union associations, in which ministers of the various sects assembled for fraternal conference and prayer.

Episcopacy and popery were suppressed by statute, because they were esteemed peculiarly inimical and dangerous at that time; yet there were supporters of both systems whom the Protector generously befriended. He treated Brownrigg, bishop of Exeter, with great respect; saved Dr. Barnard's life, and made him his almoner; invited Archbishop Usher to visit him, evinced a warm and sincere regard for his many virtues, and when that excellent prelate died, commanded his interment in Westminster Abbey, and contributed two hundred pounds to his funeral.*

Even Romanists were kindly treated if they

* Stoughton, Neale, Macauley, Forster.

conducted themselves with propriety. Sir Kenelm Digby, a well-known papist, was lodged by Cromwell at Whitehall; and the penal code against priests was often suspended under his hand and seal.* "I should think my heart not an honest one," wrote Sir Kenelm to Secretary Thurlow, "if the blood about it were not warmed with any, the least imputation upon my respect and duty to his highness, to whom I owe so much."†

Such is the glowing record which impartial history makes of the broad and Christian toleration of the great Puritan "usurper." Yet this very latitude, one of the best evidences of his high, Christian principle, has been made the basis of a sneer at his religious sincerity. "How little religion was the concern, or so much as any longer the pretence of Cromwell," says Bishop Kennet, "appears from this, that in the large instrument of the government of the Commonwealth, which was the *magna charta* of the new constitution, there is not a word of churches, synods, ministers, nor any thing but the Christian religion in general, with liberty to all differing in judgment from the doctrine, worship, or discipline, publicly held forth."‡

To mature thinkers, this fact, here stated as a fault, is the best title-deed to immortality which Cromwell could desire.

Under the Protectorate very great attention

* Stoughton, Neale, Macauley, Forster.

† Ibid.; Ludlow's Memoirs, etc.

‡ Cited in Neale, vol. 2, p. 362, 363.

was paid to the cultivation of letters; schools and school-masters abounded; and the universities were kept under the careful supervision of the government.*

Oxford especially was tenderly nurtured. That classic old town had been strictly royalist in the earlier years of the civil war, and the king had made it his head-quarters. Study was routed; the university became a garrison. The gownsman was transformed into a military cavalier; the college cap was doffed for the steel helmet.† The *terræ filii* who continued their residence employed their wits in writing weekly mercuries and satirical pamphlets, in which the Parliament was lampooned, while the Puritan divines were scoffed at as infamous, ignorant, and hypocritical traitors.‡

But when the king's cause went down before Cromwell's "Ironsides" at Marston Moor and Naseby, the University was revolutionized. Mild measures, which were essayed by the Parliament at the outset, proved ineffectual.§ Then sharper measures were tried. All riot was forcibly repressed. The halls, shattered in the recent wars, were rebuilt, the officers and townsmen who had usurped the old scholastic chambers were expelled; the bursaries emptied in the service of the king were refilled; the plate, melted down in aid of the royalist cause, was replaced. The Oxfordians were

* Godwin, Hist. Commonwealth; Forster's Statesmen, etc.

† Wood, Hist. and Antiq. of Oxford.

‡ Neale, Wood, Stoughton.

§ Ibid.

obliged to subscribe the *Solemn League and Covenant*, which caused a great flutter in the dove-cote, but of which they were estopped from complaining by their own acts, since, in their day, scholars were obliged to subscribe the Thirty-nine Articles—and "old things became new."*

"Drab-colored" Puritanism now became the order of the day at Oxford. The Liturgy was no longer chanted in the college chapel. The surplice vanished from the desk. The altar rails were removed. The communion-table was placed in the aisle. The Genevan cloak and cap appeared in the pulpit. Images and crucifixes were removed. Even the city underwent a change. Rigid Presbyterianism suppressed the olden amusements; the theatre was closed. In the streets, instead of the slashed doublet, the love-locks, and the drooping feather of the Cavalier, the close-cropped hair, the high-crowned hat, and the plain cloak of the Roundhead became predominant.†

Strict attention to study, sobriety of deportment, and external piety were enforced.

Under Cromwell's *régime* the severity of this Presbyterian discipline was somewhat relaxed. No oath, excepting to support the government, was exacted, and a number of Independents were sprinkled among the proctors and college "dons."‡ But imperious orders were given for the promotion of

* Wood, Hist. and Antiq. of Oxford; Neale, vol. 2, chs. 19, passim.

† Ibid.; Stoughton.

‡ Wood, Neale, Whitelocke.

the interests of learning; and a diligent cultivation of literature as well as religion ensued. It was also enjoined that the greatest familiarity with the learned languages should be encouraged by the employment, at specified times, of Latin and Greek in common conversation by the fellows, scholars, and students.* These studies were held to be even more important in that age than they are in ours, because Latin especially was the vernacular of the learned world, and diplomacy itself spoke through that tongue.

In 1650 the members of the university of Oxford unanimously elected Oliver Cromwell to the office of chancellor.† "Warriors seem by no means the fittest persons for such a position," observes Stoughton, "but Oxford still retains a partiality for men of that class. The university in our time has placed Wellington in the chair once occupied by Cromwell; and we may all agree with Kahl, that 'these are the two most remarkable chancellors that Oxford ever had.' However, Cromwell had something to recommend him for that post besides his military renown and political power. He was any thing but an illiterate and tasteless fanatic. Waller the poet, who was his kinsman, says he was very well read in Greek and Latin story; and Whitelocke informs us that he was capable of holding a discourse in Latin with the Swedish ambassador. Cromwell was also a lover of the fine arts. He saved the painted windows of King's College chapel,

* Wood, Neale, Whitelocke. † Ibid., Stoughton.

Cambridge, from spoliation, carefully preserved the cartoons, and would permit no injury to be done to those noble specimens of architecture, Hampton Court and Windsor Castle. He had a rare power to control men. 'The natural king,' says Carlyle, 'is one who melts all wills into his own.' This Cromwell did; and surely the man who employed Milton to draw up his state papers, and Simon to engrave his coins, could not be destitute of taste. He was, moreover, fond of music; and when the organ was taken down at Magdalen College, he ordered it conveyed to Hampton Court, where he had it placed in the great gallery, and was accustomed to soothe the cares of politics by listening to the tones of that noble instrument. Nor should it be forgotten that Cromwell proved himself a patron of literature. His well-known permission to Walton to import paper for his noble Polyglot duty free, is one example culled from many."*

* Stoughton, pp. 198, 199.

"An inventory of sums contributed to the college library at Glasgow is preserved. The first leaf contains this memorandum: 'His majesty's contribution was graciously granted at Setoun, 14th July, 1633: Charles Rex. It is our gracious pleasure to grant, for the advancement of the library and fabric of the College of Glasgow, the sum of two hundred pounds sterling.' So much for the *promise* of Charles. The *performance* was from the privy-purse of the Protector twenty-one years afterwards, and is thus recorded: 'This sum was paid by the Lord Protector, A. D. 1654.'" Dibdin's Northern Tour, vol. 2, p. 713. Cromwell also settled one hundred pounds per year on a divinity professor at Oxford; he gave twenty rare manuscripts to the Bodleian library; and he erected and endowed a college at Durham for the benefit of the northern counties. Neale.

The moderation, the wisdom, the equity, and the consummate success of Cromwell's internal government, extort a grudged encomium even from the reluctant pen of Hume himself, who was at once a tory and a sceptic. "It must be acknowledged," he says, "that in his civil and domestic administration, the Protector displayed as great regard both to justice and clemency as his usurped authority, derived from no law and founded only on the sword, could possibly permit. All the chief offices in the courts of judicature were filled with men of integrity; amid the violence of faction, the decrees of the judges were upright and impartial; and to every man the law was the great rule of conduct and behavior. He was pleased that the superior lenity of his *régime* should in every thing be remarked."*

Baxter, who was far from being partial to Cromwell, writing after the Restoration, says, "All men were suffered to live quietly and to enjoy their properties under the Protectorate. The Lord Protector removed the errors and prejudices which hindered the success of the gospel, especially considering that godliness had countenance and reputation as well as liberty; whereas before, if it did not appear in all the fetters and formalities of the times, it was the way to common shame and ruin. When I compare these times with those, I conclude for the future to think that land happy where the people have but bare liberty to be as good as they

* Hume, vol. 2, p. 398, 399.

are willing; and if countenance and maintenance be added to liberty, as then they were, and tolerated errors and sects be but forced to keep the peace, I shall hereafter not much fear such toleration, nor despair that truth will bear down its adversaries."*

But while Cromwell's domestic administration was thus admirable, his foreign policy was no less energetic and effective. Milton, who had literally torn out his eyes as an oblation to liberty—for he contracted his blindness by over-application in the compilation of his pamphlets in defence of the revolution--was continued under Cromwell in the secretaryship of state, though he had an assistant in his excellent and devoted friend Andrew Marvel.† Sir Matthew Hale was made Chief-justice of the Common Pleas; Thurlow held the State Bureau; and Monk, who was destined one day to betray the liberties of his country, was entrusted with the government of Scotland.‡

In 1654, Ireland and Scotland were incorporated; and from that time the arms of both those nations were quartered with those of England.§

In the first months of the Protectorate the Dutch had sued for peace; and this tho fame of Cromwell enabled him to conclude without the ceremony of a formal treaty. He submitted his con-

* Baxter, Life and Times.

† Life and Times of John Milton, Amer. Tr. Society, 1866.

‡ Hume, Guizot, Godwin, Forster, D'Aubigné's Protectorate.

§ Ibid.; Harris, Life of Cromwell.

ditions. Abatements were requested. "Sign," said the imperious Protector. Holland hastened to do so, and the signature robbed her of the hard-earned laurels of a hundred years; for she stipulated to abandon the interests of Charles II.; to cede the island of Palerone, in the East Indies, to England; to pay eighty-five thousand pounds as an indemnity for British losses; to punish the murderers of British subjects at Amboyna; and, hardest of all, while Van Tromp, who had threatened to sweep the British flag from the sea with the broom fastened to the mast-head of his frigates, was hardly cold in his coffin, Holland yielded up the sovereignty of the ocean.*

Europe looked on aghast; and when the continental sovereigns witnessed this humiliating treaty, wrung from the Dutch by the haughty fiat of the Lord Protector, they hastened to compliment his highness upon his advancement and to cultivate his friendship. The king of Portugal asked pardon for receiving prince Rupert in his ports; the Danes got themselves included in the Dutch treaty; the Swedes sued for an alliance, which was concluded with their ambassador;† and the French ambassador, who was received by Cromwell at Whitehall with all the state of a crowned head, having made his obeisance, and mentioned his royal master's desire to establish a correspondence between his domin-

* Hume, Guizot, Godwin, Forster, D'Aubigné's Protectorate; Harris, Life of Cromwell; Neale, vol. 2, p. 369.

† Vaughan's Protectorate of Oliver Cromwell, Godwin, Forster.

ions and England, proceeded to say, "The king my master communicates his resolutions to none with so much joy and cheerfulness as to those whose virtuous actions and extraordinary merits render them even more conspicuously famous than the largeness of their dominions. His majesty is sensible that all these advantages do wholly reside in your highness, and that the divine Providence, after so many calamities, could not deal more favorably with these three nations, nor cause them to forget their past miseries with greater satisfaction, than by subjecting them to so just a government."*

The flunkey crowned heads of Europe would have gone even further than they did had Cromwell expressed the wish, and ordered their *savants* to hunt up a *jus divinum* as a basis for the Protectorate, from some forgotten record of the past.

Towards the Romanist powers Cromwell assumed an attitude of complete and fearless liberty, unmarked by prejudice or ill-will, but equally devoid of courtship or flattery, showing himself disposed to maintain peace, but always leaving open the prospect of war, and watching over the interests of his country and of Protestantism with stern and uncompromising haughtiness.†

It was in 1654 that Cromwell's celebrated intervention for the Vaudois—

> "E'en them who kept God's truth so pure of old,
> When all our fathers worshipped stocks and stones"—

* Neale, vol. 2, pp. 369, 370. † Guizot, vol. 2, pp. 78, 79.

occurred. The duke of Savoy, spurred thereto by his duchess, by the pope, and by the Italian princes, undertook to massacre the feeble remnant of those hunted mediæval reformers who had been driven out of France to the shelter of the Piedmont valleys.* Fearful cruelty was exercised, and the wail of the slaughtered saints echoed from the Alpine mountains to Whitehall. Cromwell moved all Europe to intervene; and when Mazarin, who had succeeded Richelieu in the government of France, made excuses and hesitated, the iron Puritan thundered his war cry, and proposed to go personally to the rescue. So great was Cromwell's reputation that this was not necessary: the massacre ceased; Savoy made amends; the continental sovereigns poured contributions into Piedmont; collections were taken up throughout the united kingdoms of Great Britain; the Protector himself headed the subscription-list, and for once authority compelled an act of poetic justice.†

"To strike further terror into the pope and the petty princes of Italy," says Neale, "the Protector gave out that, forasmuch as he was satisfied that they had been the promoters of the Vaudois persecution, he would keep it in mind, and lay hold of the first opportunity to send his fleet into the Mediterranean to visit Civita Vecchia and other ports

* Hist. of Huguenots, Amer. Tr. Soc., 1866; Thurlow's State Papers.

† Milton, Prose Works, vol. 5, pp. 247–258; Vaughan's Cromwell, vol. 1, p. 158; Morland, Hist. Evang. Church in Piedmont.

of the ecclesiastical territories, and that the sound of his cannon should be heard in Rome itself. He declared publicly that he would not suffer the Protestant faith to be insulted in any part of the world; this procured liberty to the reformed in Bohemia and France; nor was there any potentate in Europe so hardy as to risk his displeasure by denying his imperious requests."*

One of the secrets of Cromwell's European influence was, that it was known that his threats were not *vox et præterea nihil.* If he talked high, he acted higher.† Some years after the Vaudois intervention, he did indeed dispatch a squadron of thirty ships, under that stern republican Admiral Blake—whose fame, like the Protector's, was now spread over Christendom—into the Mediterranean. "No English fleet," remarks Hume, "except during the crusades, had ever before sailed in those seas; and from one extremity to the other there was no naval force, Christian or Mohammedan, able to resist them. The Roman pontiff, whose weakness and whose pride equally provoked attack, dreaded invasion from a power which he had fatally offended, and which so little regulated its movements by the usual motives of apparent interest and prudence. Blake, casting anchor before Leghorn, demanded and obtained reparation from the duke of Tuscany for some losses which English commerce had formerly sustained from him. The fleet next sailed to

* Neale, vol. 2, p. 406.

† Guizot, Vaughan, Ludlow's Memoirs.

Algiers, and compelled the dey to make peace, and to restrain his piratical subjects from further violence on the English. Blake next presented himself before Tunis, and having made there the same demand, the dey told him to look to the castles of Porto Farino and Galetta, and do his utmost. The fiery admiral required no second bidding; and drawing up his ships close to the castles, tore them to pieces with his artillery. He sent a detachment of soldiers in their long-boats into the harbor, and burned every vessel that lay moored there. This bold action, whose very temerity perhaps rendered it safe, was executed with little loss, and it filled all Christendom with the renown of English valor,"* and with dread of the Protectorate.

Such was the foreign record, in so far at least as it affects the Puritans, of England under Cromwell: bound by sincere friendship to all the Protestant states, in active alliance with the most powerful Romanist sovereigns—everywhere present, respected, influential, and feared.†

Foreign visitors, accustomed to the soft, effeminate graces of the continental courts, could never quite comprehend the earnest sternness of the Protector's government. "I am now in England," wrote the Venetian ambassador Giovanni Sagredo, who had come to London from Paris in October, 1656, and now sent back his impressions in the

* Hume, vol. 2, p. 396; Russell's Life of Cromwell.

† Guizot, vol. 2, p. 244; T. Cromwell's Life and Times of Cromwell.

peculiar style of his age and country; "the aspect of this island is very different from that of France: here we do not see ladies going to court, but gentlemen courting the chase; not elegant cavaliers, but cavalry and infantry; instead of music and ballets, they have drums and trumpets; they do not speak of love, but of Mars; they have no comedies, but tragedies; no patches on their faces, but guns on their shoulders; they do not neglect sleep for the sake of amusement, but severe ministers keep their flocks in incessant watchfulness. In a word, every thing here is full of disdain, suspicion, and rough, menacing faces."*

Probably the Italian diplomat missed his wonted revels and his love-sick haunts, and his chagrin bubbled over in epigrams. It may certainly be conceded that England, under the Protectorate, sober, earnest, devout, was scarcely calculated to be the *beau ideal* residence of a roystering and ribald cavalier.

Still the pictures of the Puritans of that age have been sadly distorted. They were not savage, fanatical iconoclasts, bent on the demolition of all that was beautiful in architecture and in letters. Parliament, in its act for the removal of *popish badges*, introduced an express clause for the preservation of works of art, and provided that their ordinance "should not extend to the mutilation of any image, picture, or coat of arms, in glass, stone, or otherwise, in any

* Lettere Inedite di Messar Giovanni Sagredo, p. 29; Venice, 1839.

church, chapel, or church-yard, set up or engraven for a monument of any king, prince, nobleman, or other dead person, not commonly reputed or taken for a saint."* And that this statute, even with its limitation, was never fully carried out, is obvious from the fact that multitudes of statues and other Romanist monuments still stand in towns and hamlets where the Parliament had full sway.†

"It is common," remarks Stoughton, "to represent Puritanism as a grovelling spirit, which crushed the seeds of genius and literature. So far as genius was occupied in the investigation of religious and political principles, and so far as literature was employed in diffusing their results, it is very unfair to charge Puritanism with being the enemy of either. As it was seen in the doings of the leading men at Oxford, it appeared as the friend of both. It animated many of them to an intense study of divinity, with such an application of the aids of philology, criticism, the fathers, the schoolmen, and modern writers, as might well shame numbers of the theologians of later times. The works which some of the leading Puritans produced under the Protectorate are monuments of their talents and attainments, as well as of their piety. Baxter, Owen, Hume, Charnock, and many more, for depth of thought, compass of intelligence, and occasional power and even felicity of expression, will bear comparison with the most boasted names among the divines of any country.

* Parl. Hist.; Statutes of the Realm. † Stoughton, p. 194.

"As a class, the Puritans can by no means be said to have cultivated the forms of poetry; yet they were poets in spite of themselves. They scorned the tales of romance, but their imaginations were pictured over with the facts of Scripture. They cared little for Olympus and the haunts of the muses, but they daily visited the hill of Zion, and talked with prophets and apostles. They frequented not the scenes of classic story, but they were familiar with scenes more exquisitely beautiful, more awfully sublime. Homer, Pindar, and Virgil perhaps they might not often study, but Isaiah, Jeremiah, and Ezekiel were poets whose rich and divine utterances were on their lips as household words. The theatre they abhorred; their condemnation of its impure accessories prejudiced them against the richest creations of the dramatic muse, but they themselves trod an infinitely nobler stage, in the presence of 'a great cloud of witnesses.' They felt that they were a spectacle to the world and to angels. Others have written wonderful dramas; they *acted* one more wonderful than was ever penned. They lived much in another world, and there they walked by faith in the highest realm of poetry. 'Truly their lives were a great epic.' Nor did that soul of poetry which dwelt within them fail to express itself in their writings and conversation. There are multitudes of passages in their books to which perhaps some critics would point as teeming with enthusiasm, which are in fact redolent with the genuine spirit of poetry;

and their ordinary speech, so often ridiculed, would sometimes glitter with scriptural allusions instinct with poetic fire.

"As to the lower classes among the Puritans, they were, to say the least, as intelligent as their compeers on the other side. If they were ignorant of elegant literature, they knew something about the Bible, and were well versed in the writings and sayings of popular divines—knowledge which, even in a literary point of view, it seems a desecration to compare with the loose songs and scraps of ribald wit which formed the staple of Cavalier learning among the lower orders.

"But after all, did Puritanism altogether lack sons who walked in the paths of polite literature? Were not Harrington and Waller and Vane and Marvel Puritans and Commonwealthsmen? Did they not meet with other wits and poets of the day in true literary conclave at the Turk's Head in Palace-yard, to speculate on the profoundest themes, or playfully to chat together in conversation seasoned with a salt as pungent as any Attic wit? And have they not written works of literary renown which all parties have since combined to praise? Was not Milton a Puritan? Does not his genius tower above all other men's since the days when Shakspeare wrote? For the solitary grandeur of his muse, and for all its wayward aberrations too, he may be likened to his own

"'Wandering moon,
Riding near his highest noon,

Like one that hath been led astray,
Through the heaven's wide, pathless way.'"*

The Puritans of the Protectorate then were no horde of vulgar fanatics, no herd of tasteless, gloomy ascetics—*consumere fruges nati*—born only to eat. No; they had a work, and God graced them with the talent and the culture as well as with the dauntless courage necessary to its performance.

In 1656, good Bishop Hall expired. "His practical works," says Neale, "have been held in great esteem among dissenters. At the beginning of the troubles between the king and the Parliament, Dr. Hall published several treatises in favor of diocesan Episcopacy, which were answered by *Smectymnus* and by Milton. He was afterwards imprisoned in the tower with the rest of the protesting bishops: upon his release he retired to Norwich; the revenues of which bishopric being soon sequestered, together with his own real and personal estate, he was forced to be content with the fifths. The parliamentary soldiers used him severely, turning him out of his palace, and threatening to sell his books, which they would have done had not a friend given a bond for the money at which they were appraised. Dr. Hall complained very justly of this usage in a pamphlet, entitled, 'Hard Measure.' At length Parliament made him some amends, voting him forty pounds a year; and when the war was ended his estate was restored to him, and he

* Stoughton, pp. 224–228.

lived peaceably ever after, spending his solitude in acts of charity and in divine meditation. He has been frequently called the English Seneca, for the pureness, plainness, and fulness of his style."*

In September, 1657, Parliament, a "shrew" now "tamed" into Cromwell's peaceful help-meet, confirmed the *de facto* government, and proffered the crown to the Lord Protector.† Although tendered in the most solemn manner, it was refused, some say because Cromwell's own stern republican rectitude withheld him from the assumption of royalty;‡ others, because he feared that his acceptance would alienate the affection of the army, always democratic in its principles, and bitterly opposed to the name of king.§ "Most historians," remarks Hume, "are inclined to blame the Protector's choice; but he must be allowed to be the best judge of his own situation. And in such complicated subjects, the alteration of a very minute circumstance, unknown to the spectator, will often be sufficient to cast the balance, and render a determination, which in itself may be ineligible, very prudent, or even absolutely necessary to the actor."‖

The last years of the Protectorate were as prosperous and glorious as its opening months. The war with Spain was grandly successful. Blake blockaded the harbor of Cadiz, sunk the Spanish

* Neale, vol. 2, pp. 417, 418.

† Parl. Hist.; Godwin, Hist. Commonwealth; Guizot.

‡ Forster, Carlyle, Headley. § Clarendon, Hume, etc.

‖ Hume, vol. 2, p. 403.

fleet, and captured plate to the value of two million pounds, which was brought to London from Portsmouth in carts, and coined in the tower.* Wintering on the coast of Spain, Blake, in the summer of 1657, repeated his exploit with still greater *éclat*.† The island of Jamaica, in the West Indies, had been previously conquered,‡ and the record of a glorious year was fitly rounded into perfect symmetry by the capture of Dunkirk by Cromwell's pikemen, assisted by the French battalions of Turenne.§ Mazarin intended to retain that strong-hold in his own hands, contrary to an existing treaty. Cromwell's spies acquainted him with the design, and sent him Mazarin's secret order to that effect. The French ambassador was sent for; when he reached Whitehall, the Protector mentioned the intended breach of contract; the diplomat denied it; whereupon Cromwell took from his pocket the cardinal's private directions, and desired the astounded ambassador to let his eminence know that if the keys of Dunkirk were not delivered to his ambassador Lockhart within an hour after its capture, he would come in person and demand them at the gates of Paris. It is needless to add that Lockhart took possession within the hour.‖ This conquest added fresh lustre to the Protector's administration, since it was no empty trophy, but gave the English a foothold on

* Thurlow's State Papers; Clarendon's Hist. Reb.; Godwin.

† Ibid.

‡ Hume, vol. 2, p. 396.

§ Hist. et Mem. du Vicomte de Turenne, vol. 2, pp. 360–375; Godwin; Clarendon; Mem. Historiques, vol. 1, p. 167, et seq., etc.

‖ Godwin, Neale, Forster.

the Continent, and made them masters of both sides of the Channel.

At about this same time Cromwell had an opportunity of redressing the wrongs of the Huguenots, as he had already redressed those of the Vaudois Piedmontese. On being apprized of certain *ultramontane* tumults at Nîsmes, which the court of Louis XIV. intended to make the pretext for a general onslaught upon the reformed, the Protector dispatched an express to Mazarin vetoing the crusade; and he at the same time instructed the English ambassador to insist upon the cessation of all hostile movements, and in case his eminence did not comply, to demand his passports and to quit the court. Mazarin complained of this as high and imperious; but so great was his awe of Cromwell, that he hastened to stop the expedition, and to reëstablish the *entente cordiale.**

This intervention, like that for the Vaudois, was bruited throughout Christendom, and foreign Protestantism felt itself strengthened and vivified when sheltered beneath the august ægis of the Protectorate. In those days England dictated law to the whole Continent. Whitehall did not then stoop to to be the lackey of the Tuilleries.

But the end approached. The Protector's health, broken by excessive toil and advancing age, began to fail. At length, on the 3d of September, 1658, the anniversary of his triumphs at Dunbar and at Worcester,† the cord of life snapped, and the Puri-

* Neale, vol. 2, p. 416. † Carlyle, Godwin, Forster.

tan soldier and statesman, then in his sixtieth year, lay dead in his palace at Whitehall.*

His last words were a prayer, like himself, unique, unprecedented, sublime: "Lord, I am a poor, foolish creature: this people would fain have me live; they think it best for them, and that it will redound much to thy glory; and all the stir is about this. Others would fain have me die. Lord, pardon them, and pardon thy foolish people; forgive their sins, and do not forsake them, but love and bless and give them rest, and bring them to a consistency; and give me rest, for Jesus Christ's sake, to whom, with thee and thy Holy Spirit, be all honor and glory, now and for ever. Amen."†

* Carlyle, Godwin, Forster, Vaughan.

† Neale, vol. 2, p. 438; Carlyle, Vaughan.

CHAPTER XXIX.

JUDAS.

THE death of the Protector conjured up chaos. A smiling but treacherous calm of five months duration did indeed ensue. It took so long for England to shake off the spell of Cromwell's genius. The Protector's son and heir, Richard Cromwell, was proclaimed. Congratulatory addresses greeted the new government; the Presbyterians, who had been hostile to the father, were friendly to the son; and "all went merry as a marriage-bell."

But Richard Cromwell resembled his father only in name. Weak, inefficient, retiring, the best that can be said of him is, that he was a gentleman, and that he could pass a chair or hand a dish with rare grace.* These are not the qualities which constitute a statesmanship skilled and able to hold the helm in boisterous times; and the new Protectorate soon drifted on the rocks.

Parliament, divided between secret royalists and open republicans, began a factious opposition to the continued existence of the abnormal situation.† The army, also split into two factions, Commonwealthsmen and Presbyterians, began to bicker and to chafe. The democrats, headed by a cabal of

* Burnet's Own Times; Neale, Whitelocke.

† Hume, Burnet, Godwin.

officers, dragooned the Protector into dissolving the Parliament, his main support.* A council of military men assumed authority. The feeble pigmy who masqueraded as Protector, perplexed and terrified, at once resigned his dignity, and after a reign of eight months, sank into congenial obscurity.†

In the mean time Monk, who commanded in Scotland, began to move. The Puritan regiments in the north witnessed these revolutions with an indignation which resembled that of the Roman legions posted on the Danube and the Euphrates, when they learned that the empire had been put up to sale by the prætorian guards. It was intolerable that certain squadrons should, merely because they chanced to be quartered at Westminster, take on themselves to make and unmake several governments in six months. If it were fit that the state should be regulated by soldiers, then those soldiers who upheld the English ascendency on the north of the Tweed were as well entitled to a voice as those who garrisoned the Tower of London.‡

Thus, while the army rose against the Parliament, the different corps of the army rose against each other. Without a head, society itself dissolved. The people everywhere refused to pay taxes. The title-deeds of the magistrates were questioned. Sect raved against sect; party plotted against party.§

* Hume, Burnet, Godwin.

† Burnet's Own Times, Vaughan, etc.

‡ Macauley, Hist. Eng.; Guizot, Clarendon.

§ Ibid.

Monk advanced and entered London in 1659. A painful hush succeeded. He was felt to be the arbiter of the national fate. The republicans besought him to confirm the Commonwealth; the royalists urged him to declare for the king; the Presbyterians, forming an alliance with the Cavaliers, cried Amen to this programme, but spoke of terms, and wished to secure the establishment of their discipline in England, as the *sine qua non* of the return of the exiled Stuarts.* Neither of these parties dared initiate a movement in support of their plans. The dread of that invincible army was the spell which tied all hands; and even though divided and betrayed, it was still irresistible. Monk's importance grew out of the fact that he controlled so many disciplined regiments.†

At last Monk acted; the "Rump" Parliament was convened. "Those Presbyterian members of the House of Commons who had many years before been expelled by the army returned to their seats, and were hailed with acclamations by great multitudes who thronged Westminster Hall and Palace-yard. The Independent leaders no longer ventured to show their faces in the streets, and were scarcely safe in their own dwellings. Temporary provision was made for the government, writs were issued for a general election, and then that memorable Parliament which had, during twenty years, experienced every variety of fortune, which had triumph-

* Neale, vol. 2, chap. 4, passim; Godwin, Baxter.

† Clarendon, Burnet, etc.

ed over its sovereign, which had been enslaved and degraded by its servants, which had been twice ejected and twice restored, solemnly decreed its own dissolution."*

The army, without a leader, the sport of a dozen restless and aspiring officers, looked on in sullen, ominous, but despairing discontent. The republicans made a last rally, and Milton issued a pamphlet, in which he pointed out the "ready and easy way to establish a commonwealth," and expressed the hope that what he said might not prove "the last words of expiring liberty."†

These efforts were all vain. The people—some mad with love of change, some from self-interest, some from a longing for a stable government, some from disgust at the excesses of the past, and some from real attachment to the ancient monarchy—the people pronounced in favor of the restoration of the Constitution. "It is to be noted," remarks Macauley, "that the two great parties of the Roundheads and the Cavaliers had never been the whole nation; nay, that they had never, taken together, made up a majority of the nation. Between them had always been a great mass which had not steadfastly adhered to either, which had sometimes remained inertly neutral, and had sometimes oscillated to and fro. That mass had more than once passed, in a few years, from one extreme to the other and back again. Sometimes it changed sides merely because

* Macauley, Hist. Eng., vol. 1, p. 115.

† Milton, Prose Works, vol. 6.

it was tired of supporting the same men, sometimes because it was dismayed by its own excesses, sometimes because it had expected impossibilities, and had been disappointed. But whenever it had leaned with its whole weight in either direction, resistance had for the time been impossible."*

The elections proved that one of these spasmodic social revolutions was now occurring. The new Parliament consisted of a coalition of Cavaliers and Presbyterians. The Lords once more reëntered that hall from which they had been excluded through eleven years.† Then the two houses proceeded to invite Charles Stuart to stop hunting in the bogs of France, to cease skulking through the courts of Europe, to quit the arms of his continental mistresses sufficiently long to come to England and reascend the throne of his fathers.‡

The great quarrel which liberty has with this action and with Monk's approval of it is, that no guarantee was demanded, no terms were made, no limits were imposed on this *roué* sovereign who was *invited* to reign, at a time when all might have been and should have been exacted. A simple declaration, made at Breda, in Brabant, while he was yet a fugitive, in which Charles promised, among other things, "such liberty for tender consciences that no man should be called in question for religious opinions *which did not disturb the state*,"§ was the silly

* Macauley, vol. 1, p. 73.

† Since the inauguration of the Commonwealth, in 1649.

‡ Parl. Hist., Hume, Clarendon.

§ Clarendon, vol. 3, p. 772; Whitelocke's Memorials, p. 702.

bait which caught these gudgeons. The Presbyterians swallowed it whole, overlooking the last clause, which was a sufficient warrant for the suppression of Presbyterianism itself, on the plea that it was inimical to the government. They even expected that Charles would adopt their discipline as the national creed.* And so the Parliament, encouraged by the Presbyterians and by the aid of Monk, the Judas of British politics, without casting one glance at the past or requiring one stipulation for the future, threw down the freedom of three kingdoms at the feet of the most frivolous and heartless of tyrants.

On the 26th of May, 1660, Charles II. landed at Dover. Three days later he rode in triumph through the jubilant metropolis to the palace of Whitehall.† Foolish England went mad with joy. At night the sky was reddened by countless bonfires; there was an incessant peal of bells; the gutters ran with ale.‡

"Then came those days never to be recalled without a blush, the days of servitude without loyalty, of sensuality without love, of dwarfish talents and gigantic vices, the paradise of cold hearts and narrow minds, the golden age of the coward, the bigot, and the slave. The king cringed to his rival that he might trample on his people, sank into a viceroy of France, and pocketed with complacent

* Neale, vol. 2, pp. 464–469; Baxter's Life and Times.

† Whitelocke's Memorials, p. 702; Evelyn's Diary, vol. 2, p. 148; Clarendon, Hume.

‡ Evelyn's Diary, Whitelocke's Memorials, Clarendon.

infamy her degrading insults and her more degrading gold. The government had just ability enough to deceive, and just religion enough to persecute. The principles of liberty were the scoff of every grinning courtier and the anathema maranatha of every fawning dean. In every high place worship was paid to Charles and James, Belial and Moloch; and England propitiated those obscene and cruel idols with the blood of her best and bravest children. Crime succeeded to crime, disgrace to disgrace, until the race, accursed of God and man, was a second time driven forth to wander on the face of the earth, and to be a by-word and a shaking of the head to the nations."*

* Macauley, Essay on Milton.

CHAPTER XXX.

THE RESTORATION.

UNDER the Restoration, the theology, the manners, and the dialect of the Puritans became a scoff and a reproach, and the outcry was swollen by the voices of those "lewd fellows of the baser sort" who had been roughly repressed by the precisionists. To a certain extent the Puritans had brought upon themselves this storm of unpopularity. The people had been vexed by the interdiction of their favorite games, and fretted by a legal code which enforced the subversion of all the most popular amusements. May-poles were hewn down; rope-dancing, puppet-shows, bowling, horse-racing, wrestling-matches, theatricals—every diversion, from masks in the manor-houses to grinning-matches on the village greens, was placed under a judicial ban.*

The Puritans meant in this to subserve the interests of morality, but their indiscrimination balked them of success, and covered them with odium. Recreation is essential both to happiness and to health; therefore it is eminently necessary to distinguish between proper and improper amusements; and while we discountenance the one, we

* Statutes of the Realm; Godwin, Hist. of Commonwealth; Clarendon.

ought to encourage the other. The Puritans did not make this distinction.

Then, again, the church as a church has no coercive authority. It may and it should use every moral weapon in its warfare against vice. It may and it should rest its lever upon every spiritual fulcrum in its effort to lift the world out of criminal sloughs. But when the church attempts to compel men to be moral by civil penalties, it quits its legitimate domain and usurps the sword. Its members may, as citizens, bar out immorality and all incitements to vicious ways; but in this, while the motor power is religion, the agency is statesmanship; and Christians should achieve their purpose not through ecclesiastical, but through political forms. Undoubtedly the state is armed with authority to suppress vice; for liberty is not license, and the social compact presupposes the existence of a reserved right to protect society against the insidious encroachments of the abettors of immorality. The civil magistrate is under bonds to God and man to see that vice, that protean sapper of social order, is not left to flaunt unchecked.

We do not plead therefore for the immunity of immorality; for immorality, whatever garb it may put on, is a crime entitled to no terms; we simply deny the authority of the church as a church to wield a sword which legitimately belongs to the civil magistrate.

Besides, while thus busied in correcting the public morals, not legitimately by exhortation and by practice, but by penal legislation, Puritanism suffered in its own. It has been well said, that "the ordinary tendency of sects is to attain a high reputation for sanctity while they are oppressed, and to lose it in prosperity; and the reason is obvious. It is seldom that a man enrolls himself in a proscribed body from any but conscientious motives. Such a body therefore is composed, with scarcely an exception, of sincere persons. The most rigid discipline that can be enforced within a religious society, is a very feeble instrument of purification compared with a sharp persecution from without. We may be certain that very few persons, not seriously impressed by religious conviction, applied for baptism while Diocletian was vexing the church, or joined themselves to Protestant congregations at the risk of being burned by Bonner. But when a sect becomes powerful, when its favor is the road to riches and dignities, worldly and ambitious men crowd into it, talk its language, conform strictly to its ritual, mimic its peculiarities, and frequently go beyond its honest members in all the outward indications of zeal. No discernment, no watchfulness on the part of ecclesiastical rulers can prevent the intrusion of such false brethren. The tares and the wheat must grow together. Soon the world suspects that the godly are not better than other men, and concludes that if not better, they must be worse. In no long time all those signs which were formerly regarded as the characteristics of a saint, are regarded as the characteristics of a knave."

So it was with Puritanism; ambitious men, licentious men imitated the sober dress, straight hair, the speech interspersed with quaint texts, the aversion to comedies, which were the badges of the parliamentarians; and then, after their villany had helped to bring "the good old cause" to ruin, turned about and loaded it with abuse as a refuge of dissenting mountebanks.

The injury which Puritanism thus suffered in its *morale,* together with the ultra-strictness of its *régime,* brought it into general contempt at the Restoration. Profane wits levelled their epigrams at it; Cavaliers cursed it in their drink; and the people, long compelled to an extreme of austerity by statute, now rushed to an extreme of license from choice. England became a haunt of bacchanals. "Drab colored" Puritanism was succeeded by scarlet colored profligacy. Oxford was once more revolutionized. Its own partial historian makes this record: "The hope of the Restoration made the scholars talk loud, drink healths, and curse Meroz in the very streets; insomuch that when the king came in, nay, when he was voted in, they were not only like men in a dream, but like men out of their wits—mad, stark, staring mad. To study was fanatical; to be moderate was downright rebellion."* Neale adds these touches to Wood's picture: "There was a general licentiousness of manners among the students; the sermons of the younger divines were filled with encomiums

* Anth. Wood, Hist. and Antiquities of Oxford.

upon the olden rule, and with satire against the Puritans; the evangelical doctrines—faith, charity, and practical religion—were out of date."*

In every respect "the times which followed the Restoration were the reverse of those that preceded it; for the laws which had been enacted against vice for the last twenty years were declared null, the magistrates were changed, and men set no bounds to their licentiousness. The loyalty of loose and riotous Cavaliers consisted in drinking healths and railing at all who would not join in their revels. The king was at the head of these disorders; he had given himself up to pleasure, and devoted his time to lewdness. His bishops and chaplains complained that he came from his mistresses' apartments to church, even on sacrament days. Two theatres were erected in the neighborhood of the court. The most lewd and obscene plays were enacted, and these Charles graced with his presence. The court became an incarnate revel, and nothing was seen but feasting, hard drinking, and amorous intrigues, which engendered the most atrocious vices. From the court the contagion spread like wild-fire among the people, insomuch that men threw off the very profession of virtue and piety. Under color of drinking the king's health, all kinds of Cavalier debauchery revived; and the appearance of religion which remained with some, furnished matter of ridicule to libertines and scoffers."†

* Neale, vol. 2, pp. 543–554.

† Ibid., p. 477.

The Puritans, out of date and covered with abuse, looked on these scenes grief-stricken. The Independents had little to hope. They had been Cromwell's peculiar friends. The Baptists were strongly republican; they had opposed the Protector's government at the outset, but gradually the great body of their churches made their submission, and enjoyed the esteem and protection of the yeoman prince.* The most then that these sects ventured to petition for was toleration.†

The Presbyterians had higher hopes. They had opposed Cromwell; they had been most influential in restoring the Stuarts; and their egregious credulity led them to believe that the Establishment would be stretched to embrace them.‡

At the outset the court encouraged this belief. The Presbyterians were soothed and caressed; several of their most eminent clergy were added to the list of the king's chaplains in ordinary, and Calamy and Baxter each preached once at court.§

The fact should seem to be that in the disputes which divided his Protestant subjects, the king's conscience was not at all interested, for his opinions then oscillated in a state of contented suspense between infidelity and popery; he was an infidel when well, and a Romanist when sick. Macauley paints this portrait of the monarch: "Charles pos-

* Crosby's and Ivimey's Hist. of the Baptists.

† Newell, Baxter, Clarendon, Neale.

‡ Neale, vol. 2, pp. 475–486; Newell, p. 323.

§ Ibid.; Evelyn's Diary; Whitelocke.

sessed social habits, polite and engaging manners, and some talent for lively conversation; he was addicted beyond measure to sensual indulgence, fond of sauntering and of frivolous amusements, incapable of self-denial and of exertion, detested state business, was without faith in human virtue or human attachment, without desire of renown, and without sensibility to reproach. According to him every one was to be bought. But some people haggled more about their price than others; and where this haggling was very obstinate and very skilful, it was called by some fine name. The chief trick by which clever men kept up the price of their abilities was called integrity. The chief trick by which handsome women kept up the price of their beauty was called modesty. The love of God, the love of country, the love of family, the love of friends, were phrases of the same sort, delicate and convenient synonyms for the love of self. But though the king's conscience was neutral in the quarrel between Episcopacy and Presbyterianism, his prejudices and his tastes were by no means so. His favorite vices were precisely those to which the Puritans were least indulgent. He could not get through a day without the help of diversions which the Non-conformists regarded as sinful. Besides, as a man eminently well bred, and keenly sensible of the ridiculous, he was moved to contemptuous mirth by the oddities of Puritanism."* Indeed he was accustomed to say, "Puritanism is a religion

* Macauley, Hist. of England, vol. 1, pp. 133, 134.

unfit for a gentleman."* He was right; it was unfit for a gentleman of that day, for it was a religion of the people. Still, Charles wished to lay asleep old controversies. He also desired to tolerate that Romish creed towards which he already leaned. This he could not hope to do unless he proclaimed a general toleration. To this purpose he now lent himself with a kind of lazy nonchalance.

The moderate Presbyterians of the school of Baxter were anxious to effect a compromise with the moderate Episcopalians of the school of Usher. The moderates of one party admitted that a bishop might lawfully be assisted by a council; the moderates of the other acknowledged that each provincial assembly might lawfully have a permanent president, and that this officer might be styled a bishop. In Baxter's mind the *desideratum* was a revised liturgy which should not exclude extemporaneous prayer, a baptismal service in which the sign of the cross was optional, a communion at which the faithful might sit, if their consciences forbade them to kneel.†

These concessions would have permitted the formation of a scheme of comprehension, under which the Presbyterian clergy might retain their ministry and their livings in the Establishment.‡

The king, hating dissension, abhorring sober

* Evelyn's Diary; Whitelocke.

† Baxter, Life and Times; Macauley, Clarendon.

‡ Newell, p. 323; Neale; Burnet's Own Times.

things, anxious always to escape from the cares of state to the sensuality of the seraglio, favored this programme, since he thought it made for peace. He gave its originators an audience. Baxter was the spokesman of his party; and that great divine painted a glowing picture of the advantages certain to accrue to his majesty, to the state, to the church, from such a union. Charles listened with exquisite urbanity, nodded approval at the close of every sentence, requested the Presbyterians to draw up their proposals, dismissed the delegation with a gracious smile,* and when they were gone, sighed wearily and wondered whether that stupid conference had not kept him too late for his appointment with Nell Gwynne.

Baxter and his *confréres* withdrew from the royal ante-chamber only to assemble again at Zion college, where they were reinforced by as many of their coreligionists as they could collect. Here, after a weighty and prolonged debate, a paper framed on Archbishop Usher's model of church government was adopted.† With this the Presbyterians returned to court, where they expected to meet the bishops and hold a conference in which a definitive settlement should be arranged. What was their disappointment when they found that the churchmen had declined a conference, and empowered the lord-chancellor, who met them, to hand

* Newell, p. 323; Burnet's Own Times; Neale, vol. 2, pp. 480, 481.

† Burnet's Own Times; Reliquiæ Baxterianæ, pt. 2, p. 259.

them an elaborate paper of objections to the scheme of union.*

The fact should seem to be, that "the great body of old Cavaliers listened to this talk of compromise with no patience. The religious members of that party were conscientiously attached to the whole system of their church. She had been dear to their murdered king. She had consoled them in defeat and penury. Her service, so often whispered in an inner chamber during the season of trial, had such a charm for them that they were unwilling to part with a single response. Other royalists, who made little pretence to piety, yet loved the English ritual because it was the foe of their foes. They valued a prayer or a ceremony not on account of the comfort it conveyed to themselves, but on account of the vexation which it gave the Roundheads; and were so far from being disposed to make concessions, that they objected to concessions chiefly because they tended to produce union."†

Thus, from one cause or another, the severities of former years began to be revived. Old laws were put into execution against those who did not use the Liturgy. Clergymen who had been sequestered under the Long Parliament, under the Commonwealth, under the Protectorate, flocked to court, and obtained a royal order for their reinstatement in their former livings.‡

* Burnet's Own Times; Reliquiæ Baxterianæ, lib. 1.
† Macauley, Hist. of Eng., vol. 1, p. 125.
‡ Neale, vol. 2, pp. 474, 482; Burnet, Evelyn's Diary, Whitelocke.

The leading Presbyterians at once waited upon the king. They did not deny that those preachers who had just lost their livings as a punishment for malignancy and old disaffection, were righteously ousted; but they prayed that those who were friendly to the Restoration, and who had succeeded clergymen ejected for scandal, might retain their benefices.*

Charles was, as usual, complaisant. He said, "I will endeavor to give you all satisfaction, and to make you as happy as myself."† In October, 1660, he published a *pronunciamento*, in which the existing mixed ecclesiastical establishment was ordered to be maintained until the convention of a united assembly of Presbyterian and Episcopalian divines. This assembly was to meet five months later at the lodgings of the bishop of London, at the Savoy, and its settlement was to be definitive.‡

Meantime, under the declaration, Reynolds accepted a bishopric; Baxter was offered one, but declined for reasons other than ecclesiastical;§ and Calamy was pressed to accept the see of Litchfield, but this he refused to take until the declaration should be enacted into law.‖

Soon the declaration was presented to Parliament for their sanction. The bill passed one reading, but court intrigue defeated it on a second.¶

* Newell, p. 327; Neale, vol. 2, pp. 474, 482. † Ibid.

‡ Burnet's Own Times, Whitelocke, Baxter's Life and Times.

§ Baxter's Life and Times, Neale.

‖ Neale, vol. 2, p. 483; Newell.

¶ Hume, Macauley, Neale, Newell, Baxter, etc.

This at once opened the eyes of the self-cozened Presbyterians, and they began to prepare for persecution.*

But while this stir was afoot among the ecclesiastics, the politicians were busy. At the head of the new ministry, Hyde, Lord Clarendon, was placed. He was a man of fine talent, but rusty in politics from long exile, and prejudiced in religion by misfortune. The first political move of the Restoration was to pass an act of indemnity; this buried past offences in oblivion, and excepted from its grace only such criminals as should be designated by Parliament.†

This act has been smothered beneath the panegyrics of six generations of admiring critics; but when it is remembered that Charles came back to England by no prowess of his own, but on the free invitation of a forgiving people, the fact that he did not instantly assume the port of a successful conqueror and breathe forth fire and slaughter loses much of its attributed lustre. Had the Stuarts returned by conquest, violence and bloody reprisal might have been in place. But we apprehend that, sitting enthroned as the guest of the nation, the king's action was, from the very outset, sufficiently high and arbitrary.

The indemnity act was far from being pure rosewater. Parliament excepted all the regicides by name; it attainted Cromwell, Ireton, Bradshaw, and others who then slept in the coffin; it excepted

* Neale, Newell.

† Hume, vol. 2, p. 432.

Lambert and Vane, though neither of these had any hand in the execution of the king, and though Vane had never countenanced the Protectorate, but had lived in peaceable retirement since the downfall of the Commonwealth; it denied its benefits to St. John and seventeen others, should they attempt to hold any office; and it disabled all who had sat in an illegal court from ever accepting any public employment—banning thereby the whole judicial bench.*

Most of those who, either from prominent connection with the recent *régime* or from republican principles, were peculiarly obnoxious to the resuscitated royalty, had secreted themselves when the clouds began to gather. Three of the regicides had quitted England for America.† Richard Cromwell had passed beyond the sea.‡ Milton, old, blind, and infirm, but still serene with the patience of a great soul, had sought an asylum with a friend, where he still continued

"To sing and build the lofty rhyme."§

But all who could be found were seized. Even the grave was rifled. The bodies of Cromwell, Brad-

* Hume, vol. 2, p. 432. Mr. Hume thinks these severities very mild, considering that they followed such furious civil wars and convulsions; a conclusion from which we dissent for reasons recited in the text.

† Bancroft, Hist., vol. 1; Wilson, Pilgrim Fathers. etc.

‡ Burnet's Own Times. Richard Cromwell died at Theobalds, in 1712; Neale.

§ Life and Times of John Milton, Amer. Tract Society, 1866; Todd's Life; Ivimey.

shaw, and Ireton were dug up; and with a malice as pitiful as it was blasphemous, these were drawn on hurdles to Tyburn gallows, where they hung from sunrise to sunset; then they were huddled into one hole at the foot of the scaffold:* Blake, who had carried the thunders of the British cannon "from Ganges to the icebergs," and enthroned the navy mistress of the seas, was disturbed in his last sleep;† and the body of Mrs. Claypole, the Protector's daughter, was likewise insulted in the grave.‡ Lambert was sentenced to perpetual imprisonment at the isle of Jersey. Ten of the regicides suffered death with Christian firmness.§ The political pamphlets of Milton were called in by proclamation, and burned by the common hangman.‖ A little later, Sir Harry Vane, whom the king had promised on his honor to pardon, was sacrificed to the ghost of the earl of Strafford.¶ He sleeps

> "In peace, with kindred ashes
> Of the noble and the true;
> Hands that never failed their country,
> Hearts that never baseness knew."

Now the papists, emboldened by the patronage of the king, began to creep from their corners; and

* King James' Memoirs; Kennet's Register; Parl. Hist.

† Ibid. ‡ Headley's Cromwell; Carlyle, etc.

§ State Trials, Hume, Neale.

‖ Neale, vol. 2, p. 488; Milton's Lives.

¶ Neale, vol. 2, p. 514. Vane would not petition for his life, but said, "If the king has no greater regard for his word than for my life, he can take it." He died with serene composure. At the scaffold he was not allowed to speak; on which he said, "'T is a sorry cause which cannot bear the words of a dying man." Neale.

with the craft and patience peculiar to their system, they gradually wormed themselves into the confidence of the government, wriggled into office, and eventually made converts of the duke of York and of Charles himself.*

Through all these changes there was no disturbance; England, sick of war, seemed willing to consent to any thing for the sake of peace. The only thing that looked like an *émeute* was a crazy foray of two or three score fifth-monarchy men, who avowed their determination to upset the Restoration in favor of king Jesus.† This was of course easily suppressed, and the storm exploded in a laugh.

Nevertheless this mad raid of forty heated fanatics was made a pretext for an invasion of the recent royal declaration of indulgence, and an order of council forbade the assembly of the sectaries except at stated seasons and at specified places.‡ The Independents, the Baptists, and the Quakers petitioned the king against this mandate, and asserted their desire to live quietly and acquiescently under the Restoration. But the prayer of these despised sects went in at one ear and out at the other of the scoffing monarch.

In 1661, renewed revelry and debauchery were occasioned by the king's marriage with the Infanta of Portugal. "This match," says Neale, "was pro-

* Burnet's Own Times; Hallam, Cons. Hist.; King James' Memoirs; Harris, Life of Charles II.

† Hume, vol. 2; Neale, vol. 2, p. 490, etc.

‡ Crosby's and Ivimey's Hist. of the Baptists; Neale, Burnet, Harris.

moted by Monk and Clarendon. It was reckoned very strange that a Protestant chancellor should advise the king to marry a papist princess, when a Romanist king proposed at the same time a Protestant consort. But Clarendon had further views, for it was the general gossip among the merchants that the Infanta could have no children; in which case the chancellor's daughter, who had been privately married to the king's brother, must succeed, and her issue by the duke of York, afterwards James II., would become heirs to the throne, which actually happened in the persons of queen Mary II. and queen Anne."*

But while these intrigues were provoking comment at court and on 'change, the "Convention parliament," as it was called, because it had met without the sanction of the royal writs, was dissolved. Its members had been elected before the Restoration, and while the Presbyterians were dominant; consequently it had been a check on the exuberant loyalty of the Cavaliers, and it had long ceased to reflect public opinion.†

Early in 1661 a new election was held, and the most zealous and fiery Cavaliers were returned to the House of Commons; indeed it has been justly said that they were more zealous for royalty than the king, and more zealous for Episcopacy than the bishops. With the action of this parliament we shall presently become acquainted.

* Neale, vol. 2, p. 493.

† Burnet's Own Times; Harris, Charles II.; Hume, Hist. Eng.

CHAPTER XXXI.

"BLACK ST. BARTHOLOMEW."

ON the 25th of March, 1661, the famous Conference was commenced at the Savoy. Each party was represented by twenty-one disputants; and the professed object was, to advise upon and review the Book of Common Prayer, for the purpose of giving satisfaction to tender consciences, and to maintain the unity of the church.*

A prolonged and able debate ensued. The Episcopal cause was defended by Gunning, a man of large reading and a subtle reasoner. The Presbyterian argument was pleaded by Baxter.† "Things were carried on at the Savoy with great sharpness and many reflections," remarks Burnet. "The Conference broke up without doing any good. It did rather hurt, and heightened the asperity that was then in people's minds to such a degree that it needed no addition to make it higher. The bishops insisted on the laws as they were still in force. The Presbyterians laid their complaints before the king; but little regard was had to them. And now all the concern that seemed to employ the prelates' thoughts was, not only to make no alteration in easement of the Liturgy, but to make the terms of

* Reliquiæ Baxterianæ, part 2; Neale, Newell, Burnet.

† Baxter's Life and Times.

conformity much stricter than they had been before the war."*

Fresh from the sanction of the bishops at the Savoy, the Liturgy was dispatched to the Convocation then in session with the Parliament, and the Episcopal divines were directed in their turn to review it, and to make such additions and amendments as they thought proper. "Some lesser alterations were made," says Burnet; "they took in more lessons out of the Apocrypha, in particular the story of Bel and the Dragon; new offices were also made for two new days, the 30th of January, called King Charles the Martyr, and the 29th of May, the day of the king's birth and return; but care was taken that nothing should be changed as it had been moved by the Presbyterians."†

When this was done, the Convocation returned the Prayer-book to the king, who immediately sent it to the Parliament.‡

The Commons had commenced their session by voting that each member should, on pain of expulsion, take the sacrament as prescribed by the old Liturgy, and that the Covenant should be burned by the hangman in the Palace-yard. Next an act was passed which declared that in no imaginable extremity could the two houses be justified in resisting the royal authority by force. A statute was framed which compelled every corporation officer to take an oath to the same effect. The bishops

* Burnet's Own Times, p. 124. † Ibid., p. 125.

‡ Baxter, Hume, Neale, Burnet.

were restored to their seats in the upper house. And now, on the receipt of the revised Prayer-book, a biting Act of Uniformity was passed, which for the first time made Episcopal ordination an indispensable qualification for church preferment. St. Bartholomew's day, August 24, 1662, was fixed as the date when the new law should be put into execution.*

At length the blow had fallen. Non-conformity, sad and worn, had done its utmost, and made a gallant fight; but it now met its Waterloo.

The authorities did not wait for the time appointed to arrive before commencing their campaign, though no overt act was yet committed. The doctrine of passive obedience was once more preached.† The most inveterate high-churchmen were preferred to bishoprics.‡ The sequestered revenues were again collected.§ Clergymen, bewildered and ofttimes crazed by the return of prosperous days, employed themselves, like Milton's mammon, in piling up gold, careless of judgment, righteousness, and the world to come, if only they might make the heap high and massy. "What the bishops did with their great fines"—these are Burnet's words—"was a pattern to the lesser dignitaries, who generally took more care of themselves than of the church. The men of service were loaded with many livings and dignities. With this ac-

* Macauley, Hume, etc.

† Neale, vol. 2, p. 484; Burnet, Hallam, Macauley.

‡ Ibid. § Ibid.

cession of wealth there broke in upon the Establishment a flood of luxury and high-living on pretence of hospitality; and with this overset of gold and pomp which came upon men in the decline of life, those who were now growing into old age became lazy and negligent in spiritual interests."*

In this *interim* the church of Scotland was revolutionized. Episcopacy was established on the north side of the Tweed; and a few months later Ireland also accepted the English Establishment.†

At length black St. Bartholomew arrived. "The Presbyterians remembered what a St. Bartholomew's had been at Paris ninety years before," and they compared the days. This *formula* was tendered to every rector, lecturer, and clerk in the island: Re-ordination, if not already episcopally ordained; a declaration of unfeigned assent to all and every thing prescribed and contained in the ritual of the Established church; the oath of canonical obedience; the abjuration of the League and Covenant; the abjuration of the lawfulness of taking arms against the king, or any one commissioned by him, on any, the most weighty, pretence.‡

To these terms of conformity, severer than those prescribed by Laud himself, no Puritan could subscribe. The result was, ejectment. Two thousand clergymen, on this one black day, were expelled from their livings, and reduced to beggary. "No provision," observes Burnet, "was made for the main-

* Burnet's Own Times. † Ibid., Hume, Clarendon, etc.

‡ Statutes of the Realm, Parl. Hist., Neale, Hume.

tenance of the sequestered preachers; a severity neither practised by Elizabeth when she enacted her Liturgy, nor by Cromwell in ejecting the royalists, in both which cases a fifth part of the benefice was reserved for their subsistence. Here were many men much valued, some on better grounds and some on worse, who were now cast out of the Establishment ignominiously, reduced to pinching poverty, provoked by much spiteful usage, and cast upon those popular practices which both their principles and their circumstances seemed to justify, of forming separate congregations, and of diverting men from the public worship, and from considering their successors as the lawful pastors of those churches in which they had served."*

The pecuniary bight came here: the payment of each year's tithes fell due on Michaelmas; St. Bartholomew's day came before it, and all Non-conformists would lose a twelve-months' income, which to these poor husbands and fathers was absolute ruin.† Still a beggared purse was better than an undone conscience; and these spiritual heroes accepted their fate as serenely as they could had they been bidden to a feast. Some of the parishioners of these clergymen could not understand their scruples. "Ah," said one countryman to the vicar of Ormskirk, as that pastor stood in the door-yard of

* Burnet's Own Times, p. 126.

† Ibid. Stoughton, Neale, Newell. Burnet states that the Commons fixed on St. Bartholomew's day for that very purpose, p. 126.

his tranquil home—his no longer—and gazed with a heavy but patient heart at the dear, familiar landscape, "Ah, sir, we would gladly have you still preach in our church." "Yes," was the reply, "I would as gladly preach as you can desire it, if I could do it with a safe conscience." "Oh," retorted the man, "many nowadays make a *great gash* in their consciences; can't you make a *little nick* in yours?"*

But they could not; and such self-sacrificing heroism was more eloquent than their sermons; it was an afflatus of the Spirit of that gentle Jesus who whispered from the accursed tree, "Father, forgive them; for they know not what they do."

Thus closed "black St. Bartholomew;" and the day is linked for ever in English history with a pathos which is near akin to its bloody interest in the annals of mediæval France. In one country it was a holocaust of corpses; in the other it was a massacre of stricken souls.

> "Good Heaven, what sorrows gloomed that parting day,
> That called them from their native walks away;
> When the poor exiles, every pleasure past,
> Hung round their bowers, and fondly looked their last.
> With loudest plaints the mother spoke her woes,
> And blessed the cot where every pleasure rose,
> And kissed her thoughtless babes with many a tear,
> And clasped them close, in sorrow doubly dear,
> While her fond husband strove to lend relief,
> In all the silent manliness of grief."

The spirit of the Bartholomew act was that of haughty and vindictive retaliation, beneath the dig-

* Stoughton, Spiritual Heroes of Puritan Times, p. 291.

nity of statesmen, and unworthy of the character of Christians. The Puritans, and especially the Presbyterians, had, in the day of their power, undoubtedly given cruel provocation. They ought to have learned, if from nothing else, yet from their own discontents, from their own struggles, from their own victory, from the fall of that proud hierarchy by which they had been so heavily oppressed, that in England, and in the seventeenth century, it was not in the power of the civil magistrate to drill the minds of men into conformity with any prescribed discipline.* Some of the Puritan sects did learn and practise this lesson; but even so fine a character as Baxter plainly told king Charles, after the Restoration, that he did not believe in the toleration of Papists and Socinians.†

Still this does not excuse the Act of Uniformity. "I must own," says Fuller, "that in my judgment, however both sides have been excessively to blame, yet that the severities used by the church towards the dissenters are less excusable than those used by the dissenters towards the church. My reason is, that the former were used in time of peace and a settled government, whereas the latter were inflicted in times of tumult and confusion; so that the plunderings and ravagings endured by the churchmen were owing, many of them at least, to the rudeness of soldiers and the chances of war; they were plundered, not because they were conformists, but Cavaliers; but no mercy was shown these un-

* Newell, Macauley.

† Neale, vol. 2, p. 476.

happy sufferers, though it was impossible on a sudden to fill up the gap that was made by their removal."*

One of the worst features of this act was, that it gagged preachers of that same Protestant faith which its framers professed, and drove from the pulpits, which could not then be adequately filled, men who had been faithful to their consciences; nay, it harassed them with cruel persecution if they lifted up their voices for the instruction and consolation of the bereaved and insulted people on whose free-will offerings they were thrown.†

At this very time the author of "The Five Groans of the Church," a very strict conformist, complained that above three thousand ministers were admitted into the church who were unfit to teach because of their youth; that fifteen hundred debauched men were ordained; that illiterate men were preferred to benefices; and that out of about twelve thousand livings, three thousand were impropriate, that is, granted to laymen; and four thousand one hundred and sixty-five were *sinecures*.‡

Bad as it was, the Act of Conformity did not stand alone, an isolated monument of folly and wicked tyranny. In 1663 it was reinforced by the *Conventicle Act*, which condemned all persons frequenting "any meetings under color or pretence of any exercise of religion other than is allowed by the Liturgy of the church of England" to heavy fine for

* Fuller's Worthies. † Newell, p. 333.

‡ Cited in Neale, vol. 2, pp. 520, 521.

the first offence, to fine and imprisonment for the second offence, to banishment to the American plantations—other than New England and Virginia, where they would find coreligionists—for the third offence.* At the same time, all persons refusing peremptorily to attend the Established church were condemned to banishment; and on return, to death without benefit of clergy†—statutes which, for cold-blooded malignity, surpass the code of Draco. The Act of Uniformity was to this as "Hyperion to a satyr." That expelled men from the benefices of the church; this ejected them from the privileges of society. Half the kingdom was outlawed. A reign of terror was inaugurated, rivalling that which, in a later age, frenzied the Parisian populace. Spies lurked in every corner; informers leered from behind every blind. Men guilty only of loving their Creator were torn from their families, imprisoned, ruined by fines, tortured in the pillory, banished from their homes, or hanged upon the gallows. To attend a conventicle became a damning crime, and it required the cleverest precaution. The catacomb days of English Christianity were revived. The Puritans met in dark alleys, in upper garrets, or in the woods at midnight. In some seasons the forests were a favorite sanctuary; and "beneath the shades of lofty pines or overhanging elms, or round the gnarled trunks of oaks that had stood for ages, forming temples of God's own build-

* Statutes of the Realm; Parl. Hist.

† Ibid.; Neale, vol. 2, pp. 531, 532; Hallam,

ing, the hunted and peeled brotherhood assembled to hear the word of God."*

At other times, when the eye of human observation was sealed by sleep, they would steal into an upper chamber; and having entered, they would make fast the door, and close the window-shutters, and even extinguish the candle, lest its glimmer might be discerned by some prowler through a crevice. Then the night would be spent in prayer, until the ray of morning light, struggling down the chimney, announced the time to disperse. Thus men learned that darkness hideth not from God, but the night shineth as the day; and that "the Father, who seeth in secret, shall reward us openly."†

Often, however, all precautions proved futile: the jails were soon crowded; families were divided and distracted; yet no breach of the peace occurred.

"I saw several of these poor people," writes Pepys, a high-churchman whose heart was touched by these scenes, in his diary, under the year 1664, "carried by constables for being at a conventicle. They go like lambs, without any resistance; and would to God they would either conform or be more wise, and not be catched."‡

"*Fiat justitia, ruat cœlum*," said an enthusiastic Presbyterian royalist, when conversing with an Independent friend in regard to bringing in Charles II. "*Ruit cœlum*," remarked this friend on meet-

* Stoughton, p. 303.

† Pearsall's Outlines of Congregationalism, etc., p. 94.

‡ Cited in Stoughton, p. 304.

ing him after the passage of the Uniformity and Conventicle acts.*

The king at this time claimed a *dispensing power*, which enabled him to suspend at his pleasure all these harsh penal codes.† This was never exerted for the benefit of the Puritans; but by this shallow trick the Papists were often eased; and now in these fierce times they had the good fortune to be covered under the wing of the prerogative.‡

Some of the old Cavaliers had some compunctions of conscience when they beheld such wide-spread consternation and distress. But in this weakness Clarendon and Sheldon, the twin authors of the persecution,§ did not share. When the earl of Manchester told the king that the terms of conformity were so strict that he feared many of the ministers could not comply, Bishop Sheldon made this reply: "I have been afraid they would; but now that we know their real minds, we will post them all as knaves if they do conform." "Yet after all," said Dr. Allen, "'t is a pity the door is so strait." "'T is no pity at all," responded the proud churchman; "if we had imagined that so many would conform as have done so, we would have made it straiter; these sects must be crushed."‖

This shows the *animus* of the court. Listen now to the wise words of Locke, in his "Third Letter on

* Palmer's Non-conformist Memorial, vol. 2, p. 432.

† Neale, vol. 2, p. 528.

‡ Ibid., p. 532; Hume, Macauley.

§ Burnet's Own Times, p. 126.

‖ Cited in Newell, p. 331.

Toleration:" "They who talk so much of sects and divisions, would do well to consider whether those are not most authors and promoters of sects and divisions who impose creeds, ceremonies, and articles of men's making, and make things not necessary to salvation the necessary terms of salvation; who narrow Christianity within bounds of their own making; and often, for things by themselves confessed indifferent, thrust men out of their communion, and then punish them for not being in it."*

We commend this page from Locke to the thoughtful consideration of the Sheldons of our century.

It has been well said, that this whole chapter of circumstances is disgraceful to all parties excepting the sufferers. The king was convicted of dissimulation, the leaders of the church of treacherous cruelty, and the Parliament of grossly neglecting, in the heat of their passionate loyalty, that justice which was due to every subject of the realm, and those grand principles of liberty which are at once the ornament and the safeguard of nations. These abhorrent statutes, instead of promoting unity and cementing peace, multiplied the divisions of the conscientious, and gave a bribe to discord.

* Locke's Letter to a Person of Quality.

CHAPTER XXXII.

THE HEROES OF THE EXODUS.

It is a high speech of Sir Philip Sidney, that "the great, in affliction, bear a countenance more princely than they are wont; for it is the temper of the highest hearts, like the palm-tree, to strive most upwards when most burdened." Discrowned Puritanism, now buried in the "valley of humiliation," is at once a vindication and an illustration of this apothegm. Yet the voice of its apostles was

> 'Unchanged
> To hoarse or mute, though fallen on evil days,
> On evil days though fallen, and evil tongues;
> In darkness, and with dangers compassed round,
> And solitude."

They did not murmur, nor did they covet the "pleasant places" in which the "lines" of their persecutors had fallen. "An English merchant that then lived in Dantzic," says old Firmin, "once went to a convent and dined with some friars: his entertainment was very noble. After he had dined and saw all, the merchant fell to commending their pleasant lives. 'Yes,' said one of the friars, 'we live gallantly indeed, had we anybody to go to hell for us when we die!'"* Men who are sure of "the 'all hail' hereafter," may calmly pocket the affronts and the privations of the scornful present.

* Firmin, The Real Christian, p. 63; London, 1670.

Let us now quit for a moment the highway of our history, and wandering in the by-paths of the story, reverently gather up a few of those anecdotal and biographical incidents which vivify and individualize the exodus of 1662.

One of the central figures of that epoch was Richard Baxter. Born in 1615, his life covers the larger part of the seventeenth century.* Though always resting under broken health, his life was an active apostleship, and he lived to see his seventy-seventh year.† Baxter was the argumentative and speculative representative of Puritanism. One of the most voluminous writers of any age,‡ his clear, bold, incisive doctrines early pushed him into the leadership of his party, and secured for him the active and persevering hostility of the ultramontanists. Never was the alliance of soul and body formed on terms of greater inequality than in his person. "It was like the compact in the fable, where all the spoils and honors fell to the giant's share, while the poor dwarf put up with all the danger and the blows. The mournful list of his chronic diseases renders almost miraculous the mental vigor which bore him through exertions resembling those of a disembodied spirit. But his ailments were such as, without affecting his mental powers, gave repose to his animal appetites, and

* Reliquiæ Baxterianæ; Orme's Life and Times of R. Baxter, vol. 1.

† Ibid.; Tullock, English Puritanism and its Leaders, p. 287.

‡ See Orme's account of Baxter's writings in vol. 2 of his Life.

quenched the thirst for all the honors and emoluments of this life. Death, though delaying to strike, stood continually before him, ever quickening his attention to that awful presence by approaching the victim under some new or varied aspect of disease."* Under this influence he wrote and spoke. It was the secret of his power; and he has himself said, in his immortal couplet,

"I preached as never sure to preach again,
And as a dying man to dying men."

Baxter was one of the earliest, as he was one of the most illustrious sufferers under the Act of Uniformity; and at the age of forty-seven, bowed down beneath infirmities, he was driven from his cure at Kidderminster, to spend the remnant of his days alternately in citations before abandoned magistrates, from Jeffries down to the lowest pot-house justices, in filthy jails and precarious hiding-places.†

Yet such was Baxter's zeal, that despite the vigilant repressive hand of the law, it still bubbled over into channels of multifarious activity. Soon after the ejectment, he took up his residence in the city of Coventry, and here he was accustomed to lecture in a private house on a neighboring common, near the hamlet of Berkswell. He spoke generally at a very early hour, sometimes before the day opened its eyes. On one occasion he left Coventry in the evening for the purpose of delivering

* Brewer, Men of the Exodus of 1662, pp. 38, 39.

† Reliquiæ Baxterianæ, Brewer, Orme.

the usual lecture in the grey of the next morning. As the night was dark, he lost his way, and after wandering at random for some hours, he paused at a way-side mansion to inquire the road. The servant who came to the door informed his master that a person of very respectable appearance had lost his way. The gentleman told the servant to invite him in. Baxter readily complied, and met with a very hospitable reception. His conversation was such as to give his host an exalted idea of his good sense and extensive information.

Baxter's entertainer, wishing to know the quality of his guest, said, after supper, "As most persons have some employment or profession in life, I have no doubt, sir, that you have yours." Baxter replied with a smile, "Yes, sir, I am a man-catcher." "A man-catcher," said the host, "are you? I am very glad; you are the very man I want. I am a justice of the peace in this district, and I am commissioned to secure the person of Dick Baxter, who is expected to preach in this neighborhood early to-morrow morning. You shall go with me, and I doubt not we shall easily apprehend the rogue."

Baxter very prudently consented to accompany the justice. Accordingly they both set out in the early dawn for the Puritan rendezvous. On their arrival, a number of persons were observed hovering about; but seeing the carriage of the justice, and suspecting his intention, they would not enter the house. "My friend," said the justice to Baxter, "I fear they have obtained some information of my design. Baxter has probably been apprized of it, for you see the people will not assemble. I think that if we extend our ride, our departure may induce them to collect, and on our return we can fulfil our commission."

They rode on; when they returned they found their efforts useless, for the people still appeared unwilling to enter the house. The magistrate, thinking he should be disappointed in his object, remarked to his companion that, "as the people were much disaffected to the government, he would be much obliged to him if he would address them on the subject of loyalty and good behavior." Baxter replied, "Perhaps that would not be deemed sufficient; for as they have assembled for religious service, they would not be satisfied with advice of such a nature; but if the magistrate would begin with prayer, I make no doubt that they would listen to our remarks, and I will endeavor to say something to them." The justice, putting his hand to his pocket, said, "Indeed, sir, I have forgotten my prayer-book, or I would readily comply with your proposal. However, I am persuaded that a person of your appearance and respectability would be able to pray as well as talk with them. I beg therefore that you will begin with prayer."

Baxter assented; then alighting from the carriage, they entered the building, and the people, hesitating no longer, followed them in.

Baxter commenced the service by prayer, and prayed with that seriousness and fervor for which he was so eminent. The magistrate was soon melted into tears. The great divine then preached in his accustomed lively and zealous manner. When he had concluded, he turned to his host of the previous night, and said, "I, sir, am that Dick Baxter of whom you are in pursuit. I am entirely at your disposal."

The magistrate had felt so much, and had seen things in so different a light in the solemn service of the grey dawn, that he laid aside all enmity to the Non-conformists, was ever after their firm friend, and became a sincere Christian.* Was not that a sweet and blessed *ruse?*

John Howe, though fifteen years the junior of Baxter, was that great theologian's friend and fellow-laborer. He was one of the most noble, spiritual, and gentle of men. His lofty soul was bottomed on combined earnestness and refinement. To the glow of the Puritan religious feeling, he added a chastened taste and a singular radiance of imagination.†

Howe was one of the most persuasive of preachers. Others might rouse more by their vehemence and attract more by their doctrine, but none approached him in dignity and a certain mixture of sweetness and sublimity of sentiment. Especially when he descanted on the glories of heaven, and his large imagination found room to expatiate amid

* Independency in Warwickshire, by J. Sibree and M. Caston.

† Tullock, Palmer, Brewer.

its felicities, he rose into a pictured eloquence which was wonderfully impressive.*

In happier days Howe had been chaplain to Cromwell;† but weary of the court, he had prevailed upon the Protector to dismiss him to his quiet parish at Torrington; and it was while "doing the work of an evangelist" in this retired nook that the Act of Uniformity was passed.‡ *Apropos*, a fine anecdote is told which illustrates at once Howe's catholicity and one of its results.

It happened in Cromwell's time that the office of "Principal" in Jesus college, Oxford, became vacant, and Dr. Seth Ward was a candidate for it. Knowing Howe to be high in favor, Ward went to him and solicited his influence with the Protector to obtain the appointment. Howe introduced him to Cromwell, and so strongly recommended him that, though the place had been already promised another applicant, Ward obtained an equivalent annual allowance. Since Ward was an avowed Episcopalian, this exhibits Howe's broad and tolerant spirit.§ Under the Restoration, Ward was preferred to the bishopric of Exeter, and Howe's parish was embraced within his diocese. A few days after the passage of the Act of Uniformity, as Howe was returning to his rectory from some neighboring chapel, he was told that an officer had been

* Tullock, Palmer, Brewer.

† Baxter's Life, Brewer, Coleman, English Confessors, etc.

‡ Stoughton, Church and State Two Hundred Years ago.

§ Brewer, p. 46.

to his house armed with the episcopal authority to arrest him as a non-conformist. Howe went straight to Exeter, not to remind him of former obligations, but " to await his lordship's pleasure." The bishop contented himself with attempting to induce his sometime benefactor to conform, and that failing, he stayed all proceedings.*

A few years later, however, Howe was ejected from his living and imprisoned.† Afterwards he lived in exile during five years. He then returned to London, and became the pastor of a congregation of dissenters who worshipped in Silver-street chapel.‡ Here he lived on intimate terms with many of the dignitaries of the English church, and especially with Tillotson, afterwards archbishop of Canterbury.§ His virtues and eloquence disarmed enmity, and he might have gained a bishopric by conforming. But he remained true to his convictions, and breasted whatever opposition he could not placate until sheltered beneath the ægis of king William's toleration in 1688.‖ Howe's life touched the year 1705; then, having " served his generation by the will of God, he fell asleep, and was gathered to his fathers." Howe's most famous work, "The Blessedness of the Righteous," is the fit companion of Baxter's "Saints' Everlasting Rest"—*par nobile fratrum*—both Christian classics.

* Brewer, p. 46. † Stoughton, Coleman.

‡ Brewer, p. 49.

§ Williams, Story of the Two Thousand of 1662.

‖ Ibid.; Brewer.

Owen was another of the great men of that time. If Baxter was the copious defender, if Howe was the contemplative idealist, Owen was the theologian of Puritanism. "The main interest of his life and all the interest of his writings is theological. Whatever is most characteristic and essential in Puritan divinity is to be found in his works. A bolder, more unflinching theorist never trod the way of those sublime revelations which 'slope through darkness up to God.' Along with scholastic earnestness, profound devotion to scriptural studies, and a life of eminent spirituality, we find in Owen a combined practical sense and business faculty which make him to resemble Calvin his prototype. He had the same administrative power, the same patience and coolness of purpose, with a far higher courtesy and tolerance of feeling. Hard and somewhat dogmatic in intellect, he was genial and gentle in his temper. Resolute in his own views, and ever ready to contend for them with his unresting pen, he had none of the meanness of bigotry. He protected Pocknock in his Hebrew professorship from the interference of the parliamentary triers when vice-chancellor of Oxford, and he left the prelatists unmolested when they assembled opposite his door to worship according to the Prayer-book."*

Of course the simple "I say so" of the government was powerless to coerce such a man as Owen into conformity; and when despotic intolerance

* Tullock, pp. 282, 283.

proffered him ease and honor with a gag, and fealty to conscience with stripes, and cried, "Choose," he did choose, and with a brave and trustful heart bore and forgave

> "The spurns
> That patient merit of the unworthy takes."

Although the ill-usage of John Bunyan began before the enactment of the Bartholomew act, the persecution which hunted him into Bedford jail was the offspring of the same bigotry which gave birth to the misshapen progeny of 1662—was an elder imp of the same vile brood. The honored tinker of Elstow therefore properly falls into rank beside the heroes of the exodus. It has been well said, that "in the character and history of John Bunyan, the great Head of the church seems to have provided a lesson of special significance and singular adaptedness for the men and the strifes of our own time. Born of the people, and in so low a condition that one of his modern reviewers, by a strange mistake, construed his self-disparaging admissions to mean that he was the offspring of gypsies; bred to one of the humblest of handicrafts, and having but the scantiest advantages as to fortune and culture, he yet rose, under the blessings of God's word and providence and Spirit, to the widest usefulness, and to an eminence that shows no tokens of decline."*

* W. R. Williams, D. D., in Prefatory Notice of "Riches of Bunyan," Amer. Tr. Soc., 1851.

Born at Elstow in 1628, Bunyan's youth was spent in wild and reckless profanity. But eventually his soul was clutched "from the body of that death," and a little later he attached himself to a religious society of the Baptist persuasion in Bedford, where he received the seal of his apostleship.* Soon he began to preach; and the plain speaking of which he was enamoured, the downright sincerity of his character, and the popularity of his ministry among the people, made him obnoxious to local vigilance and jealousy.†

On one occasion Bunyan was cited before Justice Keelin for refusing to attend the Established church, and also for being an upholder of unlawful conventicles. He was obliged to listen to such words as these, uttered in the name of English justice and coming from the lips of a drunken magistrate: "Hear your judgment: you must be back to prison, and there lie for three months; and at three months' end, if you do not submit to go to church to hear divine service, and leave your preaching, you shall be banished the realm. If after such a day as shall be appointed you to be gone, you shall be found in England, or be found to come into it again without the king's license, you must stretch by the neck for it. I tell you plainly."

To this random and vindictive harangue, Bunyan replied, "As to this matter, I am at point with you; for if I were out of prison to-day, I would

* Tullock, English Puritanism, etc.; Sketch of Bunyan.

† Offor, Mem. of Bunyan; Philips, Life of Bunyan.

preach the gospel to-morrow, by the help of God."*

Bunyan was hustled off to prison. The jails of that day were very different from those of this age. Instead of being castles in miniature, they were magnificent pigsties, where pollution courted disease, and incipient wickedness was nourished into gigantic crime. The dungeon into which Bunyan was thrust at this time was twelve feet square, and built between two of the arches of the old bridge of Bedford. Being for the most part below the water's level, the walls were continually damp and sheeted with mildew. In this den Bunyan was kept twelve years, and compelled to herd with a rabble of male and female profligates and felons.†

Here it was that the "immortal dreamer" saw his beatific visions, created his own little world, peopled it with the glorious creations of his transcendent genius, and watched his "Pilgrim's Progress" up through the gate Beautiful to the Celestial City.

Seated in his moist dungeon, with the slime beneath his feet, Bunyan drew upon the Scriptures for his doctrine, and upon the memory of his own experience for his pictures, and reared on this mixed soil the grandest allegory known to human letters. The writings of the Elstow tinker were the outgrowth of his Puritanism; and a religion which could produce men like Greatheart and Honest and

* Offor, Mem. of Bunyan; Philips, Life of Bunyan; Ivimey, History of English Baptists.

† Brewer, pp. 42, 43.

Christian and Faithful and Hopeful, and of which the gentle and tender-hearted Mercy was a fair representative, had certainly features both of magnanimity and of beauty. There is a simple earnestness and a pure-minded loveliness in Bunyan's highest creations that are very touching. Puritanism lives in his pages—spiritually and socially—in forms and in coloring which must ever command the sympathy and enlist the love of all good Christians.

While Bunyan, immured in the Bedford jail, was writing himself into immortality, his brothers in the faith were ejected from the ministry of that gospel which he loved. All who refused to give their "assent and consent" to every syllable of the Prayer-book, were ousted from their cures; the moderate Episcopalians, who, with the great pastor of Kidderminster, had no objection to "a form of prayer," but who would not take a sweeping and compulsory oath;* the strict Presbyterians, who, having been inducted into the ministry by the laying on of hands of the elders, refused to accept episcopal ordination; the Independents, headed by John Owen, who, though broken and in disgrace, "bated no jot of heart or hope;" and the Baptists, led by such worthies as Henry Jesse, Mr. Symonds, who was ejected from Southfleet, in Kent, and who—according to Edwards,† an author of those times who endeavored to accomplish by abuse

* Tullock, Reliquiæ Baxterianæ, etc.

† Author of Gangræna.

what *Hudibras* was written to accomplish by satire—actually propounded the strange doctrine of religious liberty, favoring "toleration and freedom for all men to worship God according to their consciences," and by Thomas Hardcastle, who afterwards became pastor of the far-famed Baptist chapel, Broadmead, Bristol.*

Far and wide over the land, in crowded city churches, in county towns, in rural villages, the same sad scene was enacted. Thomas Goodwin, formerly president of Magdalen college; Flavel of Dartmouth, whose thoughtful learning, exemplary piety, and impressive zeal formed the crown and the laurel of his ministry; Edmund Calamy, whose week-day lecture "was attended by many persons of the greatest quality, there being seldom so few as sixty coaches," and who, when preaching before General Monk after the Restoration, on "filthy lucre," said, "And why is it called 'filthy,' but because it makes men do base and filthy things? Some men," and he tossed his white handkerchief towards Monk's face, "will betray three kingdoms for filthy lucre's sake;"† Stephen Charnock, whose sound judgment, vivid imagination, and affecting appeals secured him a well-deserved popularity; Joseph Alleine, "tall and erect, with countenance sprightly and serene," to whose "lively seriousness" Baxter bears testimony, as also to his "great ministerial skilfulness in the public explication and

* Brewer, pp. 34, 35,

† Williams, Story of the Two Thousand, p. 57.

application of the Scriptures—so melting, so convincing, so powerful," of whom Newton tells us that he had "a holy heart that boiled and bubbled up with good matter;"* Thomas Vincent, the intrepid pastor who preached in the pulpits of clergymen who fled for their lives when London wailed under the plague; Annesley, a name so revered that John Wesley thought it an epitaph and a eulogium to write on the tombstone of his mother, "She was the youngest daughter of Dr. Annesley;"† Dr. Thomas Manton, for ten years incumbent of St. Paul's, Covent Garden, whose ministry was attended by many in high places in church and state, and who exercised a beneficent and wide-reaching Christian influence; Matthew Poole of St. Michael's Queen, in London, the annotator, whose "Synopsis," in five folio volumes, is an amazing treasure-house of learning; Gale, of wondrous scholarship;‡ John Ray, the celebrated naturalist; Philip Henry, the father of the well-known Matthew Henry the commentator, who was stopped in his godly labors by a series of acts as oppressive as they were dishonorable:§ these, and a host besides, "whose works do follow them," men of marvellous strength of intellect, depth of learning, devotedness of spirit, and effective piety, were saying or had said a calm, a tender,

* Williams, Story of the Two Thousand, p. 58.

† Southey, Life of Wesley; Brewer.

‡ Williams, Story of the Two Thousand, p. 58.

§ Brewer, p. 52; Sir J. B. Williams, Life of Philip Henry.

and a last farewell to their flocks.* As Wordsworth has hymned it:

> "Nor shall the eternal roll of praise reject
> Those unconforming, whom one rigorous day
> Drives from their cures, a voluntary prey
> To poverty and grief and disrespect,
> And some to want, as if by tempest wrecked
> On a wild coast. How destitute! did they
> Feel not that conscience never did betray,
> That peace of mind is virtue's sure effect;
> Their altars they forego; their homes they quit,
> Fields which they love, and paths they daily trod,
> And cast the future upon Providence,
> As men the dictates of whose inward sense
> Outweighs the world, whom self-deceiving wit
> Lures not from what they deem the cause of God."†

In the memoirs of Philip Henry we are informed that "within a few miles around him there were so many ministers turned out to the wide world, stripped of their maintenance and exposed to continual and unwonted hardships, as, with their wives and children—most of them having numerous families—made upwards of a hundred who lived on Providence, and who, though oft reduced to want and straits, were not forsaken, but were enabled to 'rejoice in the Lord, and to joy in the God of their salvation' notwithstanding; to whom the promise was fulfilled, 'So shalt thou dwell in the land, and verily thou shalt be fed.'"‡ Though God frequently calls his servants to pass through severe scenes of self-denial, of trial, of suffering in the path of duty, yet he does not desert the faithful, but succors them

* Williams, p. 59. † Wordsworth, Eccles. Sketches.

‡ Cited by Williams in his Story of the Two Thousand, p. 139.

with the strong arm of his deliverance. Though many of these clergymen were brought very low, had many children, were harassed by persecution, and though their friends were generally poor and unable to support them, yet one of the foremost of them solemnly affirmed that "in all his acquaintance he never knew nor could remember to have heard of any Non-conformist minister being in prison for debt."*

There are many well-authenticated anecdotes illustrative of this phase of the exodus. Let us cite one or two, and take these as fair specimens of all.

Mr. Henry Erskine, who had been minister at Cornhill, in Northumberland, suffered much after his ejectment, and had several remarkable interpositions in his behalf. He resided for a time at Dryburgh, where he and his family were often plunged in distress; once in particular, when the "cruse of oil and the barrel of meal" were entirely spent, so that when they had supped that night, there remained neither bread, meal, meat, nor money in the house. In the morning the young children began to cry for their breakfast, and their father endeavored to divert them, and at the same time he did what he could to encourage his wife and himself to depend upon that Providence which "feeds the young ravens when they cry." While he was thus engaged, a farmer knocked at the door, and called for some one to come and help him off with his

* Sir J. B. Williams, Life of Philip Henry.

load. Being asked from whence he came, and what he would have, he told them he came from the Lady Reburn, with some provisions for Mr. Erskine. He was told that he must be mistaken, and that his load was most likely for another Mr. Erskine who dwelt at Shirfield, in the same town. The man replied, "No, I know what I'm about; these things were sent to Mr. Henry Erskine. Come, some one, and help me off with the load, else I will throw it down at the door." He was assisted in carrying the sack into the house. On opening it, it was found to be filled with meat and meal. This incident gave the pious pastor no small encouragement to rely upon his bountiful Benefactor in all future straits of a kindred nature.*

At another time this same clergyman was in Edinburgh, and he was so reduced that he had but three half-pence in his pocket. As he walked about the streets, not knowing what to do, or what course to steer, he was accosted by a countryman who asked if he was not Mr. Henry Erskine. "Yes," said the minister. "Then," said the man, "I have a letter for you," which he accordingly delivered. In it were enclosed seven Scotch ducatoons, with these words written: "Sir, receive this from a sympathizing friend. Farewell." There was no name; and when Mr. Erskine turned to question the messenger, he was gone.†

Mr. Oliver Heywood, ejected from Coley, in

* Coleman, Two Thousand Confessors, p. 144.

† Ibid., ut antea.

Yorkshire, also suffered greatly after the loss of his income. On one occasion his children became impatient for food, and he called his servant Martha, who would not desert the family in their distress, and said to her, "Martha, take a basket, and go to Halifax: call upon Mr. North, a shop-keeper there, and desire him to lend me five shillings. If he is kind enough to do so, buy such things as you know we most want. The Lord give you good-speed; and meantime we will offer up our petition to Him who 'feedeth the young ravens when they cry.'" The girl went, but on reaching the house of Mr. North her heart failed her, and she passed and repassed the door again and again without going in to tell her errand. At length Mr. North himself coming to the shop-door and witnessing her strange behavior, called her to him and asked her if she was not Mr. Heywood's servant. When she told him that she was, he said to her, "I am glad to see you, as some friends have given me five guineas for your master, and I was just thinking how I could send the money." Upon this Martha burst into tears, and told her story. He was much affected, and told her to come to him if the like necessity should again return.

Having procured the necessary provisions, she hastened back to them, when, upon her entering the house, the children eagerly examined the basket, and the father, hearing the servant's story, smiled and said, "The Lord hath not forgotten to be gracious; his word is true from the beginning:

'They that seek the Lord shall not want any good thing.'"*

One of the most marked traits of these heroes of the exodus was their *irrepressibility*, if we may coin a word. No suffering could break the heart of their faith, no despotism could choke their gospel. They were "instant in season, out of season," in proclaiming the truth which God had given unto them. They uttered it from the pulpit so long as they were permitted to do so; when driven thence, they proclaimed it in unsympathizing courts, shot it from beneath their prison bars, and scattered it in benedictions from the scaffold itself. When one channel was blocked up, they discovered or created new ones. When they could not preach, they wrote, and the press became a broader pulpit. Many were the shifts to which they were put in the prosecution of their purpose. Mr. Thomas Jollie, after his ejectment, preached in his own house. To avoid being informed against—for he was a man of prudence as well as zeal—he adopted this contrivance: there being in the common sitting-room a staircase with a door at the bottom, he stood to preach on the second step; the door was cut in two, and while the lower part was shut, the upper part, being fastened to the other by hinges, would fall back on brackets, so as to form a desk. To this was fixed a string, by which he could easily draw it up on intelligence being given of the approach of informers by those who were appointed

* Coleman, Two Thousand Confessors, ut antea.

as sentinels to give notice; he then immediately went up stairs, so that when the enemy entered the room, they could not prove that he had been preaching.*

Mr. Henry Maurice, ejected from Strettin, in Shropshire, was once preaching in a private house, when a constable entered and commanded him to desist. The undaunted clergyman charged him in the name of the great God, whose word he was preaching, to forbear molesting him as he would answer for it at the last day. The officer hereon sat down, trembling, heard the preacher patiently till he concluded, and then quietly departed.†

These instances show that the story of the sufferings of the ejected, gloomy as is its general tone, is not unrelieved by gleams of romantic adventure and marvellous interpositions. It must have been a singular spectacle which one of these conventicles presented, when hundreds would assemble in some obscure lane, at dead of night, to listen to some beloved pastor, in an old-fashioned chapel, fitted with secret doors, leading to the roofs of the adjoining houses, so that, on the approach of the enemy, at the signal of the sentinels placed at the entrance, the whole congregation would vanish in a moment, and the astonished constables would find nothing within but empty benches.‡

Such was the life which the Non-conformists led

* Coleman, Two Thousand Confessors, pp. 148, 149.

† Ibid.

‡ Story of the Ejectment, lecture by Rev. T. McCrie, D. D.

under the Act of Uniformity, and under what was termed the "Five-Mile Act," which prohibited all ejected ministers from residing within five miles of their own cures, and which Burnet pronounced "a step in the progress of intolerant cruelty which only just fell short of the stake and the fire."*

The faithfulness of these men to conscience, their faith in God, their meekness, their devotedness to their life-work—these were the traits which lifted them above their persecutors, which crowned them with undying fame, which made them walk upon the stars. Ere long the indignity with which they were treated created a popular sympathy and indignation which helped largely to necessitate the revolution of 1688. 'T is only the universal history. The framers of unjust laws punish themselves; the contrivers of cruel and wicked acts are pursued by a just avenger, and their treatment of others made to recoil upon themselves.

> "Nec lex est justior ulla,
> Quam necis artifices arte perire suâ."

The more prominent of these sufferers have had their epitaph written by the muse of history; but that noble army of "obscure martyrs" who toiled not for the "all hail hereafter," but were content with the simple performance of their duty, these

> "Have no place in storied page,
> No rest in marble shrine;
> They are past and gone with a perished age,
> They died, and 'made no sign.'

* Burnet's Own Times.

But work that shall find its wages yet,
And deeds that their God did not forget,
  Done for the love divine—
These were their mourners, and these shall be
The crown of their immortality.

"They healed sick hearts till theirs were broken,
  And dried sad eyes till theirs lost sight;
We shall know at last by a certain token
  How they fought and fell in the fight.
Salt tears of sorrow unbeheld,
Passionate cries unchronicled,
  And silent strifes for the right;
Angels shall count them, and earth shall sigh
That she left her best children to battle and die."*

* Edwin Arnold's Obscure Martyrs.

CHAPTER XXXIII.

THE SCOURGES.

England now became a Pantheon of impiety. Religion was puritanical; virtue was disloyalty; honor was treason. Good men were hunted when alive, and disturbed when dead. Those Puritans who, in happier days, had been interred in Westminster Abbey, in Henry VIIth's chapel, or within the precincts of the collegiate church of Westminster, of both sexes and all ranks, were dug up and thrown into one pit in St. Margaret's church-yard.* Even the grave is no protection from the ghoul.

Profligate wits slobbered over decency with obscene jests. Never had public morality been at so low an ebb. "I remember," says Sir Matthew Hale, "that when Ben Jonson, in his play of the 'Alchemist,' introduced Anartus in derision of the Puritans, with many of their phrases taken out of Scripture, in order to render that party ridiculous, the comedy was detested because it seemed to reproach religion itself; but now, when the Puritans were brought again upon the stage in their peculiar habits, and with their distinguishing phrases of Scripture, and exposed to the laughter of spectators, the show met with approbation and applause."†

* Neale, vol. 2, p. 514; Pepys' Diary, 1667.

† Cited in Neale, vol. 2, p. 547.

The story of the wild men and manners of that age reads like a chapter culled from the pages of an obscene romance. Even the homage of hypocrisy was no longer paid to virtue. The play-houses were nests of prostitution.* The king, the queen, the courtiers wandered through the streets of London masked, noisy, and profane. The houses of quiet citizens were entered by these titled masqueraders, and indecencies were committed whose very memory paints the cheek with blushes. The ladies of the court hounded on these abhorrent revels; they were carried about in hackney chairs, preceded by footmen waving flaming flambeaux; and once, 't is said, the queen's chairman, not knowing who she was, left her at midnight to return to Whitehall in a cart.†

Not only did licentiousness taint the manners and corrupt the hearts of the aristocracy of the Restoration, it poisoned the letters of the epoch. From Dryden down to Durfey, the common characteristic was hard-hearted, swaggering sensuality, at once inelegant and inhumane.‡ The omnipresent profligacy of the plays, satires, songs, and novels of that day is a plague-spot, marked, ineffaceable, on English literature. Nothing was more characteristic of the times than the care with which poets contrived to put all their loosest verses into the

* Neale, vol. 2, p. 547.

† Rochester's Trial of the Poets, Jeremy Collier, Dryden's Life, etc.

‡ Shiel's Life of Southern; Some Account of the English Stage.

mouths of women. The compositions in which the greatest license was taken were the epilogues. These were always recited by favorite actresses; and nothing charmed the depraved play-goers so much as to hear lines grossly indecent repeated by a beautiful girl who was supposed to have not yet lost her innocence.*

Jeremy Collier broke many a stout lance against this reckless Jezebel of English comedy; but even he could not effect much against the spirit of his age; and, disgusted with his effort at reform, he might have recited those matchless words which Milton puts into the mouth of his chaste lady in the Mask of Comus:

> "Enjoy your dear wit and gay rhetoric,
> That hath so well been taught her dazzling fence;
> Thou art not fit to hear thyself convinced;
> Yet should I try, the uncontrollèd worth
> Of this pure cause would kindle my rapt spirit
> To such a flame of sacred vehemence,
> That dumb things should be moved to sympathize,
> And the brute earth would lend her nerves to shake,
> Till all thy impure structures, reared so high,
> Were shattered into heaps o'er thy false head."†

"The servile judges and sheriffs of those evil days," observes Macauley, "could not shed blood so fast as the poets called for it. Cries for more victims, hideous jests on hanging, bitter taunts on those who, having stood by the king in the hour of danger, now advised him to deal mercifully and generously by his vanquished enemies, were pub-

* Macauley; Pepys' Diary, 1667; Walpole's Anecdotes.

† Milton's Poetical Works, Mitford's edition, vol. 2, p. 259.

licly recited on the stage; and that nothing might be wanting to the guilt and the shame, were recited by women who, having long been taught to discard all modesty, were now taught to discard all compassion."*

God now sent a scourge, ghastly, awful, unprecedented, to choke these impious revels, and to cleanse this lazar-house. In 1665 the plague appeared. The terror had visited England before—once in the days of king James, and once before that—but never before had it spread its wings and swooped to such a desolating banquet. In the winter of 1664 it clutched its first victims.† Two men sickened in Drury Lane. Headache, fever, a burning sensation in the stomach, dimness of sight, livid spots upon the chest, these were the symptoms.‡ Gradually the dread disease spread; the weekly mortality lists told the freezing story. Through the spring it slyly crept, ever increasing its depredations, until by June, 1665, it threw off all disguise, opened its ghastly court, and in imitation of the aristocracy, held its revels, and laughed in a hideous carnival. In one night four thousand died; and in one month, ten thousand.§ Men fled in terror. All who could quit the smitten town made haste to do so; but multitudes tied by poverty or by duty to the city pavements might not leave.‖

"One shop after another was closed; one dwell-

* Macauley, Hist. of Eng., vol. 1, p. 317.

† Palmer's Non-conformist Memorial, sec. 6; Hume.

‡ Pepys' Diary. § Ibid. ‖ Ibid.

ing after another was robbed of its inmates. The long red cross, with the words, 'Lord, have mercy on us,' inscribed upon the door, indicated that within death was at work. The watchmen appointed by the magistrates stood at the entrance, armed with halberts, to prevent all communication between the inmates and outsiders. Instead of the busy crowds that once lined the thoroughfares, a few persons might be seen walking cautiously along the middle of the path, afraid of each other's touch. 'The highways were forsaken, and the travellers walked in byways.' A coach was rarely seen, save when, with curtains closely drawn, it conveyed some plague-smitten mortal to the pest-house. The wain, laden with timber and other material, had disappeared; men had no heart to build, and the half-finished structure was left to premature decay. The cart bearing provisions came not within the city-gate; the market was held in the outskirts, where the seller feared to touch the buyer, and the money was dipped in vinegar before passing from hand to hand. The London cries, the sound of music, the gay laugh of thoughtless pleasure, the din of trade had ceased.

> "'Life and thought had gone away side by side.'

The deep, unbroken solitude of the great city was overwhelming. Whole streets were desolate, doors left open, windows shattered with the wind, houses empty.

"Suddenly did the disease smite the sufferers.

Sometimes they dropped down in the streets; others perhaps had time to go to the next stall or porch, 'and just sit down and die.' The man who drove the death-cart expired on his way to the huge pit dug for the reception of thousands, or fell dead upon the heap of corpses that he was tumbling into that rude sepulchre. A person went home hale and strong; 'at evening there was trouble, and before morning he was not.'"*

Filled with awe, great numbers crowded to the churches, crying, "What shall we do to be saved?" Many of the parishes were deserted; all worldly priests deserted their posts in this crucial hour. Some of the Established clergy remained, "faithful among the faithless found," but the large majority fled in wild terror.† Then the Non-conformists replaced them; the ejected ministers broke the bread of life to these hungry and smitten souls; and all parties have since united to praise the faithful philanthropy which characterized their efforts.‡

"People flocked to preaching," says Vincent, one of the most tireless of the Puritan laborers through the plague, "and every sermon was unto them as if it were their last. Old Time seemed now to stand at the head of the pulpit with his great scythe, saying with a hoarse voice, 'Work while it is called day; at night I will mow thee down.' Grim Death seemed to stand at the side of the pulpit with his

* Stoughton, pp. 307, 308.

† Neale, vol. 2, p. 534; Stoughton.

‡ Ibid., Pepys' Diary, etc.

sharp arrow, saying, 'Do thou shoot God's arrows, and I will shoot mine.' The Grave seemed to lie at the foot of the pulpit, with dust in her bosom, croaking,

"'Louden thy cry
To God,
To men,
And now fulfil thy trust;
Here thou must lie;
Mouth stopped,
Breath gone,
And silent in the dust.'*

One hundred thousand victims glutted the maw of the pestilence; and it did not cease its ravages until the fall frosts nipped its sting."†

Strange to say, the weight of this calamity did not stun the drunken court into sobriety. "It will amaze all posterity," affirms Neale, "to learn that, in a time both of pestilence and when the Puritan ministers were jeoparding their lives in the service of the souls of distressed and dying citizens of London, the prime minister and his creatures, instead of mourning over the nation's sins and meditating a reformation of manners, should pour out all their vengeance upon the Non-conformists, in order to make their condition more insupportable. One would have thought that such a judgment from heaven, and such a generous compassion in the ejected clergy, should have softened the hearts of their most cruel enemies; but the Puritans were to

* Vincent, God's Terrible Voice in the City.

† Pepys' Diary, Stoughton, Neale, Hume.

be crushed in defiance of the rebukes of Providence; and as if the judgment of Heaven was not heavy enough, nor the legislation sufficiently severe, the bishops threw their weight into the scale; for in the very midst of the plague Archbishop Sheldon sent orders to the several diocesans of his province to return to him the names of all ejected non-conforming ministers, with their places of abode and manner of life. The design of this inquiry was, to gird the laws yet closer upon the dissenters, and by depriving them of their already slender means of livelihood, to starve them into exile or conformity.

"The vices of England not being sufficiently punished by pestilence and by war, which then raged with Holland, it pleased Almighty God, in 1666, to suffer the city of London to be laid in ashes by a dreadful conflagration, which blazed through three days, and consumed thirteen thousand two hundred dwelling-houses, eighty-nine churches, among which was St. Paul's, and many public structures, schools, libraries, and stately edifices.* Multitudes lost their goods and merchandise; the whole town changed its face; many of the nobility lost the greater part of their substance, and some few people lost their lives. The king, the duke of York, and the courtiers witnessed the desolation, but had not the power to check its progress, till at length it ceased almost as wonderfully as it began.

* Most of the antiquities of old London were lost at this time, and the city as rebuilt was essentially different from the London of the Tudors.

Moorfields was filled with household goods; the citizens were forced to lodge in huts and tents; and many families who were in the last week in prosperity, were now reduced to beggary, and obliged to commence the world again."*

The plague was the offspring of profligacy and total neglect of all sanitary laws. Sensuality was its father, and filth was its mother. The great fire is said to have been lighted by Jesuit incendiaries; and one of these was executed on his own confession.† Between these scourges Puritanism gained a brief respite, and gasped for breath. "But none of these calamities had any further influence upon the court prelates than that they dared not persecute the preachers so severely for the present."‡

* Neale, vol. 2, pp. 535–539. † Ibid. ‡ Ibid.

CHAPTER XXXIV.

THE LAST REVEL.

FOLLOWING hard upon the plague and the great fire came the downfall of Clarendon, premier of England. He lost the seals through his haughty insolence and opposition to the plainest maxims of constitutional law.* Clarendon was a bitter hater, and he used every wile to compass the destruction of Puritanism. "It was a great ease that befell good men when he was impeached and banished," says Rapin; "for he was wont to decoy those whom he hated into conspiracies or pretended plots, and then upon those rumors innocent people were laid in prison, so that no one's life was safe."†

Burnet informs us that "the king was highly offended at the unnatural behavior of the bishops. Sheldon and Morley, who kept close by Lord Clarendon, the great patron of persecuting power, lost the royal favor: the former never recovered it; the latter was sent from court into his diocese."‡

Meanwhile the rectitude, the diligence, the patience of the dissenters placated popular resentment; pity bred proselytes; and under the fiercest frown of oppression, their numbers visibly increased.§ Not only so, a nobler generation of church-

* Hallam, Hume, Macauley.

† Rapin, Hist. Eng., vol. 2. ‡ Burnet's Own Times.

§ Palmer's Non-conformists' Memorial; Neale.

men now came on the stage. Attempts were made from time to time to abate the rigors of those statutes which pressed conformity; and the threatening aspect of foreign affairs gave constantly increasing authority to these efforts. Protestantism was menaced on the Continent. Louis XIV. was in the full flush of his career of conquest. Spanish Flanders, overrun by the French armies, had just been yielded in full sovereignty to that haughty monarch who had said, "*L'état c'est moi!*"

Charles II., bribed by Louis' gold and cajoled by his French mistresses, looked on unconcerned;* but England was alarmed. The moderate churchmen and the moderate Cavaliers began to think that it was time to initiate a reform. Awed by the critical situation abroad, and spurred by the growing insolence of the Romanist party at home, such lawyers as the lord-keeper Bridgman and Chief-justice Hale, and such bishops as Tillotson and Stillingfleet, did their utmost to curb intolerance; esteeming it folly to batter brother Protestants with whom they disagreed on minor points, when the common enemy, Rome, thundered at the gate.†

Parliament too had changed. The Commons were weary of voting supplies which were lavished in debauchery; and they were disgusted with the feeble part which England now played in the European drama. Many a Cavalier recalled the iron days of the Protectorate, and sighed when he contrasted

* Harris, Life of Charles II.; Vaughan, Hist. of Eng.; James II., Mem.

† Rapin, Burnet's Own Times.

that time with this degenerate age, when the island stooped to be the paid lackey of a neighbor court.

These things made wise men anxious to secure peace and amity in the Protestant camp; and the moderates even went so far as to draw up a programme of comprehension.* Then the party of the past made a rally. The House of Commons was won to vote that no such proposition should be made on its floor. The jubilant bishops hurried to the king, and bothered him into the issue of a proclamation which directed the strict enforcement of the penal code against the Puritans.†

We have said that the king was *bothered* into this action: perhaps he was *bought;* for the "gift" of a sum of money would, notoriously, purchase the royal spendthrift's signature to any document.‡ At all events, it is certain that Charles favored a toleration, because he desired to permit the Romanists, whose coreligionist he secretly was even now, to secure a prestige which they could not gain while under the ban. So far however as their personal security went, they were, and had been, safely sheltered under the prerogative. The court swarmed with them. The duke of York was an open and energetic Jesuit. The chapels of the foreign ambassadors welcomed them to the interdicted service, and the mass was chanted at Whitehall by the confessors of the queen.§

* Carrel's Counter Revolution in England; Neale, Burnet.

† Rapin, Neale, Hume.

‡ Harris, Carrel, Neale, etc.

§ Baxter's Life and Times; Palmer, Rapin, Burnet.

Yet at such an hour, menaced from abroad, insidiously assailed from within, certain bishops of the Established church inaugurated a new persecution. Conventicles were forbidden; Non-conformists were once more hunted, and such men as Baxter and Taverner were flung into Newgate. The Conventicle Act expired in 1670; but it was galvanized into new life by a vote of the Commons, and made even more vicious than before, by the addition of two clauses—one of which bound all magistrates, under fine, to its stern execution, and thereby drove many honest and able judges from the bench;* and the other of which provided that the act should be construed most largely and beneficially for the suppression of conventicles, and for the encouragement and justification of all persons employed in its execution.†

This at once armed a multitude of informers, who took on as many shapes as Proteus, and who were as mischievously active and vindictive as Satan in Milton's poem.

Still the dissenters braved the act. Indeed, the Quakers made no attempt at concealment, meeting, with imperturbable heroism, at their accustomed hours and places. When dragged to prison, they made no resistance, and would pay no fines: and when their term of confinement expired, they went again to their wonted resorts. All this was done

* Neale, vol. 2, p. 549.

† Statutes of the Realm; Parl. Hist.; Carrel.

without bravado, but with the calm dignity of martyrdom.*

Parliament at length became alarmed at the increase of popery; and the Commons, after cementing an alliance with Sweden and Holland, known as "the Triple Alliance,"† proceeded to petition the king for the banishment of the Jesuits and the suppression of the Romanist worship in England.‡ Charles equivocated; the Commons persisted. Then the *debonnair* monarch dissolved the Parliament; and calling to his assistance five councillors—called, from the initial letters of their names, the CABAL§—undertook to govern by the prerogative.

Charles was bribed into this course by the bright *Louis d'or* of France and by the still brighter eyes of several new French mistresses.‖ If he aimed at absolute government, he would not trouble himself sufficiently to gain his goal, and was amply satisfied when his corrupt ministers acquired liberty to enact their pleasure. Whatever occurred, he was not to be troubled. His idea of monarchy was, ability to draw without limit on the national treasury for the gratification of his private tastes; wealth and honors with which to hire persons to help him kill the time; and "friends" willing to assist him, when the state was brought by maladministration to the depths of

* Sewel's Hist. of the Quakers; Neale.

† Sir William Temple's Memoirs. ‡ Parl. Hist.

§ Lord Clifford, a papist; Astley Cooper, afterwards Lord Shaftsbury; the duke of Buckingham, a debauché; Earl Arlington, a concealed papist; and Lord Lauderdale.

‖ Memoirs of James II.; Carrel, Rapin.

humiliation and the brink of ruin, in keeping the unwelcome truth from the purlieus of his *seraglio*.*

His new councillors were precisely to his taste. One was an avowed papist; another was a concealed one; still another was a *debauché;* and the last was an atheist.† And now both king and council became the puppets of France, mere echoes of Louis XIV. Seven hundred thousand pounds in French gold were poured into the pockets of this junto of profligates within twenty-four months—a very handsome retaining fee. Then Louis sent his programme across the channel: the gradual introduction of popery, under the guise of absolutism; two steps immediately to be taken, the marriage of the duke of York, recently a widower by the death of Clarendon's daughter, and the dissolution of the Triple Alliance by a war with Holland.‡

This mandate was obeyed. James married the princess of Modena, an Italian papist;§ and a few scurrilous medals, struck at the Hague, to satirize Charles' amours, served as a pretext for war with the Dutch.||

Then the grateful council, thinking that Louis had paid them sufficiently well to warrant some extra, uninspired zeal, hatched a notable scheme. It was proposed, under cover of the *dispensing power*, to enlist the Puritans against the church, and under

* Macauley, Hist. Eng. † Ibid.; Neale, vol. 2.

‡ Sir William Temple's Memoirs.

§ Ibid.; Memoirs James II.; Neale.

|| Motley's Dutch Republic.

the banner of the court, by offering them the protection of the crown, and proclaiming a general toleration, in which the Romanists should be included.*

Against this scheme Lord-keeper Bridgman protested, not because he did not favor toleration, but because he denied the constitutionality of such an act; and his protest cost him his office.†

"The Protestant Non-conformists," says Neale, "disliked the *dispensing power*, and were not forward to accept of their liberty in that way. They were sensible that the indulgence was not granted out of love for them, nor would continue any longer than it would serve the interest of popery."‡ Nevertheless many ministers availed themselves of the indulgence. Vast crowds flocked to the dissenting chapels, and a cautious and moderate vote of thanks was presented to the king; but all trembled for the result.§

At the same time the Papists, who already rivalled the Protestants in numbers as they surpassed them in craft, thronged from every corner of the metropolis, audacious, insolent, menacing. Churchmen were challenged to dispute with them; they threatened to assassinate all who denounced their creed; and pointing to the court, and jingling their foreign gold, they seemed already to regard the island as their own.

In 1673 Parliament met. The dissatisfaction

* Neale, vol. 2, p. 554.

† Ibid.; Russell's Life of Russell. ‡ Neale. § Ibid.

was general. The king was out of funds. The House refused to vote a shilling, until the king surrendered the *dispensing power*. The Cabal urged Charles to make a bold stand for the prerogative, and promised him success. But it was not in him to make a persistent stand for any thing; and since his mistresses required money, he was easily persuaded by the tearful fair ones to *sell* that usurped authority to the Commons.*

By this action, the Non-conformists and the Romanists stood alike uncovered and exposed; but the passage of the *Test Act*, a few days later, which confined all places of profit or trust to conformists alone, was a severe blow at the Papists, since many of them held high office, and it at once broke the Cabal.†

Now once more the Puritans entered the dark valley. The whole pack of informers were again unleashed. Dissenters of all creeds were united in the bond of a common misfortune. True to the genius of their faith, the Romanists began to plot. James was a bigot and a zealous proselyter. He was heir apparent. Charles was a papist; but he was soft, purposeless, and inefficient, more devoted to his amours than to his creed. Rome needed a king who should be made of sterner stuff. It was therefore resolved to assassinate one brother, and to enthrone the other; and this purpose got fresh vitality from the conclusion of peace with Holland, which occurred in 1678. From these feelings sprang

* Rapin; Carrel; Mackintosh, Hist. Revolution 1688. † Ibid.

the *Rye-House Plot.* Rumors of a conspiracy reached the court. Those in the secret professed to laugh; the king gave the reports no credit. "It is not probable," said Charles to Lord Halifax, as their chat turned one day upon these sayings, "that papists should conspire to kill me; have I not always been their countenancer?" "Yes, sire," returned his lordship, "you have been too kind to them; but they know that you will only *trot*, and they want a prince that will *gallop*."*

When the plot was discovered, the king was pensive for some time; but England did not recover from the shock so quickly as did the thoughtless and giddy Stuart. Now, as before in the case of the gunpowder-plot, great exertions were made to connect the Puritans with the exploded conspiracy: but unhappily for the success of this project, a little book was discovered in a meal-tub in the house of a prostitute, which contained the whole scheme of the fiction; and this bob to the larger kite was called the *Meal-tub Plot.*†

Through all these years the alliance between the moderate churchmen and the Non-conformists grew closer and closer. Religion was dear to both; the legends of liberty stirred the blood of either; they were united by common opposition to the Roman tenets; they looked with the same alarm upon the gloomy portents of the time; and they clasped hands over minor differences, in an effort to rescue

* Mackintosh, Hist. Revolution 1688.

† Ibid.; Neale.

their country from the abyss towards which the Stuarts hurried it.*

In the elections of 1679, all parties exerted themselves. The low-churchmen and the dissenters made common cause; the high-churchmen and the tories did the same. When Parliament met, its tone was so independent that Charles prorogued it. Assembled again in 1680, the liberalists were still more prominent; the two great parties assumed the historic names of *Whigs* and *Tories*, names still in vogue; and the Whigs clutched their first trophy in the triumphant passage of these two resolutions, which marked an epoch:

"*Resolved*, That it is the opinion of the Commons, that the acts of Parliament made in the reigns of Elizabeth and king James against popish recusants ought not to be extended against Protestant dissenters.

"*Resolved*, That it is the opinion of this House, that the prosecution of Protestant dissenters upon the penal laws is at this time grievous to the subject, weakening to the Protestant interest, an encouragement to popery, and dangerous to the public peace."†

The Parliament at the same time attempted to change the succession, by setting aside the duke of York on account of his inimical creed.‡

Upon this, Charles abruptly dissolved it. In

* Russel's Life of Russell; Lord Lonsdale's Memoirs.

† Parl. Hist., Statutes of the Realm, Mackintosh, Neale.

‡ Mackintosh, Neale, Macauley.

1681 another Parliament assembled at Westminster Hall; but the king, learning that the *Bill of Exclusion* was to be again brought in, angrily dismissed this also, after a session of seven days.*

This was the last Parliament that Charles ever faced. The old laws still stained the Statute-book. The resolutions of the Commons had been declaratory, not judicial; and the court, sore and ruffled, hastened to put the merciless machinery once more in motion. Charles had a double motive for his old abhorrence of the Puritans: they were now Whigs in politics, as well as dissenters in religion; so the persecution which he now set afoot knew no cessation, and was without relief.

Sadly closed the record. In February, 1685, Charles II., struck by apoplexy, dropped the sceptre from his nerveless hand. His mistresses lavished their tenderness upon him to no purpose. Lingering through four days, he apologized to those who stood about his couch, and said with a wan smile, "I have been an unconscionable time dying; but I hope you will excuse it."† A priest was brought, the room was cleared, the royal penitent was absolved by Roman hands, and on the 6th of February, a piece of crape laid over a cold form announced that Charles Stuart had danced through the revel of his life.

* Mackintosh, Neale, Macauley. † Pepys' Diary, Macauley.

CHAPTER XXXV.

THROUGH THE WILDERNESS TO CANAAN.

In a former century, England, by the death of Edward VI. and the accession of Mary Tudor of bloody memory, had been lassoed to the feet of Rome. History seemed about to repeat itself. Charles II. was now succeeded by his brother James II.—" Belial by Moloch."

The two most prominent traits of the new king's character were bigotry and absolutism;* he was under the complete dominion of those congenial twins. Bishop Burnet, who was intimately acquainted with James, says that "he was very brave in his youth, and so much magnified by Monsieur Turenne, that, until his marriage lessened him, he really clouded Charles, and passed for the superior genius. He had a great desire to understand affairs; and in order to that, he kept a constant journal of all that passed. The duke of Buckingham once gave a short but severe character of the two brothers; it was the more severe because true. 'The king,' said he, 'could understand things if he would, and the duke would understand things if he could.' James had no true judgment, and was soon determined by those he trusted; but he was obstinate against all other advices. He was bred with

* Clarendon's Autobiography, vol. 1, p. 122; Hume, vol. 2, p. 564.

high notions of the royal authority, and laid it down as a maxim, that all who opposed the king were rebels in their hearts. He was perpetually in one amour or another, and was not very nice in his choice; so that Charles used to say, 'I believe that my brother has his mistresses given him by his priests for penance.'"*

The new monarch's initial move was to utter a solemn lie; but it served its purpose and cozened England. Assembling the privy-council while Charles lay dead in an adjoining room, he affirmed that he had no purpose but to maintain the existing laws, civil and ecclesiastical—that he planted himself upon the *statu quo*.†

This declaration surprised and delighted the island, and copies of it were scattered far and wide. Yet James was so awkward a dissembler, that on the first Sunday after his accession he went openly to mass, still an illegal act;‡ he publicly announced that his royal brother had been shriven, and had died an avowed Romanist;§ he even sent Caryl on an embassy to Rome to negotiate with the pontiff for the readmission of England into the bosom of the holy see.‖ Indeed so hot and reckless was his conduct, that pope Innocent XI. cautioned him against his precipitate zeal, and urged him to

* Burnet's Own Times, p. 114.

† Dalrymple, Mem. of Great Britain, vol. 1, pp. 162, 163; Life of Lord North; Hume, vol. 2, p. 564; Clark's Life of James II.

‡ Hume, vol. 2, p. 564; Dalrymple.

§ Evelyn's Diary, Barillion's Memoirs.

‖ Mackintosh, Hist. of Revolution of 1688; Hume.

"make haste slowly."* Ronquillo, the Spanish ambassador at the English court, also ventured to remonstrate with the king, and to advise him not to assent too readily and openly to the dangerous counsel of the priests who thronged his court. "Is it not the custom in Spain," queried James, "for the king to consult with his confessor?" "Aye," was the reply, "and 't is for that very reason our affairs succeed so ill."†

When Parliament met, in May, 1685, James demanded the settlement of a revenue upon him for life, and insinuated that he would not depend upon the precarious grants of the grudging Commons. He also had the impudence to reiterate his promise to preserve the existing government in church and state; whereon the cajoled Parliament voted him a life annuity of two million pounds, and then presented an address requesting him to issue a proclamation for the strict enforcement of the penal code against dissenters from the English ritual.‡

In so far as the laws which the Parliament had invoked bore upon Protestant non-conformists, James hastened to give their execution his cordial assent; but the magistracy, never before so servile as now, were aware of the king's predilections, and while the Puritans were given no quarter, they refused to issue any process against Romanists.§

An event now occurred which armed the king

* Mackintosh, Hist. of Revolution of 1688; Hume.

† Hume, vol. 2, p. 564.

‡ Dalrymple; Fox, Hist. of the Reign of James II.

§ Neale, Mackintosh, Dalrymple, Evelyn's Diary.

with a new pretext for severity. The more prominent movers of that parliamentary bill of exclusion, which had been framed to exclude James from the throne, and which had provoked such ill-feeling between Charles and the Commons in the recent reign, fearing that James would sacrifice them to his resentment, had quitted England on his accession, and sought an asylum on the Continent.* Here they began to plot. The duke of Monmouth, a natural son of Charles II., was given the leadership in a conspiracy to dethrone James by rallying the Scottish Presbyterians and the English dissenters to the support of the insurrection. The Quixotic attempt was made. Argyle landed on the north side of the Tweed; Monmouth landed on the west coast of the island. Bands of ill-armed, undisciplined, and foredoomed guerillas were collected, and a crazy effort was made to unseat a sovereign who had not yet forfeited the loyal good-will of the people. Parliament, then in session, voted to adhere to James; passed a bill of attainder against Monmouth; equipped an army; and on the 5th of July, 1685, met and routed the insurgents, and captured its chiefs. Argyle was executed at Edinburgh; Monmouth was beheaded at London; and James, elated and vindictive, determined to wreak his cruel vengeance on the disaffected, and to lay the heavy arm of a conqueror upon the Puritans at large.†

* Life of Lord North; Macauley, Hist. of England.

† Palmer, Non-conformist Memorial; Neale; Evelyn's Diary.

Jeffries was at this timo Chief-justice of the King's Bench, a position won by those atrocious traits which have made him immortally infamous. Charles had never liked him. His insolence and cruelty provoked the merry monarch's scorn and disgust. "The man has no learning, no sense, no manners, and more impudence than ten carted street-walkers," cried he one day. But a fellow-feeling drew James towards him. His lack of reverence for law, his insensibility to shame made him a useful tool; so the court bought his "forehead of brass and his tongue of venom;" and a beast so habitually drunk that he was said to have climbed up every lamp-post and lain in every gutter in London, was installed in the chief-justiceship of England as the successor of that consummate and unspotted lawyer Sir Matthew Hale.

This wretch was dispatched into the insurrectionary district, and every step he took was on a corpse. His atrocious circuit is to this day the scoff and the execration of the English bar.*

James was emboldened by this success to resume his schemes for the naturalization of Romanism. Like all despots, he preferred the abnormal forces to the legal forces of society. He wished to back his absolutism by bayonets. The recent *émeute* was an excellent pretext; and on the plea that the security of tranquil government necessitated it, he announced his determination to maintain a stand-

* A long account of this circuit is given in Dalrymple and in Macauley.

ing army.* Then, when this point was gained, he threw off the mask. His council was packed with papists; the most obnoxious prerogatives of the crown were usurped anew; the dispensing and suspending powers began to be in daily use; the court of High Commission was dug up, and it was filled with Romanists; all the offices of state were usurped by papists; elections were subjected to his arbitrary will; charters of corporations were annulled; judges were displaced if they ventured to refuse to play the parrot and repeat the sentence of the court; petitions even the most modest, and from persons of the highest rank, were treated as seditious and criminal; buildings of all kinds, churches, chapels, colleges, seminaries, were erected for the Romanists at the national expense; Scotland was harried into popery; Ireland was surrendered wholly to the domination of that creed; the English universities were revolutionized; Magdalen college became a pocket edition of the Sorbonne; a gigantic effort was made to leash England to the pope's triumphal car.†

Astounded at this "Punic faith," Protestantism could at first find no voice even to protest. The dissenters were effectually gagged and thinned by the legal campaigns of Jeffries, and their destruction was a part of the plan for the strengthening of

* Rapin, Hume, D'Araux; Life of Lord North; Memoir of James II.

† Ibid.; Dalrymple, Neale; Declaration of the Prince of Orange; Fox, Hist. of the Reign of James II., etc.

the Romish horde.* But the church of England was as yet unbound; it could protest. Startled into prodigious activity by this assault upon what was most loved and revered in England, the bishops did exert themselves. They began to preach against the Roman tenets. The king forbade even this mild opposition. The bishops persisted. James summoned Dr. Sharpe and the bishop of London before his High Commission, and had both suspended.†

And now, feeling the importance of allying himself with the dissenters in the war against the church which he was inaugurating, James suspended the penal laws, declared it to be his purpose to tolerate all sects, affirmed that he had only consented to the recent persecution of the Non-conformists because obliged to do so by the Episcopal bench; indeed he used every wile in order to ingratiate himself with the Puritans and gain their aid against the Establishment.‡

Of course the Non-conformists did not scruple to avail themselves of the liberty now granted, but they understood the motives of the king, and they were not cozened by the toleration into silence or content.§ Patriots as well as Christians, they could not but look with reprobation upon a despotism bolder than that of Elizabeth, meaner than that of Charles.

* Memoirs of James II., Dalrymple, Evelyn's Diary, Borillon, Neale. † Hume, Dalrymple, Macauley, Mackintosh, Fox.

‡ Ibid. § Neale, vol. 2, p. 607.

When the Puritans reviewed the record of a quarter of a century, and counted two millions of pounds wrung from them since the Restoration by illegal fines; when they remembered their mutilated persons, their wrecked prosperity, their scattered families, and their outraged neighbors; when they collected lists of their brother sufferers, and reckoned eight thousand who had died in prison, and sixty thousand who had suffered since the recall of the Stuarts, as martyrs for conscience,* they were in no mood to listen with patience to the homilies of a Jesuit king whose utterances, as all knew, went no deeper than his lips.

But while he coquetted with the Puritans, James carried on a vigorous war against the churchmen. Six prelates were arrested in 1688, and flung into the Tower for refusing to acknowledge the legality of the dispensing power.† "When the people," says Hume, "beheld these fathers of the church brought from court under the custody of a guard; when they saw them embarked in vessels on the Thames and conveyed towards the Tower, all their affection for liberty, all their zeal for religion blazed up at once. The whole shore was covered with crowds of prostrate spectators, who at once implored the blessing of these holy pastors, and addressed their petitions to heaven for protection during the extreme danger to which their country

* Delaune's Plea for the Non-conformists; cited in Neale, vol. 2, pp. 607, 608.

† Mackintosh, Fox, Neale, Evelyn's Diary, Burnet.

and their faith now stood exposed. Even the soldiers, seized with the contagion, flung themselves upon their knees, and craved the benediction of those criminals whom they were appointed to guard."*

When the trial of these prelates occurred, the same imposing ceremony of grief and veneration was exhibited by the sympathetic populace; and when it was announced that they were acquitted, the wildest enthusiasm was displayed.†

This haughty insult, offered by James to the English church, divorced its affection from him, and rendered all future reconciliation impossible. Yet he did not pause. Claiming to be above the law, grasping prerogatives which had brought his father to the block, he strutted with heedless, blundering haste towards the achievement of his plot—the conquest of the island, and the submission of its torn and strangled liberties to Rome. For this, *magna charta* was torn in pieces and scattered to the winds. For this, Protestant officers were cashiered in the army.‡ For this, Hull and Portsmouth, the two principal sea-ports of England, were seized and held by Romanist conspirators.§ For this, Irish papists were welcomed to Whitehall in shoals, and sent to garrison important towns.‖ For this

* Hume, vol. 2, p. 582.

† Burnet's Own Times, Borillon, D'Araux, State Trials.

‡ Fox, Hist. of Reign of James; Dalrymple, Hist. des Revolutions d'Angleterre, liv. 11.

§ Life of Lord North; Bramston's Memoirs; Mackintosh, etc.

‖ Neale, vol. 2, p. 617; Burnet's Own Times.

the court of England stooped to beg the king of France to advance his accursed gold. For this, Whitehall became a stipendiary of Versailles, and Louis XIV. poured into England more than three million *Louis d'or.** For this, that puissant nation, which had been the arbiter of Europe, sank to be the spaniel of petty continental princes, and competed in political importance with the duchy of Savoy.

But even in those directions in which James flattered himself that he had made most progress, incidents which constantly cropped out showed that he had made the least. He was accustomed to "encamp the army on Hounslow-heath, that he might both improve their discipline, and by so stern a spectacle overawe his mutinous metropolis. A popish chapel was openly erected in the midst of the camp, and every effort was made to bring over the soldiers to that communion. It was time wasted; the few converts the priests made were treated by their brothers in arms with such contempt and ignominy as deterred others from similar renegadism. Even the Irish officers whom the king introduced into the army, served rather, from the aversion borne them, to weaken the royal influence. It happened, on the very day that the trial of the bishops was triumphantly concluded, James had reviewed the troops, and had just retired into the tent of Lord Feversham their commander, when he was surprised to hear a great uproar in the camp,

* Borillon; Macauley, Hist. of England; Dalrymple.

attended by the most extravagant symptoms of tumultuous joy. He inquired the cause, and was told by Feversham, "'T is nothing but the rejoicings of the soldiers over the acquittal of the bishops.' 'Do you call that nothing?' replied the irritated monarch; then he added darkly, 'But so much the worse for them.'"*

Every day the battle between the king and the people increased in fierceness and in venom. Romanism strutted in the royal purple, and clutching the stolen liberties of England, leered and mocked from the very throne. There was but one bright spot in the leaden horizon: James was as yet childless; his daughter Mary was heir presumptive; she was a Protestant; and in 1677 Charles II. had given her in marriage to the prince of Orange at the conclusion of a bitter war with Holland, as a sign of amity and the seal of peace.† The hope of a juster rule under her auspices, gave England patience to endure this night of tyranny and to await the dawn of a jocund morrow.

One day this ray of hope was quenched. It was announced that a son had been born to James.‡ This event, which the king and his cabal had always regarded as certain to garland their cause and insure success, proved fatal. The royal babe was pronounced to be supposititious. It was af-

* Hume, vol. 2, p. 583.

† Evelyn's Diary; Dalrymple; Fox, Reign of James II.; Hist. des Revolutions d'Angleterre.

‡ Dalrymple; Diary of Henry, Earl of Clarendon; Burnet.

firmed that a monarch who had scrupled at no crime in his career of bigotry, would hardly balk at the sacrifice of his heretic daughter when she threatened to thwart his passionate determination to anchor the island in the Latin faith.*

A coalition was formed. Secret negotiations were opened with William of Orange. The churchmen and the aristocracy, both robbed and trodden under foot by the royal madman at the helm of state, were the first movers in this dangerous diplomatic game, and they used every imaginable argument to win recruits.† It was esteemed momentously important to secure the active support of the non-conformists. Lloyd, bishop of St. Asaph, held frequent consultations with their clergy. The secret of the Dutch negotiations was cautiously communicated, and Lloyd said, "I hope the Protestant dissenters will concur in promoting the common interest; you and we are brethren: we have indeed been angry brethren, but we have seen our folly, and are resolved that we will keep up our domestic quarrels no longer."‡ These words were not the empty wind of a desperate schemer anxious to inveigle dupes into his plot; they echoed not the unanimous, but the most authoritative voice of the English church.§

The Puritans, anxious for the future, thrilled by the glowing legends of the past, earnest, patriotic, joined the coalition; trusting more, however, to the

* Hume, vol. 2, p. 584; Burnet; Evelyn's Diary.

† Ibid.

‡ Neale, vol. 2, pp. 621, 622.

§ Ibid., Mackintosh, Fox.

tolerant principles of William of Orange, a prince who had been educated in their creed, than to the caresses of their inveterate foes.*

The Whigs opposed James precisely as Hampden and Pym had fought his father; in their eyes the rights of the commonwealth were not to be balanced by the usurped prerogatives of a thrice-perjured king.

The Tories, frightened into inconsistency, no longer embalmed the slavish dogma of passive obedience in matchless panegyrics, but, spurred by the instinct of self-preservation, they too deserted the court, and took on their lips the watchwords of the revolution.

Faction was put in the cradle and rocked to sleep; England at large united to invite the intervention of the Dutch stadtholder.†

William of Orange was the most remarkable man of that epoch. A scion of the princely house of Nassau, which had stood conspicuous among the noblest of the ruling families of Germany from the dawn of modern history, he was early initiated into the mysteries of the cabinet and the subtle tactics of war. Domestic broils sharpened his wits, and he studied politics under the consummate administration of De Witt. His first laurels were won in defending his country against the French standards of Turenne and the great Condé; and now, at thirty-nine, he governed the United Netherlands

* Hume, vol. 2, p. 588.

† Mackintosh, Fox, Dalrymple, D'Araux, Burnet.

with an *éclat* which rivalled the brilliant days of the republic's birth.*

Thoughtful, of ungovernable spirit, persuasive though taciturn, of simple character, yet maintaining due dignity and becoming magnificence in his official station, an able captain, a wise statesman, a tolerant Christian, William of Orange was the preserver of his own country, the head of the Protestant interest in Christendom, and the asserter of the liberties of Europe.†

With habitual caution, he took time to consider the invitation of the English coalition, but finally he decided to intervene. An army was equipped, ferried across the Channel, landed in England; and with William and Mary at its head, it trod in triumph from Torbay to the metropolis.‡

In the mean time, James, as inefficient in a crisis as he was haughty in a calm, played the meanest comedy in which a crowned head ever figured. Without an effort, without a struggle worthy of the name, he skulked out of England into France, and sued for an asylum at the foot of Louis XIVth's throne.§

The royal dastard was solemnly declared to have deserted the throne; William was voted the crown jointly with queen Mary, and the glorious

* D'Estraeb's Memoires de la Hollande; Vanderrynkt; D'Araux; Temple, in United Netherlands, chs. 4, 5, passim.

† Mackintosh, p. 395; Dalrymple, vol. 2, book 5, p. 2.

‡ D'Araux; Evelyn's Diary.

§ Ibid., Mackintosh, Fox, Borillon, Pardoe's Court of Louis XIV.

revolution of 1688 was accomplished—*victoria sine clade.*

On the 21st of December, 1688, three days after the arrival of the prince of Orange at St. James', the bishop of London, accompanied by a mixed delegation of churchmen and dissenters, waited upon the liberator and congratulated him on his success.* Two weeks later a distinct body of nigh one hundred non-conformist clergymen were introduced to William, and to their cordial address he made this reply: "Gentlemen, my great end in this expedition has been the preservation of the Protestant religion, and with the Almighty's assistance and permission, so to defend and support it as might give it strength and reputation throughout the world, sufficient to preserve it from the insult and oppression of its most implacable enemies, and that more immediately in these kingdoms of England, Scotland, and Ireland. I will use my utmost endeavors so to settle and cement all different persuasions of Protestants in such a bond of love and community as may contribute to the lasting security and enjoyment of temporals and spirituals to all sincere professors of that holy religion."†

The echo of this speech was the bill of toleration, passed early in 1689, and which excused dissenters from attending the Established church, and removed the ban from separate conventicles.‡

* Burnet's Own Times; Neale.

† D'Araux; Burnet's Own Times; Neale's Puritans.

‡ Burnet's Own Times, pp. 529-532; Grey's Parl. Debates.

Here, beneath the benediction of this toleration, ends the distinctive history of the English Puritans. Even under the Restoration, *Puritan* had begun to be merged in *Dissenter* and *Non-conformist*. Now the good old name was dropped in Britain; but not so the spirit. That still lives, and animating twice five thousand pulpits, it is fadeless, immortal.

The revolution of 1688 marked that age and moulded the future: William of Orange was its chief; to that illustrious statesman, under God, Puritanism owes temporal and spiritual liberty, and we may agree with Cromwell, that "he sings sweetly who sings a song of reconciliation between those interests."

If now, under the shelter of this toleration, we pause to weigh the spoils and count the trophies of this tremendous struggle, smeared with the blood of martyrs, dignified by the sufferings of saints, we shall find that the triumph of Puritanism was the result of its rigid attachment to the moral forces. The hair of this Samson was theology; shorn of that, the Philistines might easily have bound it. But no Delilah could coax it to repose its head on the treacherous lap. It knew the secret of its strength, and guarded it with austere care.

It has been well said, that the history of English Puritanism is the story of a theological movement, and of a great national struggle. These are two parts of one grand whole; they are as closely wedded to each other as Austin was to his *Nebridius*, of whom he said, "They had one soul in two bodies."

Old Firmin, in his quaint dedicatory epistle to John Barrington of Redgewood, in the "Real Christian," which Cotton Mather pronounced "a golden book," said, referring to his friend's spirit, ever active to promote the good of others, "Methinks the town is not at home while Mr. Barrington is out of town." Puritanism is not at home if its religious aspect be divorced from its political manifestations. It not only entered into and strongly colored the national life of its epoch, but, overflowing contemporaneous channels, it has spread into all lands and ages. It has not only given strength and passion to the religion, but to the literature and the aspirations of Christendom. For Puritanism is not a dead antique. It did not die under the edict of toleration; its life was not cut short by a date: passing over into modern dissent, it has toned and emphasized the ethics of later times as potentially as it did the thought and expression of the era of Hampden and of Baxter. Two results of Puritanism, the Commonwealth and the Revolution of 1688, consolidated English freedom; these produced, at a fitting interval, the independence of the Puritan colonies of our fathers in 1776. The American Revolution, in its turn, did much to precipitate the first great Revolution of France; and if, as Carlyle has said, "The eighteenth century blew out its brains in the French Revolution," the suicide was owing to a lack of Puritan principle in the leaders, juggled by the "goddess of reason," and of Puritan training in the *sans culottes* who went raving through the streets of the capital, and smeared the Parisian pavements with gore.

Yet abortive as that revolution seemed, it has accomplished much; and all the subsequent *émeutes* and attempted settlements in Continental Europe are returns of the same "irrepressible conflict," which cannot apparently find a close and a peaceful issue till the Bible of the Puritans be everywhere consulted, and the God and Redeemer of the Puritans be everywhere recognized.

Nor is the Puritan spirit "cabined, cribbed, confined" within the limits of any specific sect; it underlies and vivifies the whole evangelical movement of modern times. It is the spiritual ground which the gospel athletes of all denominations must touch to regain their strength exhausted in the struggle with materialism. Most of the famous divines of the eighteenth century were connected with the Puritans, either through blood relationship, or through the higher kinship of the soul.* Watts, the "singer

* "It is a fact not generally known, that the most remarkable men of the eighteenth century, both Conformists and Non-conformists, were the lineal descendants of the ejected clergy, or of their Non-conformist adherents. This is illustrated in the histories of Archbishop Secker, Bishop Butler, Dr. Newcome, William Burkitt, John and Charles Wesley, Matthew Henry, Jeremiah Jones, Dr. Doddridge, John Priestley, Dr. Nathaniel Lardner, and Dr. Watts. Of these, Secker, Butler, Jones, and Chandler, were all trained as dissenting ministers by Mr. Samuel Janes of Gloucester; and it was at the age of twenty-one, and while under Mr. Janes' roof, that Butler gave the first indication of that power which appears so conspicuous in the 'Analogy of Religion.' Secker, afterwards archbishop of Canterbury, first essayed his powers as a preacher as a candidate for the Non-conformist ministry at

of Israel," imbibed their spirit with his mother's milk as she suckled him on the stone steps of the jail where his father, a Non-conformist, was incarcerated. Wesley's mother, to whom he owed so much, was a daughter of Dr. Annesley, a clergyman who was ejected from St. Giles', Cripplegate, London, in 1662; and his *Methodism*, which was greeted by the ribald sneers of giddy Oxford, was, in an important sense, the flowering out of those austere Puritan tenets with which he became familiar when a boy. Whitefield, though not of Puritan descent, still valued the distinctive principles of Owen, of Howe, and of Calamy, and it is said that he read Matthew Henry's "Commentaries on the Scriptures" through upon his knees.

The influence of Puritanism has been and still is most marked in the evangelical movement within the English Establishment. The "low-church" stands almost upon the plane of Baxter; and Wilberforce, in his "Plea for Religion," commends the perusal of the Puritan writers with emphatic earnestness. So in the awakening within the Scotch established Presbyterian church: Chalmers, whose phrase conjured the wondering stars to disclose

Boston. Newcome, archbishop of Armagh, whose various theological works reflect so much credit on his learning and industry, was a descendant of the Rev. Henry Newcome, M. A., ejected from Manchester. William Burkitt, whose 'Expository Notes upon the New Testament' have passed through almost as many editions as the 'Pilgrim's Progress,' was the son of Miles Burkitt, M. A., ejected from Neatishead, in Norfolk, for Non-conformity." Brewer's Men of the Exodus of 1662, pp. 64, 65. London, 1862.

their virgin mysteries, placed the highest value upon the Puritan *doctrinaires*, exhibited the greatest relish for their works, and was tinctured by their tone and method.

Puritanism, crossing the water with the Pilgrims, created Edwards and inspired Brainerd. It was the soul of the revivals of the colonial epoch. It nerved the hearts and strengthened the hands of the men who jeoparded their "lives, their fortunes, and their sacred honor" in the days of 1776; and in our second Revolution of 1861, the grand providential result of which has been to stereotype into active law that liberty, equality, and fraternity of which our fathers dreamed, the war-cry was the same that rang over Naseby and Marston-moor. Foote and Mitchell were regular Cromwellians dug up from beneath the scaffold of Charles I. And if we recross the water, we shall find Montalembert, himself a Frenchman and a Romanist, referring to Havelock as a "resurrected Puritan."

Puritanism is to a great extent the soul of modern missions; and with the Bible in it and behind it, it strikes, through the pulpit and the press, the key-note of the progressive civilization and the Christian enlightenment of the nineteenth century. It has its million voices; and loud above the babble of materialistic philosophy, it shouts the glorious watchwords of what Milton loved to call "the good old cause."

Let us reverently thank God that Puritanism is a living and a growing power of our epoch; for it is an unimpeachable historic fact, that those communities which have been moulded by principles essentially Puritanical, have always written *excelsior* upon their foreheads in the race of material progress, and clasped the highest moral standards to their hearts. This the most opposite scholars have conceded. Mozley, in his "Augustinian Doctrine of Predestination," and Merivale, in his "Constitution of the Northern Nations," admit it at length; yet neither of these thinkers is a Puritan. High views of God, and stern judgments as to man's dependence and demerit, have ever, in Britain, in Scotland, in Holland, in Protestant Germany, in Huguenot France, in our United States, and in the older Geneva, produced a decency, a gravity, a firmness, and a delicacy of moral character which cannot be excelled, and which perhaps may not be paralleled elsewhere.

The cause of the Puritans was the cause of spiritual Christianity. Their whole career was colored by their radiant faith. They "trusted God, and kept their powder dry." It is this trait which has given them so wide and so beneficent an influence on either continent. It is this which has detached men from childish devotion to mere forms, and has won them to grasp at the essence of their principles. It is this which has persuaded the highest thinkers to protest against the grovelling tenets of materialism, and which has taught society to appeal from the present to the eternal. Religion, stripped of its presumption, cleansed from its impurities, announces its dependence upon God, lifts its sweet face to the stars, and the Father kisses it upon its forehead.

As regards the Puritans, "the odious and ridiculous parts of their character," as Macauley has told us, "lie on the surface. He who runs may read them; nor have there been wanting attentive and malicious observers to point them out. For many years after the Restoration, they were the theme of unmeasured invective and derision. They were exposed to the utmost licentiousness of the press and of the stage, at the time when the press and the stage were most licentious. They were not men of letters; they were, as a body, unpopular; they were therefore abandoned without reserve to the tender mercies of the satirists and dramatists. The ostentatious simplicity of their dress, their sober aspect, their nasal twang, their detestation of polite amusements, became the game of the laughers. But it is not from the laughers alone that the philosophy of history is to be learned.

"The Puritans were men whose minds had derived a peculiar character from the daily contemplation of superior beings and eternal interests. Not content with acknowledging in general terms an overruling Providence, they habitually ascribed every event to the will of the Great Being, for whose power nothing was too vast, for whose inspection nothing was too minute. To know him, to serve him, to enjoy him, was with them the great end of existence. They rejected with contempt the ceremonious homage which others substituted for the pure worship of the soul. Instead of catching occasional glimpses of the Deity through an obscuring veil, they aspired to gaze full on his intolerable brightness, and to commune with him face to face. Hence originated their contempt for terrestrial distinctions. The difference between the greatest and the meanest of mankind seemed to vanish, when compared with the boundless interval which separated the whole race from Him on whom their eyes were constantly fixed. They recognized no title to superiority but His favor: and confident of that favor, they despised all the accomplishments and all the dignities of the world. The Puritan was made up of two different men: the one all self-abasement, penitence, gratitude, and sacred passion; the other proud, calm, inflexible, sagacious. He prostrated himself in the dust before his Maker, but he set his heel on the neck of his king. The intensity of his feelings on one subject made him tranquil on any other. One overpowering sentiment had subjected to itself pity and hatred, ambition and fear. Death had lost its terrors, and pleasure its charms. The Puritan had his smiles, his tears, his raptures, his sorrows, but they were not for the things of this world. Piety had cleared his mind from every vulgar passion and prejudice, and raised him above the influence of danger and of corruption."

But if the Puritans were oblivious of the *otium cum dignitate* of life, they were never unmindful of its stern duties or of its necessities. Above all, they were *actors;* they were not speculators in divinity; they were not hucksters in politics; they did not take upon their lips unmeaning oaths, as little to be trusted as the "By these hilts" of an Alsatian dicer; they did not mimic the outward sanctity of the Italian faith, and become as constant at prayers as a priest, as heedless of God as an atheist; they did not attempt, like Jewish pedlars, to trade in the relics of by-gone saints, or to masquerade in the garb of their fathers' piety. But if their principles lay scattered broadcast in the centuries behind them, their application was all their own; and we read their history "in the broad, legible steps of lives whose polar star was duty, whose goal was liberty, and whose staff was justice." Before their time, men had been creeping along the Mediterranean of thought, from headland to headland, in their timidity; the Puritans launched boldly out into the Atlantic, and trusted God.

The results of this militant faith soon appeared in a renovated church and a liberalized state. The English Constitution is largely indebted to Puritanism for many of its grandest checks on despotism. That element first sketched out the boundary line between liberty and the prerogative in the "debatable land" of the British polity. Liberty regulated by law is the secret of Anglo-Saxon progress, and we owe it to Puritanism.

Common-schools were born of that democracy of which the Puritans were enamoured; and these, with piety, are the divine sheet-anchor of all commonwealths. The Puritans saved the seventeenth century from a relapse into popery; and it was owing to their steady, unshrinking faith that when Loyola organized Jesuitism and made his reactive assault upon the Protestant idea, Western Europe came out of the ordeal triumphant.

Of course the Puritans had faults; they were men, and they shared the imperfections of humanity. There are no angels in the records of our race. Wherever we may search, we shall find at best but sinful men; still "we find men to whose might, piety, daring, and disinterested suffering for those about them, the succeeding generations owe the larger share of their blessings."

Nor is it just to measure the Puritans of the middle of the seventeenth century by the standards of the middle of the nineteenth. Measured by the tests of their own epoch, they need not balk the trial; indeed they tower above their contemporaries as mount Blanc towers above its brother Alps.

Still, after all, the Puritans are to be regarded *in posse*, not *in esse*—in the possibilities which lay wrapped up in their epoch. The children are the glory of the fathers. The best tribute to the Puritans is a civilization bound, if possible, to be better than the past—bound to be what Vane and Baxter and Latimer would be, were they alive to-day and surrounded by our opportunities.

'T is said that, when some one sent a cracked plate to China as a pattern for a new tea-set, the stupid Chinese imitated the original so exactly that each plate in the new set had a crack in it. Such imitation is not discipleship. But in that unshrinking love of liberty which characterized the devotees of the "good old cause;" in that stern, uncompromising faith which was the cloud by day and the pillar of fire by night, which led our fathers in the tangled way through the wilderness unto the Celestial City; in that faithful proclamation of the gospel, that love of God, that affection for the only begotten Son, the Saviour of mankind, which inspired our illustrious sires--in these, the beatitudes of life, we are solemnly called to imitate the Puritans, who were the impersonation of God's order and God's law, moulding a better future, and setting for it an example.

www.ingramcontent.com/pod-product-compliance
Lightning Source LLC
LaVergne TN
LVHW020917110826
845150LV00004B/700

* 9 7 8 1 4 2 5 5 5 6 1 0 5 *